From Where We Sail

A Family's

Six and a Half Year Journey

Around the World

on *Sorcery*

A Memoir

by

Dianne Lane

FROM WHERE WE SAIL

A Family's Six and a Half Year Journey Around the World on *Sorcery*

ISBN-13: 978-1979964135
ISBN-10: 1979964130

Author: Dianne Lane

Printed as a work of non-fiction in the U.S.A.

Cover design by Kari Cureton.

Layout by David Larson.

Dedication

To my family,

our fellow cruisers,

and

our beloved Sorcery *who brought us safely home*

Acknowledgments

The La Playa Writers' Workshop gave me the impetus, support, and good advice that carried this book from start to finish. Without their constant encouragement and suggestions, the book would never have been written.

My dear husband, Robb, listened to most of the manuscript as it went along, contributed important details and wording, and indulged me in putting the writing of this memoir above almost anything else for such a long time.

Daughter Annie, wearing her journalist and sailor hats, provided invaluable help by proofing and editing the manuscript, writing out some of her memories, and coming up with good ideas for multiple aspects of the book, including the cover design and name. Both she and our son Alex allowed me to read and use quotes from the journals they kept during the trip, supplying that fresh and wonderful perspective that is unique to children.

Over the years many, many friends and acquaintances urged me to write about the adventure. I thank them all for that. Also thanks to Sam Minervini for looking after our finances and coming up with suggestions that made our cruising so much more enjoyable. He urged us to install an electric windlass for raising the heavy anchor, to take along fishing equipment, and to get a dinghy and outboard motor that could reach planing speed.

Without Susan McCrocklin, the trip would not have been the same. Like an angel on our shoulders, she looked after us in so many ways: keeping scheduled radio contact, forwarding mail, checking in on my mom, taking care of business in San Diego, and sending goods of all descriptions wherever we were in the world.

How It All Began

*"If you can sail to Catalina," someone once said to me,
"you can sail around the world."
That's pretty much it. You don't have to figure out
the whole thing all at once.*

AS it turned out, we did sail to Catalina, then to Mexico three times, before venturing any farther. Long before we left on the first trip to Mexico, I worried and wondered what it would be like cruising, to be sailing all the time. My good friend and neighbor Michele, who'd cruised extensively in Mexico with her husband Phil on *Delia*, assured me, "Most of the time you're at anchor."

Such a relief, and it proved to be true. Still, throughout the years, whenever we made landfall I'd say "cheated death again" and mean it. Exploring new places enchanted me, but for the most part the mental and physical challenges of sailing intimidated and often frightened me. I felt vulnerable so far from land, which is to say, from other people who could help in the emergencies which came our way.

If the slides our marina neighbor, John on *Serenity*, photographed on his cruise to French Polynesia, hadn't captivated me, I might never have been willing to go that far, let alone keep on going. The views were stunning – Moorea, Tahiti, especially Bora Bora. Each island had a luminescent, unreal, picture-perfect quality: intense greens and blues and whites. I longed to see those islands.

Of course, sailing to the South Pacific is one thing, and sailing around the world something else, but you know how one thing can lead to another. I started out dragging my feet, but weathering the storms of boat living and family life, I tapped into my inner pioneer and came to appreciate and mostly love the unusual and thrilling lifestyle that unfolded. The entire voyage, San Diego to North Carolina, including the third and last excursion to Mexico took six and a half years – January

1992 to June 1998. To this day, that era, and our earlier two trips to Mexico, are the most treasured period of our lives.

I tried to write about our cruising experience in a general way, from the whole family's point of view. But I realized, even while we were out there, each of us was on a different trip.

Here's an early example: The first time beating up the outside of the Baja coast, when the boat was *Pound! Pound! Pounding!* over each wave, I wondered what in the world I was doing there. My husband Robb, tucked into the navigation station with a blanket and cup of tea, both of which I'd brought to him, said, "This isn't so bad, is it?"

Some people who knew us before and during the trip will wonder who Robb is in this account. Until we landed in North Carolina at the end of our voyage, he'd gone his entire life by his given name, Clyde, a name he never liked. Returning to the States meant new beginnings for all of us. What better time to change his name? "Robb" is short for Robbins, his middle name.

⚓

When I met Robb in 1985, he owned a sailboat, the lovely *Sunward*, a Columbia 50. In less than a year, he and I and our two children – his seven-year-old Alex and my three-year-old Annie – were living on the boat at Mission Bay Marina in San Diego. After getting married in 1987, we planned a five-month trip to Mexico. We did some day sailing, including a trip to Catalina Island 60 miles away. At that point, sailing around the world never crossed our minds.

To prepare for Mexico the following year, I read a lot and went to seminars on "cruising," traveling on a boat with no fixed schedule. I stocked up on school materials from an educational supply store, provisioned for food, and designed an all-you-might-need medical kit complete with reference books. Robb readied the boat, doing preventive maintenance and getting spares for everything. Alex, by then eight and already a seasoned sailor, was keen to help. Taking her primary task very seriously, four-year-old Annie marched up and down the dock armed with a clipboard, getting names and mailing addresses of friends on other boats.

The most valuable information I took away from a cruising-cooking seminar was this: Food you wouldn't dream of eating at home tastes great on a boat. The idea reassured and sustained me throughout the life that was to come.

On land, I often felt burdened by having to think of, shop for, prepare, eat, and clean up after, three meals a day for four people. What a pleasant surprise to find I didn't mind, even looked forward to, cooking while cruising. Although we had plenty to do on the boat, none of the typical distractions from the outside world vied for our attention. Also, preparing food tapped into that creative part of me that said, *Okay, this is what we've got, what can I do?*

This is an extreme comparison, but remember in the movie *Apollo 13* when the air filter system stopped functioning? Using a table full of the type of materials and tools the crew had on board, the team in Houston was able to guide the astronauts in fashioning a filter that saved their lives. Our lives were never at stake as far as food was concerned, but cruising is where I honed my crisis-cooking skills.

At my insistence, we always provisioned to the hilt: basic food that would last 52 days if the motor quit and the mainsail shredded. This tactic was based on the account of a woman we met whose boat drifted 52 days after those exact catastrophes struck.

Whenever we could buy food, we replenished not only the fresh food, but our already ample supply of non-perishables. Soups, seasonings, sauces, refried beans, anything dehydrated was the best because the packets didn't weigh much and didn't rust. We took long-life milk in quart boxes and condensed juices in little boxes, powdered milk, peanut butter, and canned goods galore – vegetables, fruit, even fabulous cheeses from the Washington State University Creamery and whole cooked chickens.

The Great Canning Adventure

Our marina neighbors, Trevor and Carrie on *Aquila*, were also preparing to cruise Mexico. Carrie said they couldn't possibly go without hamburger for their children. Although most boats had refrigerators, we all learned not to depend on them. One time I'd brought a dozen packages of Sizzlean, a delicious turkey bacon. When the fridge went out, I cooked up all the bacon and served it with every meal until it was gone: bacon and eggs, bacon in sandwiches, crumbled bacon sprinkled on practically everything. No one complained about having too much bacon.

Carrie discovered the public was allowed to use the Mormon cannery in Los Angeles and arranged for some of us to go there to can our own ground beef and turkey. She even found where to buy the meat and made all the arrangements. On the appointed day at zero-dark-thirty, as Robb would say, Trevor and Carrie from *Aquila*, Robin, Pauline, and their teenaged son Simon from *Marco Polo,* and Robb and I piled into Robin and Pauline's van for the drive.

At the factory, bags and bags of unground, uncooked beef and turkey awaited us. The facility was ours for the day and the Mormons provided a few pleasant people who unobtrusively supervised and did everything we couldn't do ourselves. They showed us how to grind the meat and cook it in huge cauldrons with oar-sized paddles.

Next, we ladled the meat into cans that wobbled along a conveyor belt to get their lids. From there we stacked the cans into giant pressure cookers. Finally, hundreds of cans got placed into dozens of boxes. The food had to be left behind for a week until the Department of Public Health could spot-check for botulism. After the long, sweaty day. we arrived home after dark, and couldn't have been more pleased with ourselves.

In 2013, the practice of allowing the public to use that Mormon canning facility was abandoned, in part because it was too expensive. They didn't charge us for the use of the facility or even for the cost of the people who assisted. Thoughts of the adventure always bring back fond memories, now even more so, since that experience can't be replicated.

We sold three or four boxes of the canned meat at cost because other cruisers begged to have some. To our good fortune, it turned out one couple didn't like it at all, so months later we were able to buy back a box or two. What a treat, as the excellent quality of the ground meat lent itself to so many recipes.

***

Making the classic cruising food, yogurt, is one of those things in life that's simple, but not easy. All of my early attempts ended up in pancakes. Each time my batch didn't set up, or "yoge," I was so devastated Robb finally said he'd pay me $5 to not bother anymore.

Luckily, he never paid up, and on the umpteenth try, it yoged – a triumphal moment. Over those years on the boat, we consumed gallons of the healthful, versatile food because we found it so delicious.

Fellow cruisers often asked me about making yogurt. One time in an anchorage somewhere in the South Pacific, I held a yogurt-making class. Sharing the technique of something I'd worked hard to learn and finally mastered felt wonderful.

A few years after we got back from the trip, Annie, who remembered the yogurt as "amazing," asked for homemade yogurt for her birthday. Alas, I'd lost the knack.

Annie and Alex aboard *Sunward*

Robin and Pauline, who are English, often invited us over for that lovely British custom, Afternoon Tea. I once asked why her tea always tasted better than mine. As a bon voyage gift, they gave us a shiny blue teapot and a seven-step recipe for making tea. Pauline added a quote from Henry James: "There are few hours in life more agreeable than the hour dedicated to the ceremony known as Afternoon Tea." We began the custom that very day on *Sunward,* and carried on even while underway, weather permitting.

Other gifts came from our neighbor and close friend, Sam Minervini on *Christel II*: a case of red wine for the adults, something fun for Alex – although what that was escapes all of us, and for Annie, a handheld flashlight/alarm clock, a treasure she kept by her bedside, even when we were back on land and still has to this day.

Within a few days of departure, I displayed outward calm for the sake of the family, but was nearly paralyzed with fear. My husband, thrilled to be going, tended to poo-poo my concerns. Needing some female support, but not from other boat women who were already cheering me on, I called my longtime friends, twins Lisa and Ellen in New York City. They never sailed a day in their lives, but I knew they could talk me back from the edge.

"Go!" they shouted in unison, "You'll have the time of your life! There's danger in staying home."

All my fears didn't fade away, but I was able to focus on what needed doing, which was plenty. To make room for what we took, we'd removed lots of things from the boat.

On the day of departure, the children were off having last visits, Alex with his mom and Annie with her grandma. Three small piles still remained on the dock: stuff on its way to the dumpster, items to be given away, and a couple of remaining objects destined for our storage locker. Suddenly, Robb cast the lines from the dock, saying we had to leave now – we'd never be absolutely ready.

"What about all this stuff?" I asked, waving my hands at the piles on the dock. "And, what about the children?"

"Leave the stuff. We'll pick up the kids at the Police Dock."

And just like that, we were off for the adventure of a lifetime.

MEXICO

Sorcery at anchor

First trip
Baja on *Sunward*
January to May 1988
Alex was eight, Annie four

L ITTLE did I know, urban person that I am, how much I'd love the outdoor adventure. Sailing per se wasn't the draw; though traveling by boat became the catalyst to opening a whole new world. By day and by night we moved through vast, glorious, and ever-changing panoramas of nothing but sea and sky. Rather than driving or flying in, we crept up on Mexico, experiencing the country from its unspoiled watery edge.

After sailing three days from San Diego, *Sunward* pulled into Cedros Island. We didn't have to wait long for our first genuine cruising experience. Before we'd even finished anchoring, Alan and Gertrud on *Carioca III*, the only other boat in the anchorage, shouted, "Come on over for a glass of wine!"

As we came to learn, they typified the gregarious, curious, warm, and energetic individuals that peopled the cruising world. He'd been a sound man for Disney, had worked on *Lady and the Tramp*, and told hilarious stories about himself and others in Hollywood in the 1950s.

One afternoon when they'd come to visit, the wind picked up. Going back to their own boat seemed unsafe, so they settled in for a while. The day happened to be both Alan's and Robb's birthday. To celebrate, Annie and I made a fruit pizza, and set a fat candle in the middle. The pizza, still requested by the family, is a fruit tart made in a pizza pan. The baked sugar cookie base gets slathered with layers of cream cheese and marmalade, then topped with a variety of whatever fruit we have on hand, arranged in concentric circles.

Before we set out from San Diego, Robb suggested I cut Annie's hair for the trip. Her waist-long mop of dark brown curls required me to sit on the floor each day with her in my lap, my legs trapping her in order to get a comb or brush through the thicket. But no, cutting her gorgeous hair didn't seem necessary. Now we faced a mini-crisis. Annie's hair, which hadn't been touched for days, was tangled beyond combing. Using a 3-inch piece of cardboard as a guide, I cut her curly locks evenly all over her head, a very cute style for her, I thought. Recently she told me how sad and angry she was at the time – though even then she remembered me telling her she'd better get to combing "or else." In the village a little boy seemed smitten. He followed her everywhere, shared a packet of sunflower seeds, and gave her a tiny cross.

* * *

One of the early events foretelling the unexpected pleasures of cruising life occurred at our next stop, Turtle Bay. A couple from another boat puttered up in their dinghy and handed us a loaf of homemade bread still warm from the oven. That act of generosity deeply moved me. We were total strangers, yet instantly welcomed into the cruising community. Someone shared food effortful to make, and which they themselves would have had no trouble eating. The offering was particularly welcome coming after a long passage, when something fresh had already become a novelty.

Speaking of bread, the problem is that it doesn't last all that long. Enter bread making. The first time a loaf came out of the oven, we gobbled down the whole thing in 10 minutes. Who can resist hot bread with butter? We often had cans of real butter from Ireland or New Zealand. From then on, making two loaves at a time became the norm. Over the years I must have made hundreds of loaves of bread on board.

Mostly we used the oven, but a few times, in especially hot weather, I made stove-top bread in the pressure cooker. An utterly marvelous English muffin loaf cooked in an unbelievable six and a half minutes in the microwave. That oven came to an end in the Marshall Islands, where the appliance succumbed to salt air, poor quality electricity, and old age.

I relied heavily on Betty Crocker's 1974 edition of *Breads*, which I now have open before me. A note-to-self inside the front cover, "Don't use chicken bouillon for salt." Each attempted recipe has detailed notes and a rating at the top. Here are two with current notes:

Mock Sourdough – "Fabulous! May '94, South Minerva Reef." Cruisers love the mystique, not to mention the actual taste, of sourdough. Every "starter" someone gave us came with a claim of having been handed down from a miner/49er. In the case of our Alaskan friends, Rodney and Katherine on *Orion*, the claim may have been true. Sometimes we had dehydrated starter, and, if my back was to the wall, I made my own. Sourdough is the one bread for which you need to plan a couple of days ahead.

Soft Pretzels – No date or place, but they were as fun to make as they were to eat. Our onboard copy of the New Columbia Encyclopedia told us, "Pretzels were invented in southern France in 610 A.D. by monks who shaped them to look like a child's arms folded in prayer."

And two from our collection of stained and ragged recipes:

Beer Bread – Alex and Annie especially liked this bread, partly because of the taste, but mostly, I believe, because of the name. What I liked is that it's truly a quick bread. Stir a can of beer into the dry ingredients and throw the pan in the oven. Quicker still were muffins, which didn't take as long to bake. We were often in a hurry and always trying to conserve propane.

Tortillas – The kids had fun rolling out the dough and hanging each amoeba shape to rest over the edge of our big aluminum mixing bowl. This flat bread came in handy for lots of meals, not just Mexican.

Back to the Trip

Farther along the coast at Los Frailes, Jim on *Dream Merchant* took the kids knee boarding, trailing a boogie board behind his dinghy. Later he invited all of us over for a potluck and to watch a movie from his collection of more than 100 VHS tapes. After dinner his wife, Joan, announced we wouldn't be watching a movie, we were going to play a game.

Since my heart had been set on a movie, I felt annoyed and determined to hate the game, even though I'd never heard of it. Pictionary, however, became one of our family's all-time favorites and was one of our first purchases back in San Diego. That evening was the beginning of the standard Girls versus Boys. Girls' turn: Joan studied the card she'd picked out blindly, before sketching a simple mountain with a hut on the side.

"Resort!" I screamed, winning the game for the Girls, and flabbergasting the Boys.

Though adults usually welcomed our children, getting them together with other kids became a priority. As we entered a new anchorage, we looked to see if any of the boats had netted lifelines – the primary clue as to whether the boat had children. If we didn't see any evidence of kids, we often tried our luck at the next anchorage, if it wasn't too far away.

At La Paz we checked into the cruisers' net, a fixed time on the radio when boaters exchange information. We invited anyone with children who wanted to get together to call us. A young girl's family responded, and Annie enjoyed a playmate for the next several days. No boys for Alex, but while we were there, he rescued our dinghy when we saw it drifting away. And once when I was swimming around the boat, the current started carrying me out to sea. Alex saw what was happening, jumped in the dinghy, and picked me up. Much later, Annie wrote, "Alex saved her but I wanted to be the one!"

Breaking away from the bustle of La Paz for a spell, we sailed 100 miles up Baja's east coast. For a couple of weeks, we moved from one charming, deserted little anchorage to another: San Evaristo, Nopolo, Los Burros, and one with no name.

"It's so quiet." Alex said with surprise the first evening.

Later on, we heard a loud, long, slow *uhhwhishhh* and then another, *uhhwhishhh* – like a giant exhaling into the other end of a telephone. "It's just a whale breathing," Robb said, "nothing to be alarmed about."

Though the sound came from fairly close by, we never saw any sign of a whale.

At each stop we tested for the quality of echoes. We'd cup our hands and holler, "Hellooooo," and wait for the satisfying response. We also rated each anchorage for the amount of bioluminescence, the light produced by certain living organisms in the water. Combining the two traits into "echo-vescence," we had one word that described two elements making a small anchorage especially appealing.

The kids played around in the water in the early evenings, and set off the organic lights with their movements. One moonless night after the kids were asleep, I invited Robb to go for a swim.

"You go ahead, I'll be on shark watch," he said.

Shark watch? Oh, well, here goes. Doing my best Esther Williams, I swirled around sending out sprays of glitter. After the show, I emerged glistening from the water only to learn that between the cover of darkness and Robb's concern about sharks, he didn't notice I'd been clothed only in sparkles.

⚓

In late June we got serious about heading for home. As bottles of wine emptied, we began sticking messages inside and throwing the corked bottles overboard. Back in San Diego, two responses waited for us. We were ecstatic. One bottle had been found by a fisherman, who took the letter to his nineteen-year-old son, the only person in his village who spoke English. In the middle of his two-page letter, Rogelio asked, "You need help, or you want to have friends?"

Phil, an American surfer, wrote at the end of his long letter, "Thanks for a true story of a message in a bottle." Getting letters back encouraged us to drink more wine. Over the years we threw dozens of bottles with messages, but only one more, as far as we know, was ever found. When we get to Australia, there's a story that goes along with that third bottle.

Technically, we should never have thrown any bottles within 12 miles of shore. But since we were scrupulous about what and where we threw other trash in the ocean, we forgave ourselves that breach for a time-honored tradition.

International law forbade the dumping of plastic anywhere in the ocean or navigable waters, so we saved plastic for disposal on shore. Restrictions for other trash – "paper, rags, glass, food, garbage, metal, crockery, and dunnage" – changed with the distance from shore. Nothing could be dumped within three miles. Between three and 12 miles out, trash had to be torn into pieces less than 1-inch square. After 12 miles, we could have thrown anything, except plastic. Nevertheless, no matter how far out we were, we designated it a kids' chore to attach their harnesses to the rail, then shred paper and poke holes in cans with an ice pick before throwing the results off the stern.

Winch Handle Meets My Jaw

Slogging upwind on Baja's west coast became a cold, wet, rugged undertaking. After two exhausting days and nights with two reefs in the main, we pulled into calm Magdalena Bay in the late afternoon. Next morning while Robb hoisted the mainsail to dry it, I fixed applesauce crepes with dollops of thick yogurt, and a sprinkling of cinnamon.

After breakfast, he asked me to come up and help take the sail down by releasing the brake on the wire-reel winch. Unfortunately, I forgot to take out the winch handle, which spun around, hit me under the jaw, and knocked me over. He found me lying and whimpering on the pile of sails.

"Where are we? Why am I still wearing my nightgown?"

Robb explained a little, but seeing my blank looks, started asking questions.

"What's your name?"

"Dianne."

"What's my name?"

"Robb."

"Do you know we're married?"

"Yes."

"How old are you?"

"I don't have to tell you that."

The funny thing is, normally I never hesitated to tell my age. Apparently, I had temporary amnesia from the blow, because I don't remember any of that conversation. Cautioning me not to move, he ran below to get on the radio for advice.

"Go up with your mom," he told the kids. "She doesn't know where she is."

"I'll take her a chart!" Alex piped up.

The first thing I remember was their little faces on the other side of an open chart, with Alex pointing and explaining where we were, where we'd been, and where we were going. Even at that age, he had excellent geographical sense – no surprise he later became a lieutenant commander in the Navy. My thought at the time was I should know what he was talking about, but really didn't.

By the time Robb shepherded us all below, a raging headache had set in, along with desperate fatigue and hunger. The doctor on the radio, a fellow cruiser, described signs to look for in a head injury, and advised no painkiller, sleep, or food for an hour or two. He'd stay on the radio, just in case. I remember planning what to eat, and berating my family for finishing off the tasty barbequed fish left over from the night before.

At the hour and a half mark, I insisted Robb call the doctor and ask when I could eat, take a painkiller, and go to sleep. All was granted. A faint yellow bruise on the underside of my jaw was all I had to show for the drama that could have been a serious, even a lethal, injury. A couple of women cruisers we didn't know stopped by to "say hello" and left a brochure on spousal abuse. The accident might have dissuaded us from further cruising, but by then, the life style had me hooked.

Though demanding in so many ways, cruising is more deeply satisfying than the law allows. One evening in an anchorage as pretty as it was peaceful, we sat in our cockpit with friends, a bottle of wine, a nosh, and village lights twinkling in the background. "I wonder what the rich people are doing?" someone asked, giving us an expression we often used while cruising, whenever we thought life just couldn't get any better.

One trip to Mexico turned into three, each a year and a half apart. All of them run together in my mind – a stimulating and endless cycle of potlucks on boats or on the beach, new friendships and old, hiking and exploring, catching and cooking fish, snorkeling, book and food exchanges, and shelling until Robb forbade further collecting.

A sand dune! Annie's favorite memory of the first trip

More on Food

At one anchorage a man traveling alone, a "single hander," showed up at a potluck with a big platter of fresh sushi – a surprising and impressive offering. He assured me it was easy to make. All I had to do was get a package of sheets of *nori*, dried seaweed, at any grocery store and follow the directions.

Our friend Susan on *Alcatraz*, based in San Diego, included some *nori* and a bamboo sushi mat in the next care package she sent down. Making sushi was a little time consuming, but such a crowd pleaser, it was worth the effort. We almost always had fresh fish, and our wide selection of canned and dried foods provided us with good, if sometimes quirky, add-ins. Of course, with enough soy sauce and wasabi there was nothing that didn't taste fabulous.

Many cruisers brought Spam because it was a good protein source and didn't require refrigeration. But then, when too far from home, some people found they just couldn't eat it – an exception to that rule about everything tasting great on a boat. But our family was always happy when cans turned up at one of our book and food exchanges. We used Spam lots of ways, but the best was sliced very thin and cooked until crisp like bacon, which in fact it resembles since it is, after all, pork.

***

My favorite recipes had maybe three or four ingredients. If we had limes of any ethnic persuasion, we made an ersatz Key Lime pie: one can sweetened condensed milk; add half a cup of fresh lime juice; blend; pour into graham cracker or cookie crust; chill for two hours. Divine. This was such a perfect cruising recipe, I assumed it had been invented by a sailor.

So it surprised me to read recently in a Trader Joe's flyer that Key Lime pie had originated in Key West, Florida in the 1850s. There was no refrigeration in the Keys until the 1930s, so the invention of the magic ingredient, sweetened canned milk, in 1853 led to the creation of Key Lime pie. Once I gave the recipe to a fellow cruiser. After a while she called on the radio to ask, "I've been stirring for a long time. When does it become green?" Oh. Third ingredient, a drop or two of green food coloring – not traditional, but nice.

Apart from fruit, most desserts were baked: cookies and cakes, fruit pizzas, eggless cupcakes. Both sweet and savory Impossible Pies were also staples in my repertoire. This cruising-friendly recipe calls for stirring together all the ingredients for both the shell and the filling, then baking the mixture in a pie pan. The flour gravitates to the bottom and sometimes a bit up the sides to form a soft crust. The best of those improbable pies I ever made and the one my family will never forget was the coconut one. I'd accidentally doubled the butter and sugar.

"It's a fine way to improve any dessert recipe," Robb said.

Our edition of *Joy of Cooking* printed in 1967 was purchased for $1 at a library used-book sale. It was an outstanding investment, and like so many things that went around the world with us, it's now a sacred family treasure. *Joy* is the sort of book you can thumb through simply for pleasure. At the end of the fish chapter there's a recipe for whale that reads, "Last, but vast. Allow half a pound per serving." Some might question whale being in the fish section, but you really wouldn't want to find it under beef, which, according to the book, whale meat closely resembles. I always thought there was an outside chance we might need the recipe.

Apart from being a solid resource for cooking information, *Joy* contains wonderful stories, like this one with the lobster recipes:

> The uninitiated are sometimes balked by the ferocious appearance of a lobster at table. They may take comfort from the little cannibal who, threading his way through the jungle one day at this mother's side, saw a strange object roar overhead. "Ma, what's that?" he quavered. "Don't worry, planes are pretty much like lobsters. There's an awful lot you have to throw away, but the insides are delicious."

We told that story just about every time we had lobster, which was pretty often. We had so many in Mexico the kids literally got fed up. "Oh, no, lobster again?" became a common refrain.

It may sound as if I'd finally understood the joy of cooking, but that was only while we were out there. Cruising cooking was something I became pretty good at, which kind of made up for my lack of sailing skills. Annie says I always managed to make something tasty and creative with such limited offerings. "We were all grateful for that, even if we didn't always tell you."

We Had Our Ship

That first trip to Mexico changed the direction of our lives. Robb had always wanted to go cruising, and the venture blew past his expectations. The children took to the life quite naturally, and, as parents, we felt good about exposing them to a different culture and new experiences. As for me, I'd swung all the way from a state of trepidation to being an enthusiast. We started looking for a boat with an interior configuration that would better suit the four of us.

"This is the boat I'd love to have," Robb said as he handed me a flyer advertising the sale of a famous old race boat.

The $250,000 price tag caught my eye, and my mouth volunteered, "I don't think so."

As if he hadn't heard me, Robb proceeded to list all the virtues a race boat would have for cruising. First and foremost, she was fast. That appealed to me mightily since I far preferred being there to getting there. By the time he came to "Can we just have a look?" I was ready.

When we saw the boat, we liked her a lot, but confessed early on we'd come under false pretenses. "We don't have anything like that kind of money to spend on a boat." The broker, who'd had the boat listed for a year without a single offer, prompted, "Well, how much do you have?" Settling on $150,000, our secret top price, we wondered even then if we'd done the right thing. It was still a whopping amount of money, and at 61 feet, a whopping amount of boat.

The ink had hardly dried on the contract when someone offered to buy the boat for more than we'd paid. Robb wanted to sell, while I argued we'd looked a long time, really liked the boat, and had gotten an exceptional one for the price.

"You don't understand," he groaned. "You're *never* able to sell a boat for more than you paid."

We turned down the offer. But what neither of us could've imagined then was that this magnificent boat would prove herself priceless many times over. To steal from Crosby, Stills and Nash in their song "Southern Cross," we had our ship and *Sorcery* was her name.

Our ship: *Sorcery*, a C&C 61, sail #4785

Second Trip
Baja and Mexican Mainland on *Sorcery*
December 1989 to May 1990
Alex was ten, Annie six

TO find out if *Sorcery* really was the boat for us, we made a second trip to Mexico. On December 11, a foggy Monday at 6 in the morning, we motored out of Mission Bay. Annie took a break from listening to her Walkman. "This wasn't a very good day to go to Mexico. Last time there wasn't this much bumps!" Alex let us know he was already bored. Oy vey.

Sorcery proved fast and stable, with far more room both on deck and below than *Sunward*. We converted the forward sail locker into a cozy cabin for Robb and me. Alex and Annie had little cabins – one starboard, one port in the aft of the boat – each just enough for a single mattress, a red-plaid flannel curtain and a small ledge with a drawer underneath. Designed for a racing crew of 12 to 16, *Sorcery* slept eight using the hot-bunk system: only half the crew slept at one time.

The boat had a shower stall, a pump-to-flush toilet, a comfortable salon, and an enviable galley. *Sorcery* needed a decent galley to produce all those meals, but by the time the boat came to us, the freezer had disappeared. The roomy refrigerator opened from the top, and when closed, provided extra counter space. Protruding into the galley at waist height, the varnished engine cover made another useable surface. Pivoted supports kept the stove level as the boat rocked from side to side.

The galley and bathroom sinks had both salt and fresh water faucets, each activated with a foot pedal that required continual pumping. The system allowed for extremely efficient use of fresh water, and was one of the reasons we easily got by carrying only 125 gallons.

The other reason: fresh water was used almost exclusively for drinking and cooking, and only a tiny amount to rinse ourselves after showering and our clothes after washing.

⚓

The second evening out, since we were between Thanksgiving and Christmas, I fixed a holiday meal, unusually elaborate for underway. If you'd been there, perhaps you'd have appreciated the moist, ground turkey pungent with sage, rosemary, thyme, oregano, garlic and onion. The dehydrated Idaho mashed potatoes had real butter, and good gravy from a packet. Mrs. Cubbison's stovetop bread stuffing, with celery, onion and extra spices, went nicely with Trader Joe's fresh cranberry/orange relish. Canned green beans were sautéed in olive oil and dill, then sprinkled with a little salt, and freshly ground pepper. I made a pumpkin pie.

Soft light came from two brass kerosene sconces in the galley, and blue cloth placemats and napkins lent a homey look. The highly varnished table was lovely, even if each person ate, as usual, with their plate, utensils, napkin and drinking glass in a rectangular metal cake pan. We never knew when the boat might lurch and things go flying. As a further precaution, the table and the counters in the galley had 2-inch-high wooden fiddle rails at the edges to prevent things from sliding off when the boat rocked.

***

From my notes on the way down, "What a delicious, peaceful time we're having. These days have been among the most pleasing in my life. Everyone is happy as a clam. We're barely moving, and have drifted to halfway between Guadalupe and Cedros islands." From the top of the 70-foot mast I took a photo of the boat's shadow in the water.

Back at the dock in San Diego, the first time Annie begged her dad to hoist her up the mast in the bosun's chair, he stopped at each spreader to check on her. "Is that high enough? Are you ready to come down?"

"No, Dad! Higher!" At the top, she yelled down, "Dad! Send me some tools! I'll fix something!" Months later in Manzanillo, she confessed to Alex she was "a little bit scared" of going all the way up any more.

The Captain Sinks to His Knees

While underway, Robb asked me to help adjust the spinnaker pole by letting out the line from a winch. He looked up at the pole 4 or 5 feet above his head and yelled for me to release the brake. Not remembering how the mechanism worked, I jerked it open rather than lift the lever carefully with one hand, while slowly feeding out the line with my other. In an instant, the line flew off the winch, allowing the 22-foot-long aluminum pole to come crashing down on Robb's head. He sank to his knees.

The rule underway is: Do Not Desert Your Post. Immobile with fear anyway, I didn't move and barely breathed. Robb said he counted to 10, then counted some more. His head hurt, but he felt sure there was no serious damage. Annie's recent memory of her reaction at the time was that she suddenly worried we might be alone out there, but realized people don't usually die in the kneeling position. A "hyena-type cackle" boiled up from her belly, and she didn't know if she'd start laughing or sobbing. With one last look at her dad frozen in pain and the sheer terror on my face, her tears just started pouring.

More philosophically, later on she wrote:

> How lucky were we? Actor Liam Neeson's wife died
> after a head injury while skiing, and she had access to medical
> care – we didn't. How did Dad not lose consciousness or
> break his neck or back? So many things happened on our
> trips that I think people will ask, why did we keep going? Part
> of it's because after a certain point you have to keep going to
> get back to where you started. The other part is, things can
> happen to anyone, anywhere, and our misadventures made up
> only a small fraction compared to the good times.

Holidays Afloat

Immersing ourselves in the sailing life and other cultures kept us busy and entertained. But when the major American holidays rolled around, they tugged at us, pulling us back to our roots. We dug into our creative resources to make these times as festive as we could. All of those cruising celebrations were special because they differed so much from the ones at home. I'd like to use the word memorable, but in truth, I can't remember them all. Halloween, one of our family favorites, just didn't travel well, and was abandoned after one or two feeble attempts. Every Thanksgiving and Christmas included watching Garfield tapes. The two holiday specials had been recorded by my mom for Annie who adored that sassy cartoon cat. We all came to love and rely on the tradition of watching them, and still do.

⚓

On this trip Robb had wanted to sail to Manzanillo on the Mexican mainland without stopping, a trip of 1,400 miles, roughly 10 days from San Diego, then head up into the Sea of Cortez. I liked the peacefulness and centeredness of being out in the middle of nowhere, but as we approached Bahia Santa Maria on the west coast of Baja, a strong urge to be at anchor and futz around for Christmas came over me.

"But we just got some wind!" Robb argued, "You never know when there'll be any more!"

"There will always be more wind," I said.

Exercising my authority as Commander in Chief, I insisted we go in for Christmas to a spot we knew and had enjoyed on the first trip. Once the decision had been made, Robb, as always, embraced the project. The beach, a sand-dollar heaven, was firm enough for Alex to ride the collapsible stainless-steel bike he'd gotten for his birthday.

Robb and the kids got busy making red and green construction paper chains for the main cabin, while I put up decorations we'd brought along. A 4-inch-wide red ribbon wound around the below-decks part of the white mast created a giant candy cane. Along with other ornaments, small white sand dollars dangled by red ribbons on our plump little fake tree. After that first Christmas, we kept an eye out in various countries for items to serve as ornaments.

When I suggested we invite people over for hot spiced cider on Christmas Eve, Robb sighed, "If only *Marco Polo* were here." Robin, Pauline, and Simon had taken off about the same time we did. Since we hadn't been in contact, it seemed like a long shot. Yet no sooner had Robb uttered the wish, than in they came – excuse enough to throw a bigger party, a Christmas Eve potluck.

The kids and I cut snowflakes out of white tissue paper, glued them onto red construction paper invitations, and delivered them by dinghy. Of the dozen boats in the anchorage, *Casteele, Destiny, Frolic, Gold Eagle,*

Golly Gee, Marco Polo, Susitna, and *Vagant* all came over. When we invited the older German couple on *Vagant,* at first they declined, insisting they always spent Christmas alone. We found, though, when our children asked for something, people had difficulty resisting. So Ussel and Friedel came after all, and regaled us with stories of their two trips sailing around the world. When asked how they managed without any way to get weather forecasts, Ussel grinned, licked his index finger and held it up, as if to test the wind.

Robin played his guitar, a welcome accompaniment to our singing. Both he and Pauline had exceptional voices, lifting our caroling to a higher standard. His sea shanty, the story of a rum boat that sank, became the children's favorite. "Again! Again!" they shouted. Robin carried on with the same gusto each round. Lively and cozy with 22 people, the evening turned into one of our happiest and most cherished Christmases. After nine days for our Christmas break and a quiet New Year's Eve, we headed for the Mexican mainland.

A Tragedy at Sea

"The temptation in recalling this trip is to make everything sound wonderful," Pauline had said to me over the holidays. "I'm going to write something about what it's really like: wearing the same clothes for two or three days during a rough sail, having cereal for dinner, that sort of thing."

Suddenly I remembered telling a friend on the radio, "Oh, yes, we had champagne and lobster for a candlelight dinner." Thanks, John and Eileen on *Serenity,* for the bubbly for our first landfall.

The whole story: Dinner was quite late, so everyone was a bit edgy. I'd forgotten the lobster preparing/eating process and had set three entire beasts on the table. Not only did we end up with innards everywhere, but they hadn't been cooked long enough. Meanwhile, the children were complaining they couldn't see anything with only candlelight, and, come to think of it, they didn't like lobster anyway.

Yes, we had bug bites and schoolwork, things that broke and things that spoiled, misplaced flashlights and misunderstandings, leaky hatches, night-long noises and stinky toilets. Here's Annie's list: leaving friends, sibling rivalries, bedtimes and nightmares, wetting beds (first trip), lice (later on), ripped sails, no wind, loud engine, cold showers, serious injuries, and hurricanes. There's more, and far, far worse.

Sometime in January, we heard that the U.S. Coast Guard, the Mexican Navy, and private boats were searching for Jan from *Golly Gee*, who'd fallen overboard. She and Don had spent Christmas Eve with us. A couple of months later Hal and Kay on *SpiceSea* told us they'd learned from Don that Jan had apparently been filming because the cord to the video camera was plugged in with the cord running forward, but no camera. Also, she had a balancing problem. We all knew accidents could happen to anyone, anytime. Although we didn't know her well, the loss left an eerie hole in the cruising community.

Whenever something horrible crept into our lives, we made an effort to remember the beauty in things. One morning as the sun rose, layers of intense fuchsia and gold on the horizon reflected in the calm water. On the opposite horizon the full moon created a shimmering silver path leading straight to our boat. As slow as our pace was, we kept scaling down. The entire Sea of Cortez slipped from our plan. Instead, we thought before heading back to Baja and home, we'd spend mid-February to mid-April between Manzanillo and Mazatlán on the mainland.

Mexican Mainland

Along 500 miles of coastline, we slowly worked our way through a slew of pleasant anchorages. The following accounts are somewhat out of order. I do know we first headed to Chamela, where we hoped to meet up with *Aquila* before she got south of us on her way to the Panama Canal. She didn't show up until another anchorage. But we happily spent our time eating seafood at a palapa on the beach, counting sea stars on the bottom of the 15 feet of clear blue water under the boat, and watching the children swim from boat to beach, and back again.

When there's as much surf as there was in Chamela, launching a dinghy from shore can be tricky. We had to watch the wave sets, then push off when we figured we could get out past where the waves are breaking before starting the outboard. Once, when the motor wouldn't start, a wave caught the nose of the dinghy and pushed it up and over, completely upside down. Everything went in the water: the four us, three bags of groceries, and stacks of clean and folded clothes we'd just picked up from the laundry. As soon as we knew everyone was okay, we righted the dinghy. Robb started the motor and took off, pushing it full throttle to flush out the saltwater. With help from a number of local people, the kids and I retrieved virtually all of our flotsam, some of which had already washed ashore.

Once back on the boat, we ran the clothes through our portable clothes wringer – the kind you see atop an old-fashioned washing machine – gave them a little freshwater rinse, and wrung them out again. Groceries in cans or well-sealed packages were salvaged. But other items, like the precious bags of potato chips were not watertight, and so a total loss. At first, figuring the extra salt wouldn't hurt, I spread the chips out on deck to dry. But the dried chips lost their satisfying crunch and tasted of the sea.

***

At the end of February, we spent three nights at Ensenada Carrizal, a small cove close to Manzanillo. *SpiceSea* came in, as well as *Bag End*, who had a parcel for us. When we cruised Mexico, my mom picked up our mail and dropped it in the Baja Express box at Downwind Marine in San Diego. That packet of letters bounced from boat to boat in our general direction until it reached us.

The kids seemed especially content there. When they weren't glued to Game Boy, they rigged and played in the hammock on the foredeck. Every day at sundown, 20 or so flapjack-sized manta rays made a great show of jumping and spinning out of the water before splashing down. The other day Annie said, "Experiences like that made the wonder of SeaWorld lose its luster forever."

***

Alex wrote a play based on actual events. *Puffy's Worst Day* concerned a puffer fish being fought over by two frigate birds before being dropped on our boat. We performed the play on deck with the kids speaking the parts of the birds, me as Puffy, Robb as the captain.

One day the kids played so well together that I let them create a fruit pizza with bananas, pears, canned mandarins, pecans and shredded coconut. Giving up control was a stretch for me, but the result looked terrific, and, more importantly, they had a blast doing it. Our fresh produce and other supplies were getting low, but with the perfect weather, none of us had any ambition to move on. One afternoon, in a satisfying exchange on both sides, three elderly fishermen in a long, old panga traded a freshly-caught Pacific sierra for a quart of motor oil.

Alex spends a morning fishin'

Since we first started traveling in Mexico, Annie had begged to have her ears pierced so locals would stop thinking she was a boy. Most Mexican females have their ears pierced when they're babies. To compound the confusion, Annie had short hair and mostly wore shorts and T-shirts.

"I've pierced a lot of girls' ears," Philomena told us. Phil owned Los Pelicanos, a palapa on the beach in the village of Melaque. As she instructed, we bought a pair of little gold starter-earrings at the *farmacia*. While the earrings soaked in a shot glass of tequila, Phil washed her hands, poured a little of the strong liquor over them, and rubbed Annie's earlobes with a tequila-soaked cotton ball. Without further ado, she jabbed the posts through the flesh. Nothing to it, though I fortified myself with a Bloody Mary. Phil told Annie it was her responsibility to keep her ears clean until they healed. That evening, our patient asked, "May I have some tequila, please?" She became a little frantic when told we didn't have any, but ultimately she became convinced that rubbing alcohol would do just as well. Not many weeks passed before our six-year-old tired of the project, and the holes in her ears closed for the next four years.

***

Friends from Mission Bay Marina came into Melaque: Susan, Drew and Elizabeth on *Alcatraz* and Carrie, Trevor and their two small children on *Aquila*. At Philomena's cruiser-friendly place, the adults could sit in the shade with a cool drink and keep an eye on the kids entertaining themselves in the sand and water. We three boats spent the next couple of weeks in the same anchorages.

Tenacatita was a super stop. Our very first stalk of bananas, kind of a cruiser's badge, hung from the spreaders. Besides *Alcatraz* and *Aquila,* the boats *Nautical Wheeler, Alia* and *Felicity* also had children. The troop of nine ranged in ages from three to thirteen. Annie noted in her journal, "This was an exciting day. Our best friends came to Tenacatita. It was fun."

Of the five days we spent there, at least one was devoted to a day-long picnic on the beach. We drilled ourselves and the children on how to avoid getting stung by the many stingrays in the shallow water: Always wear water shoes and shuffle your feet so the rays have time to scatter. Sadly, a couple of local fisherman got a kick out of torturing the animals by poking them with their own barbs. No one got stung except the unfortunate rays themselves.

Thames from *Nautical Wheeler* and I had noticed women doing their laundry in the nearby creek. One morning we settled our jugs of laundry soap and bleach, metal wringer, and bags of soiled clothing on rocks and a fallen tree in the knee-deep, slow-moving water. The experiment was fun, but not something we'd choose to repeat. At the time the thought didn't cross my mind, but wearing our swimsuits may have offended the fully-clothed Mexican ladies doing their washing a little way upstream. I wish we'd been more respectful of the culture.

***

Ordinarily, we didn't favor anchoring at resorts. However, dinghy docks, free water, and other amenities at the sprawling Las Hades hotel in Manzanillo called to us. All the kids had a rollicking good time in the various pools and feeding hibiscus flowers to the resident iguanas. I liked sitting on an outdoor patio, sipping a glass of wine, and listening to the mingling sounds of a guitar, bass fiddle, and water gurgling in a stone fountain.

One day we'd arranged a babysitting exchange with Trevor and Carrie. Robb and I began our date in swimsuits at the hotel's bar in the wading pool. Margaritas tasting like lemonade arrived at a steady pace in Styrofoam cups. *How strong could they be?* I woke up that evening back at the boat, but under a blanket in the dinghy. Just then Robb appeared to check on me. "Here, let me help you," he said coming down into the dingy. "I left you here because I was afraid I couldn't get you up into the boat."

Too soon, *Alcatraz* sailed off toward the Panama Canal. In a few days *Aquila* followed. There's something special and pleasing about spending time with people you like, and with whom you've gone through all those months, even years, of preparations: readying the boats, provisioning, seminars, ham radio licenses, first-aid classes, and an endless exchange of questions, tips, and information.

After our friends left, a flicker of discontent and restlessness passed through me. I missed consistent female companionship. I adored my husband, yet sometimes we were a bit at odds over parenting and other matters. Cooking failures became more frequent, though Alex, bless his heart, cheerfully ate almost everything. Robb reassured me he hadn't married me for my cooking or housekeeping skills. Nevertheless, I started putting more effort into our meals.

By the next anchorage, the Tres Marietas islands, I was back in cruising mode. Those islands are not to be confused with nearby Tres Marias, a penal colony, 62 miles off shore. Whales, dolphins, booby birds, and manta rays bigger than our dinghy captivated us. At Punta de Mita, as I snorkeled toward a manta with its 10-foot-wide mouth fully open, I prayed that it was true the animal preferred tiny organisms. We played chicken, the manta turning first. Mental note: Buy an underwater camera.

The explorers

Back at Chacala, the kids and I bought shrimp from a shrimp boat. At San Blas, mosquitos and no-see-ums, those nasty little biting gnats, didn't seem to notice the numerous insect coils burning in our boat's cabin. When we couldn't stand the smoke and the insects any longer, we reanchored farther out from shore, and close to *Kaselehlia* and *Galadriel*, both of whom came over for beer and chips.

Known as the Mexican Galapagos, tiny Isla Isabel is an uninhabited island full of wildlife, particularly seabirds. A local guide, Victor, walked us within touching distance of blue-footed boobies, their nests and chicks. One bright morning after an early walk, the idea of a champagne brunch, with sparkling cider for the kids, came to mind. My cobalt-blue Rose Marie Reid swimsuit and jewel-tone Club Med pareo tied around my waist made me feel glamorous. As we sat in the cockpit enjoying our fancy repast, *Kaselehlia* hummed into the anchorage, and came over to say hello. In keeping with the tone of the occasion, Kase showed up in a tuxedo T-shirt and shorts. Linda sported an off-the-shoulder black top and rolled up khakis.

⚓

At two o'clock one morning, we left for Mazatlán, our last and northernmost stop on the mainland. After sunrise, Robb called to me, "Dianne! Can you come up here? I don't understand what these fishermen want. Sounds like they're asking for pizza."

Sorcery had been doing a comfortable six knots when a Mexican fishing panga pulled up alongside and handed Robb their bow line. Three men gestured as if cutting or squeezing something, all the while shouting, "*Pinzas! Pinzas!*"

Finally, I guessed they were saying "pinchers" and needed pliers. When Robb handed them a pair, the men beamed, and one of them immediately set about fixing their motor. Since we had a spare or two and could buy more, we gave them the *pinzas.*

During our five-day stop in Mazatlán, we spent a little time with friends on *Felicity* and *Bag End*, but mostly we did city things: a trip to the Port Captain, riding the bus, lunching at the Arts and Crafts Center, shopping and provisioning, and buying a used horseshoe for good luck. Since it had performed so well all those years of cruising, later we nailed it over the back door of our house, where it's still working its magic. As we descended from a tour of the city's famous El Faro lighthouse, like a scene from an old western, the keeper's wife called after us, "*Vaya con Dios!*"

Back to Baja

The hurricane season would start in mid-June, and we needed to be back in San Diego before then. So at 5 a.m. on April 6, we set out for Baja. At noon, to celebrate our 2,000th mile on *Sorcery,* we broke open a bottle of champagne. One night at sea brought us to the Baja coast at Los Frailes.

For a couple of days, we relaxed, snorkeling, beachcombing, and fishing. Then we headed up to Los Muertos where we shared an evening campfire and potluck with *Kaselehlia, SpiceSea,* and a full moon. Kay always added a touch of class to our potlucks. She'd owned and operated San Diego's School of International Cuisine for 20 years before she and Hal began cruising. That particular time she brought Chinese dim sum packed in round, stacked bamboo boxes. At another potluck she said she'd bring stuffed grape leaves, so I made a yummy Greek *pastitsio,* using a can of our ground beef.

My moment of cooking fame came when my recipe for papaya chutney appeared in Kay's fine cookbook, *Cruising Cuisine.* The recipe called for seven or eight items over my usual ingredient limit; but the resulting six cups of chutney didn't disappear within half an hour of being prepared. Note at the end of the recipe, "Keeps without refrigeration for several months." Something only a cruiser would appreciate, or probably even try.

Back to the potluck. Building a fire on the beach almost always meant having "shoosh." We heard, and chose to believe, that Civil War soldiers made this staple in the field. They rolled bread dough into long thin snakes, curled them around rifle barrels, then held the barrels over a fire for a minute or so until the bread lightly browned. In our version, sturdy sticks substituted nicely for rifles.

***

Finally, we stayed a week at the marina in La Paz to get ready for the run back to San Diego. Lounging on the patio outside the marina office, we chatted with other cruisers. "I have a new wife, but the same old boat," bragged a man we'd met on our first trip.

Without realizing how his play on words would come out, Robb said, "Well, I have a new boat, but the same old wife!" Silence reigned as everyone's wide eyes turned to me. But I appreciated the innocent boast, and couldn't help but smile and roll my eyes.

Before leaving La Paz, we bought *Frolic's* windsurfer, a terrific purchase, especially for Alex. Alan from *Carioca III* graciously drove us around in his rental car for last-minute chores and provisioning, including, according to an old note, "batteries, antibiotics, two-cycle oil, fresh orange juice."

Except for Cabo San Lucas at the tip of Baja, and Turtle Bay, halfway home, none of the 16 stops ahead would offer much in the way of provisions, fuel, or water. We did find when supplies grew low, bringing the children with us prompted people in even the smallest outposts to remember where we might be able to get a gallon or two of water, a jug of diesel, or a chicken. In one such village, a local led us to the house that sold chickens. The proprietress pulled a package from her refrigerator. When I asked if she had another one, she nodded and stepped out the back door.

Squawk! Squawk! After several quiet minutes, she reappeared with another headless, featherless, newspaper-wrapped bird.

***

Leaving La Paz in mid-April, before starting back up Baja's dreaded west coast, we lingered as long as we dared at the familiar and spectacular beaches of Pichilinque, Los Muertos, Buena Vista, Los Frailes, and Cabo San Lucas. The morning we left Buena Vista, Robb fixed pancakes while Alex and I weighed anchor and motored out. Those lazy days saw us with *Lena, Alia,* and *Winsome* – hiking, snorkeling and having potlucks with fish prepared all kinds of ways. Sometimes people came over for popcorn and a movie. Boat work never let up for Robb. When he wasn't cleaning the bottom, he had projects like tightening up the U-shaped rail at the bow of the boat. His skill and tireless dedication to our safety can't be overstated.

Up the Baja West Coast

The nearly 1,000 miles between the tip of Baja and San Diego consumed the entire month of May. Two days and nights out of Cabo, we pulled in to Bahia Magdalena. Apparently, the trip had been rough, because we had champagne with our *huevos rancheros* for breakfast, and I slept until three in the afternoon. Robb napped before going over to *SeaRider* to help with her engine problem. At Bahia Santa Maria *Winsome* was able to pull up alongside to get some diesel, but bouncy seas prevented *Lena* from rowing over later to join us for a dinner of fresh bonito.

Stopping for a day or two, sometimes four or five, we traveled to nine more anchorages where we often met up with *Mithril, Companion, Gambit,* and other boats we knew, or got to know. After one night at Hippolito, we took a three-day break at Punta Abreojos, which means "open your eyes," and refers to the treacherous sailing conditions, and many rocks and reefs. Sometime in the 1970s, *Sorcery* herself had run aground there as she trained for races in the Pacific.

The second day at Abreojos Mike from *Mithril* and Robb made a rough, wet dash in our dinghy to the tiny village to see what they could find in the way of fresh food. By the time they returned, a package of hot dogs, four apples, and six limes had escaped the shopping bag and rolled around the wet floor of the dinghy, but were only a little worse for wear.

At the next stop, Asunción, a bunch of us sat along the curb of a dirt road savoring the best, and maybe biggest, raised doughnuts any of us had ever eaten. The delicacies had been cooked in oil heated in a metal barrel over a wood fire. We toured a small, primitive workshop that punched half-inch holes out of thick quahog clamshells. The resulting plugs traveled to Japan to be sliced thin and turned into buttons, many of which probably found their way back to the West.

After one night in Thurloe Bay, we rested for five in Turtle Bay. The first couple of nights we slept 10 hours. To get to shore, we tied the dinghy to a rickety old pier, and climbed a 20-foot metal ladder, secured vertically to the pilings with lengths of frayed rope.

The town was fun because we often ate up the hill at the Aqua Verde restaurant with sometimes as many as a dozen folks from other boats. Besides the good and inexpensive food, the young waitress impressed us by not writing anything down and never making a mistake in the order or who it was for. While Robb worked on *Sorcery's* plumbing, the kids and I made water runs, schlepping our jugs to and from the town's reverse osmosis plant.

From Turtle Bay, we headed for the San Benito Islands, but slow motoring convinced us to go in at Cedros Island for three days instead. At the next stop, Bahia San Carlos, our calendar entry proclaimed, "Slept all night!!!" Sea conditions, however, prevented us from going ashore, breaking our habit of hitting the beach soon after we anchored.

Sorcery had a flush deck and no windows in the hull, so from inside the cabin, the only openings were overhead. Our usually cozy cabin had become permeated with dampness from a big wave we'd taken through the small open hatch in the galley. And, in spite of the waterproof foul-weather gear we wore on deck, our clothes managed to become clammy.

Then, a small miracle: A warm and welcome wind, not technically a Santa Ana, blew off the plateaus, dried out the boat, and invited us to stay four more days. After San Carlos we stopped a single night at dreary overcast Isla San Jeronimo, before going on to beautiful, but rolly and noisy, San Quintin for one night.

Good Samaritans

Shortly after leaving San Quintin, we spotted a sailboat just rocking in the water. The boat, which will remain unnamed, responded to our radio call, telling us their engine had caught fire and the mainsail had ripped. The captain, with a young Mexican man he'd picked up in Acapulco for crew, dinghied over to borrow a screwdriver and a hacksaw. The captain was dressed in jeans and a warm jacket against the chill, but the young man shivered in shorts and a T-shirt.

We invited the two men for dinner and outfitted the younger one as best we could. Robb suggested we tow the boat the 15 miles or so to the next anchorage, Punta Colnett. He rigged a 100-foot tow rope connected to a "Y" shaped rope-bridle off *Sorcery*'s stern to attach to the disabled boat's bow.

Once at Colnett, an 80-foot motorsailer, which Robb had contacted, towed the boat to San Diego. From Colnett the kids and I would have liked to go into Ensenada, but Robb was frazzled and wanted to head for the barn. We motored most of the night, and arrived at the San Diego Police Dock on the morning of May 27.

The boat we'd towed was at the fuel dock. Since the captain hadn't returned or mentioned the tools or spare electric fuel pump he'd borrowed, Annie and I marched over to the boat to get them. The owner wasn't there, but the young crewman returned our things, and mentioned he hadn't gotten paid.

Let the record show that most cruisers are honorable and far more prepared.

Third Trip
The Sea of Cortez
January 1992 to April 1993
Alex was twelve, Annie eight

I N the year and a half after we returned from our second trip, we made plans to spend time in the Sea of Cortez, between Baja and the Mexican mainland, before heading to the South Pacific.

Before we left, many friends gave us delightful and useful gifts, treated us to dinners, including two or three at kid friendly Luigi's pizzeria near the Mission Beach roller coaster. Meals prepared by someone else were especially welcome those last days before a voyage, when cooking took too much time away from getting ready.

Riding on a wave of good feelings, at 3 a.m. on January 20, 1992, we motored out of Mission Bay for the last time. As Robb had calculated, by leaving in the wee hours we arrived in the late afternoon at Baja Naval boatyard in Ensenada, about 70 miles south of San Diego, for a scheduled haul out.

By the end of week two, he feared we'd be there forever, and started second-guessing himself on some of the work he'd planned. Throughout the time he focused on the boat, I kept all the other systems going: shopping, meals, laundry, emptying the bucket we used for a toilet at night, managing the trash, overseeing schoolwork, and keeping the children occupied. A clean and fresh-smelling public bathhouse close by afforded us long, hot showers.

One field trip, to the Santo Tomas Winery, was only a short walk from the boatyard. Our kids peppered the tour guide with questions, while the rest of the small group nodded and listened, perhaps waiting patiently for the wine tasting. Here's an eight-year-old's report on the excursion:

Were on our way to the winery! Finily got to the winery. It was a DREAM it was huge. I mean there was vats 25 feet high at least. And one was emtey. I look inside it was magnifisent. We had a nice guied!

Nearly every afternoon at 4, our family gathered for tea. A blue and white tablecloth I'd gotten years ago in Egypt graced a weathered folding table in the cockpit. Pretty hand-painted cups, gifts from *Alcatraz*, the blue teapot from *Marco Polo,* and a plate of goodies completed the tableau. If I hadn't made cookies, we'd have a treat from what Robb liked to call "The Used Food Store." The Canned Foods Outlet in Chula Vista sold discounted overstock and close-out products with name brands and private labels.

I'd bought dozens of items with long shelf life, perfect for cruising. For example, small, foil-wrapped loaf cakes lasted well – lovely for our afternoon teas. Today, our spice cabinet still harbors a small jar with whole nutmegs and a miniature grater from that outlet. Seeing and using the little kit reminds us of those glorious times we snorkeled, and savored butterscotch punch afterwards. Of course, the original nutmegs disappeared years ago in that warm milk drink and in anything else calling for the spice.

***

During the haul out, school requirements for each pupil consisted of writing an hour a day plus an hour of reading. Toward the end of the second week, Alex announced he was bored and asked to do some math. That prompted Annie, who always wanted to do whatever her big brother did, to ask, "Will you teach me math too?" Fortunately, we had grade-appropriate math workbooks for both of them. Right away it was clear that basic arithmetic calculations were slowing both students down. The time had come to bring out the big guns: flash cards. Using a stopwatch to keep track of their personal best times turned the exercise into a fun game, and both kids saw rapid improvement. Getting extra points once a week for beating their personal best times had the unexpected result of our children working as a team; they encouraged and drilled each other to help one another earn the bonus points.

While the yard prepped the hull for painting, Robb took *Sorcery's* shaft and propeller to Pacific Marine Propellers in San Diego to have the shaft cleaned and the pitch changed on the propeller. On the return trip, he picked up our car at the marina and drove it down to Baja Naval.

⚓

Annie had developed a minor medical issue, and, since our Kaiser health insurance would expire in three days, I decided to drive her to San Diego. On a deserted road before we reached the outskirts of Tijuana, the car broke down. I don't remember feeling afraid, but as a way of soothing us both, my daughter leaned against me while I brushed her hair.

When an old pickup truck pulled up behind us, my heart raced a little. A young woman came up to the window and asked if we needed help. Her husband was a mechanic and could have a look. He determined the timing belt was shot, and the car would have to be towed to his workshop. He asked for a $100 deposit for the tow and replacement parts. No reasonable option came to mind, and, besides, he struck me as trustworthy. The two of us rode with him, his wife and their little daughter into the back streets of the unfamiliar city.

Garage Margaro looked a bit like a junkyard; but the operation had a tiny office where Margaro let me call the doctor from his cell phone – the first time I'd ever used one. When he dropped us off at the border, he handed me a business card and said the car would be ready in three days.

Crossing on foot to the States, we jumped on a trolley into San Diego; then a taxi sped us to the doctor where my mom picked us up. The boatyard got Robb on the phone for me. Now he claims he trusted my instinct, though more than one naysayer predicted:

"You'll never see that car again."

Two days later the car was ready. Relatives Everett and Viola, visiting my mother, offered to drive us to Tijuana. As I thanked and paid Margaro, he asked if I could help him and his family get to the States. Saying no felt embarrassing and selfish, even as I explained we were leaving for a long trip with an unknown ending. Otherwise, I hope I'd have tried to do something for those good people. My family followed me in my car to Ensenada for a farewell lunch. Robb declared the car had never driven better.

In early February, the four of us made a trip to San Diego to leave the car to be sold. Ever cheerful and generous, friends Susan and Drew drove us back down to Ensenada, one of the countless ways they helped us. As cruisers, they knew all too well the complications and effort involved in getting ready.

The boat went back in the water – "splashed" as boaters say – on February 11, but we stayed on another week to double check all systems and equipment, and to stow everything securely. Besides, along with eight other boats, we were waiting for a good weather window. Robb made a run to San Diego with Miguel, the manager of Baja Naval, in his truck to pick up some last-minute items. Finally, we were on our way.

Thirteen miles out from Ensenada we passed through floating kelp paddies near Todos Santos Island, where thousands of kelp flies swarmed our deck. Armed with flyswatters, the kids went a little crazy swatting with wild abandon until their dad noticed the squashed flies were drying and sticking to the deck. He advised that a light tap was all you needed to kill them. Though half the fun had been taken away, the kids kept up the killing spree until every last trespasser was dead or gone. As usual, Mom was head of the cleanup squad.

From that battle sprang one of the whole family's best homework assignments: The Kelp Fly Project. Using our 3½-inch-thick New Columbia Encyclopedia, our equally large Webster's Unabridged Dictionary of the English Language, a children's dictionary, *Fun Facts about Creatures*, and a National Geographic, each student wrote an essay and drew a labeled, anatomically correct depiction of a fly. Did you know flies have two little stabilizing knobs on their bodies, one behind each wing? We learned that flies belong to the order *Diptera*, especially of the family *Muscidae*, which led to investigating the animal classification system.

Along the way, I wrote:
High spot: night watch, lying in cockpit listening to
Telemann's *Water Music* while looking up at the full moon

made larger by a giant hazy corona. I like night watches for the quietness, and for the beauty of the water and sky. Also, it's an opportunity to do special projects, like breakfast treats that take a little extra time.

Even Running Aground Can Be an Adventure

Hoping to find some mother gray whales and their babies, and needing to rest my back, which went out of whack periodically, we spent a week or so exploring the San Carlos Channel in Magdalena Bay. One day Robb had in his mind the tide was coming in, when actually the water was on its way out. Annie later recalled the episode like this:

> Our boat ran aground. A powerboat, passing by in deep water not 50 feet away, called on the VHF radio, "Are you okay? Do you need any help?" With the boat dramatically heeled over, the 8½-foot keel stubbornly in the sand, my dad channeled his inner Han Solo: "No, no problem. Why?"
>
> In that second, our whole mindset changed. Despite the powerlessness of the situation, we weren't in any inherent danger. We simply needed to wait for the tide to rise and release us. My mom looked at the boat, then at us kids, and then at the stretch of terrain now above water, before smiling and telling my brother and me to put on our shoes. We stepped off the boat into the mud, and spent the next couple of hours exploring the tide pools. We brought back shells, pictures and happy memories that became part of the unexpected adventures of cruising.

While the captain remained with the ship, the kids and I explored the intriguing sea life exposed on the mudflats: a jelly-pickle, a string of broken bits of shells, a necklace of egg clusters, live sea stars buried just under the mud, sea stars walking on hard sand, murexes eating clams, smooth collars of moon-snail egg cases, large live sand dollars, a clam sticking out its red tongue. I took photos of carefully arranged rocks around several inch-wide holes about 8 inches deep.

The captain stays with the ship

Weeks later, when we made yet another run back to San Diego, this time on a bus, I showed the slides of the mysterious holes with the rocks to a friend who knew Dr. Richard Brusca, curator and chairman of the Department of Marine Invertebrates at the San Diego Museum of Natural History. He hypothesized that the hole was made and the rocks placed by either an octopus or some kind of fish. "May I send your slides to my colleague at the University of Mexico?" The same answer came back: either an octopus or a fish.

When Dr. Brusca learned we were going to the South Pacific, he asked if we'd be willing to collect isopods from the Marquesas. If we discovered a new species, it would be named after me. Say no more. He supplied me with instructions and several heavy-duty watertight collection bags. I couldn't wait for us to get started on a real science project.

After the grounding, the refrigeration quit, requiring us to drink the opened milk and cook up some of the food, much ending up in a big soup. Robb rigged a little hammock for the fresh produce. The typhoid vaccine needed to be kept cold, so had to be trashed. No, we weren't going to give each other shots. If we'd heard there was a typhoid outbreak where we were going, we'd have taken the vaccine, along with our own disposable needles, to a local clinic.

***

By our third trip, the anchorages had become quite familiar, which, of course, presented opportunities for disappointment. In the four years since we first came to Baja, Los Frailes and Los Muertos, in particular, weren't the isolated, untouched places we'd known.

Digging for clams for dinner

What sounded like "Gumby" trying to reach us on the staticky radio turned out to be *Drumbeat* with good friends Dennis and his wife, Drew, from Mission Bay Marina. We met up at Los Muertos for the inevitable potluck: fish caught and brought by a friend of theirs, tortillas created by my young sous chefs, and Spanish Rice made by yours truly in our pressure cooker.

The cooker had become central to meal preparation. Using it had the dual advantage of taking less time and, therefore, less propane. Nearly every day the cooker saw rice pudding or some other rice dish, soup or a stew, vegetables, chicken, occasionally bread, who-knows-what-all.

One day at anchor in La Paz I'd used the pot to make spaghetti. After lunch, as the last bits got dumped over the side for the fish, the handle remained in my hand, but no pot. It had plunged 30 feet to the bottom. Robb immediately dropped a plumb line from the spot where I'd been standing, dove down, and recovered the pot as it tumbled along with the current. In his box of spares, he found a replacement screw for the one that had corroded away.

Drew and Dennis on *Drumbeat's* dinghy

Our Word of Honor

Our decision to go to the South Pacific was as firm as cruising decisions can be, yet we were in no hurry to leave the pleasurable cruising grounds of Mexico. At the end of our entire trip, after we'd been to scores of places around the world, we would list Mexico as one of our top favorites.

Occasionally, too much wind did come our way, but overall, sailing in Mexico was nice, even for me. There was no anchorage that didn't have its charm, and frequently we had them all to ourselves. Staying in an unnamed anchorage a day or two seduced us into feeling like explorers. We found the prices low, the rugged desert countryside spectacular, the fishing good, and the locals friendly. On our first trip to Baja in 1988, in the days before ATMs were common in Mexico, we needed to cash a check for $100. We weren't having any luck until the owner of one small shop asked for identification, followed by many questions, ending with,

"Do you give me your word of honor?

Our Log from the Sea of Cortez

On that third trip, spending time with friends old and new filled the days as we explored the magnificent Gulf of California. *The Log from the Sea of Cortez*, a worn copy of John Steinbeck's fascinating account of his trip in 1940, made its way from boat to boat. My journal noted, "Lots of good books from book exchanges. Too many. Reading and sleeping too much." Who knew reading and sleeping would become a complaint?

For a time on Mondays, Robb was net control of the Mañana Cruisers' Net in La Paz. We skipped around near that city, making forays a few miles north to Isla Espiritu Santo, Isla Partida, and dinghy trips to nearby El Mogote, a deserted sandbar sticking into La Paz Bay. One morning at 6, Robb dropped off Marie from *Samatas*, Annie, me, and a VHF radio on the far side of Mogote to look for nautilus shells. Two hours later, I started trying to call Robb, but could never get through. Around noon, after we'd been gone six hours and he hadn't heard from us, he surfaced from the project he'd been dealing with and came to see what was going on.

Apparently, because of a small hill, the two radios couldn't make contact. Apart from a treasured photo of Annie and me wearing matching white hats and sitting close to each other looking out across the water, a single piece of nautilus shell was the only evidence of our adventure. Years later, at Ashmore Reef off Australia, we finally got a whole nautilus shell when two Timor fishermen rowed up to our boat with one for trade.

***

Our friend Robin from *Marco Polo* arrived on a boat he was delivering. His crew, Minnie, and Shelly and Rick from *Dolce Vida*, all friends of ours from Mission Bay, joined us for a potluck and a swim at the Palmira end of Mogote. After the crew flew home, Robin stayed with us for a week. He'd brought music, loads of food, and T-shirts for the kids. We all enjoyed his company; the kids said they didn't feel as lonely with Robin around. Always positive, full of information, and ready for adventure, he delivered high praise,

"You're the most together cruisers I know."

One of the highlights of the journey, and maybe my life, occurred when our friend Gabrielle from Downwind Marine came to stay with us for a few days. She and I idolized the old folk songs, particularly those sung by Joan Baez, with whom Gabrielle had worked in New York City. I supplied the words to the songs I knew by heart and a dozen chords on the guitar. My friend's marvelous throaty voice brought out the best in mine, and together we harmonized the unforgettable evening away. Remembering Gabrielle's long, silver hair gleaming in the kerosene lamplight and listening to the singing, Annie said recently, "For once I didn't feel worried or preoccupied with the 'What next?' of our trip, but was happy in a way you can't pretend to be."

⚓

Late one spring afternoon at Punta Bonanza on Espirtu Santo Island, the rain came: great black clouds, and thunder. Cozy on the boat, while listening to tiny fists of rain pummeling the deck, we read, played dominos, and made hot chocolate and popcorn. To take the chill off the cabin, we created a little heater by turning a big red-clay flowerpot upside down over a lit burner on the stove.

On a sunny day, Dennis, Drew, and Mission Bay friend Chris on *Blue Serenity* met up with us there. The island was breathtaking, really. Tall cactus- and boulder-covered hills led down to blinding white sand beaches. The water color eased from bright aqua to deep blue. In the distance, purple mountains topped with banks of fluffy clouds sat beneath a perfectly blue sky. Just this year, Drew and I discovered that when we each meditate and imagine ourselves in the most beautiful, peaceful place we know, we both envision Punta Bonanza.

At calm and pretty Los Islotes, little islets, near Isla Partida, our dinghy puttered through natural arches, and drifted while we snorkeled among huge boulders, sea-fan corals, sea stars, and needle and scorpion fish. Back on *Sorcery*, I prepared our traditional after snorkeling drink, butterscotch punch, by melting butter in the pressure cooker, stirring in brown sugar, then slowly adding milk and a little vanilla. The brew was served warm with a sprinkling of nutmeg, and sometimes with a splash of rum or brandy for the adults. After we were dry and warm, we hiked up to where we could see our dinghy at anchor in shallow water over a great expanse of pebbly shore. On the transparent water, the little boat appeared to float in the air. We often thought many people would love a chance to spend even one day the way we did almost all the time.

We'd been tied up at Marina de La Paz for a spell, but left to anchor out in the bay. When we dropped the hook, the chain kept running out. Something going wrong always alarmed me – that very close sense of trouble, if not danger. "We aren't in any danger," Robb said. "A pin's come loose, but the end of the chain's tied with rope to the boat down below."

That evening, we lounged with Chris on shore at a palapa. When we went back to the boats, we were shocked to find *Blue Serenity* had drug anchor and was bouncing against *Sorcery*. Rudy on nearby *Cirrus* had seen this happening, brought over his own fenders, and spent two hours protecting our boats. He declined an offer for dinner, so I took him a plate of cookies. The kindness and selflessness of cruisers never ceased to impress us.

Before coffee the next morning, Dennis and Drew surprised us with a visit; we had no idea they were in La Paz. They invited us for a potluck on their boat before Drew flew back to the States. While she was gone, *Drumbeat* and *Sorcery* motored to our favorite spot, Punta Bonanza. A southerly came up and slopped us about, causing the wind vane attached to the stern to punch a hole in the dinghy – another repair job for the captain. Chris came over too and the men and kids spent lots of time collecting heaps of oysters and scallops which the men transformed into pan-fried shellfish and spicy ceviche.

When Drew came back, we met up in Puerto Escondido for a potluck with her and Dennis and *Tenacity*. Up and down Baja's east coast we went on photo safaris, ate out, snorkeled, and had potlucks with *Drumbeat*. After exploring the ghost town of Salinas, we spent a mellow evening. Encouraged by a little wine, I played my guitar and sang. The next day, they came over to say goodbye, then stayed for tuna salad sandwiches, and Drew trimmed my hair. Although we knew them from the marina, cruising together is what solidified a friendship which has lasted to this day.

***

Tenacity told us they'd heard whale bones had washed up on the beach at Monserrate, a tiny island to the south. When we went to have a look, we swam from the boats to the steep shore since there was no place to land the dinghies. The bones were there, not enough for a whole whale, but plenty. I longed to take one for a souvenir, but even the smallest ones were colossal, and, worse, stinky. Furthermore, I believe taking them was against the law, even back then.

***

We'd met the *Unforgettable* family, Fernando, Jan, Nathaniel and Alisha, somewhere earlier, then ran into them again in Puerto Los Gatos, an anchorage with stunning pink, soft-sculpted sandstone cliffs. For a beach party, the men and boys left early to collect wood and burn trash. A reddish sunset gave way to our fire's reflection stretching way out into the water. A bright moon watched from above the velvety black hills. I'd brought my guitar along to accompany Jan with her fabulous bluesy voice. We'd once heard her sing in a Baja restaurant, so in spite of my positive experience with Gabrielle, I didn't attempt any singing myself.

In exchange for Alex's old dive suit for Nathaniel, they gave us diving gloves for Alex and a pound of French roast coffee. I wrote out some recipes Jan wanted. Fernando got money back for us from the port captain, who'd overcharged. Nathaniel built complex card castles reaching from our galley table to the ceiling of the unsteady boat. For two days he and Alex worked on a still-unfinished article for kids about cruising. Alisha taught Annie a short, hilarious comedy routine, which starts out, "Hi, my name is Chubbie." Having an entire family so congenial with the four of us was rare.

At the end of a very hot June, John Krase and his thirteen-year-old son, Miles, bringing masses of food and a 12-volt cooler, came down from San Diego to spend a few days. Right away, John, the rigger whom Robb had hired to inspect *Sorcery*'s rigging before we left, noticed a crack in one of the fittings for the lifelines. Not one to take chances, Robb ordered and replaced all the fittings and lifelines before our Pacific crossing. We hiked, took the dinghy exploring, snorkeled, made ceviche from pen-shell clams, and cooked up *chocolatas*, the clams with dark-brown shells that lived in the sand under our boat. Finally, the weather began to cool off. For me the heat, compounded by my hot flashes, had been debilitating.

At the town of Loreto, Karen, Jerry, and son Darren on *Felicity* had Baja Express mail for us and invited us to stay for dinner. They introduced us to Lynn on *Scout*, who gave readings on the morning net of her comically entertaining *True Stories of the Constellations*.

A few days later, in a pretty little bay, just north of Loreto at Isla Coronado, Robb and I celebrated our fifth anniversary and my fiftieth birthday. Alex fixed a couple of simple meals, and was very sweet, looking after me that day.

Hurricane Hole

Somewhat belatedly in the season, mid-July, we headed for the hurricane hole of Bahia San Carlos on the mainland. Although "everyone" said the bay was hurricane safe, we had misgivings the minute we pulled in. The narrow entrance and surrounding peaks, Tetas de Cabras, "goat tits," did offer impediments, but winds at the right angle could blast into the bay. The moorings were close together, and a number of boats didn't appear to be occupied or well-maintained. Nearby marinas, perhaps not any safer, were already full. Robb thought being there was our best available option, and we secured *Sorcery* to a mooring.

The next four or five days we prepped the boat to be left while we made a trip to San Diego. We needed to take Alex there so he could fly to Chicago and spend a few weeks with his mom. Dan and Pat from *This Side Up* dropped us off at the Guaymas bus station. Almost every hour an express bus to Tijuana came through, but each one was completely full. All night long we arranged ourselves as comfortably as possible with our backpacks on hard wooden benches, and ran out to try to be first in line whenever a bus pulled up.

In the morning, when the station master reported for work, he walked up to us. "What are you still doing here?"

"All the buses going to Tijuana were full, we couldn't get on."

"Of course not! To get to TJ from here, you have to take the local bus to Hermosillo, transfer to Mexicali, then another bus to Tijuana."

You couldn't have told us that yesterday?

The local bus, also full, was big and modern. After considerable pleading on our part, the driver agreed we could ride if we were willing to sit on the clean, carpeted floor. We climbed aboard. Soon I developed a violent migraine, and, at the first stop, threw up in a trash can in front of everyone. When we reboarded, a Mexican gentleman offered me his seat in the back.

From Mexicali to the Old Town station in San Diego we took a bus, a taxi, hoofed it across the border, got on a trolley that broke down, rode a bus, then another trolley. What should have been a 16-hour trip from Guaymas took, according to Alex's journal, "27 hours and 45 minutes with little or no sleep."

For a week we ran around visiting relatives and friends and taking care of business. Then on July 29, Alex left for Chicago. Two weeks later, Robb took a bus back down to the boat. A week after that, Annie and I followed, arriving August 22.

Hurricane Lester, August 23, 1992

Earlier in the day, the weather forecast had downgraded Lester to a tropical storm, and predicted it would travel up the east side of Baja. The National Hurricane Center then turned its attention to Hurricane Andrew in the Atlantic, and we focused on settling in. So when Lester regained strength, headed to the Mexican mainland, and roared into San Carlos Bay with gusts up to 85 mph, we were disappointed, but not truly surprised.

Once the wind started picking up, the three of us put on our wet suits to provide protection and flotation in case we had to swim the 100 feet to shore. The dinghy, already in the water, would be our first choice if we had to abandon ship. I held my daughter's eight-year-old hands. "Your job is to stay safe. Keep your harness on all the time, and when you come up on deck, clip onto the lifeline right away. Mostly you need to stay below."

"But I want to help," she pleaded, "and I don't wanna be by myself."

"Okay. You can stand in the companionway where you can see us. We'll hand you things to stow below, and you can fix something for us to eat and drink when we need it. That will be a huge help."

For the next 12 hours, we hardly sat down.

The previous week, Robb had dived to check the mooring chain, and inspected all 45 feet down to where it attached to a huge concrete block. That inspection became the first of many factors working in our favor. During the hurricane, one boat broke its rusty old mooring chain and wandered off.

Thanks to being on board, we were able to prepare our boat. To cut down on windage, we removed awnings, solar panels, windsurfer boards, the roller-furled sail, bagged sails, lee cloths from the lifelines – in short, anything that might attract the wind's attention. To absorb some of the shock as *Sorcery* jerked from side to side, we lowered a string of orange Frisbee-shaped plastic discs, called flopper stoppers, into the water near the bow.

Before the wind really got going, a trimaran with Dave, a single hander, started to drag anchor. Robb loaded our stern anchor with some chain and 120 feet of heavy line into the dinghy, and motored over to help. He wanted to hand the end of the line to Dave so he could secure it to his boat. But Dave insisted Robb drop the anchor first, then bring the line back. By the time Robb had done that, the tri had dragged 5 feet past where the line could reach.

"I knew that was going to happen!" Dave barked, as if it were Robb's fault.

With no time to argue, Robb shouted over the wind and ever-increasing distance, "Do you have any line? I can tie the two lines together!"

No, Dave didn't have any line. Just then a wave broke over the dinghy, half filling it with water. Leaving the anchor behind for the time being, Robb headed back to our boat. The tri eventually broke up on the beach with Dave aboard.

***

We were deep in the bay, and therefore downwind of a fleet of 40 or 50 moored vessels, all chafing at the bit, many of them breaking free. By mid-morning, a loose boat glided past about every 20 minutes. A few hardy souls stood on shore watching the disaster unfold, but nothing could be done to help until the wind died down.

As those witnesses later confirmed, Robb and I were always on deck – Robb checking, adjusting, and repairing the four mooring and anchor lines, and me as backup help, gofer, suggestion-maker, and lookout for seafaring missiles headed our way. The driving rain made eyeglasses useless. Robb hated to go below even for a minute, but I convinced him to go and put in his contact lenses.

Shortly after noon, a 32-foot runaway bobbed toward us. Its heavy wooden bowsprit, now a ramming rod, headed for our port spreader lines. Two feet of rusty chain dangled from the bow. Primitive warriors waiting for the enemy, we armed ourselves with a 6-foot-long boat hook and our two biggest fenders, and moved toward the anticipated point of impact.

As the invader came within reach, we pushed her along with the boat hook and our bare hands before it could get entangled with *Sorcery*'s rigging. As the boat bumped along our port side toward the stern, it damaged our overboard pole and life ring. Robb scrambled to get to the back of the boat, but wasn't fast enough to prevent the spar from crashing down on our stern pulpit. The blow torqued and stretched the heavy stainless steel rail into a U-shape. We felt lucky the rail survived at all.

In the early afternoon, three men in a Boston Whaler skiff pulled alongside and asked if we wanted help setting an anchor. By that time the wind was so strong, Robb felt having an anchor would be a prudent backup in case we broke free of the mooring. So, yes, please. The rough seas caused one of the men to lose his footing and fall in the water. The other two pulled him out, and the three dropped our 110-pound Bruce anchor with 200 feet of chain about 100 feet into the wind.

"The only thing we have to worry about now," Robb said, "is a boat dragging across our anchor chain." Within the half hour, a huge trimaran did that very thing. I put fenders where the boat was hitting us. After unsuccessfully trying to fend it off with our boat hook, Robb jumped from our bow onto the deck of the tri.

"Don't go!" I screamed. Once he'd made sure the trimaran would be clear of us, he clambered back up onto our deck.

By the end of the day, 17 vessels were on the beach, some destroyed beyond repair. Of the 17, seven sandwiched up in a shallow nook not 100 feet from us. Two of the seven slowly filled with water and sank before our eyes. A heartbreaking spectacle. By that time, exhaustion and our relief that the worst had passed drained us of further emotion.

***

The next morning dawned calm and bright with pelicans floating in the water. The eerie contrast to the day before seemed a perfect expression of the natural elements simply doing what they do, neither pleased nor saddened by the damage they wrought.

After Robb recovered the anchor he'd dropped the day before, he helped untangle the pileup in the nook. The last boat in, which had taken on water through a 16- by 4-inch hole in the transom, had to be the first out. Robb spread underwater epoxy on a piece of screen to cover the hole and slow the incoming water. Then, to the amusement of the looky-loos observing from shore, he immediately started bailing with a five-gallon bucket.

"That ain't gonna work!" one hollered.

But the boat slowly rose until the hole was above the waterline. At that point, a Mexican truck with gas-powered pumps pulled up as close to the boat as it could. As the truck pumped out most of the remaining water, the boat came up enough to be moved out of the way of the six other crippled vessels.

For the next 10 days we helped where we could, tried to get some insurance money for the damage to our boat, and put *Sorcery* back together for the trip across the Sea of Cortez. Our dear friend Robin on *Marco Polo* offered to come down from San Diego to help with repairs if we needed him. Having survived the ordeal with comparatively little damage, we were grateful for the experience because of what we learned, and for the good feeling that came with fighting and winning.

Lessons:

No. 1 – It's better not to be anywhere near a hurricane.

No. 2 – Be on the boat. We absolutely believe that's what prevented *Sorcery* from joining her sisters on the beach. Of the 17 that ended up there, only one had someone on board.

No. 3 – A boat's connection to the mooring chain needs to be made of chain. Sixteen of the 17 beached boats chafed through the rope lines connecting them to their mooring chains.

No. 4 – Have a boat hook with a pole longer than 6 feet.

No. 5 – Maintain a strong belief there's always something you can do.

Annie recalls the storm this way:

What an adventure! I stood in the aft companionway and remember the wind whipping my hair. I remember Mom being scared and thinking that was so unnecessary, and that I was happy to be a kid and not have to worry.

I remember Dad springing into action, jumping from our bow onto the trimaran that had gotten entangled in our anchor line, and then getting back onto our boat having successfully saved *Sorcery*. He did the type of thing you see in the movies, but it was *my* Dad. How cool was that?!

Then Dad held off the bowsprit of another boat with the boat hook, but he couldn't quite fend it off while climbing aft through the cockpit. When the bowsprit banged down on our stern pulpit, the metal bent like plastic. It was incredible. Not in a good way, just wow. Imagine all the damage the ship could've caused had we not been on board.

Speaking of that possibility, it became real and sad for me when we heard a man from shore begging over the VHF for someone to pick him up to get to his moored boat. We ignored the call because at that point the wind was so strong we couldn't risk the dinghy ride to shore, and we didn't want to tell him no.

It became worse when we watched and counted the boats moving past us in slow motion, and running aground 100 feet away. And if that wasn't bad enough, they started to sink. Compared to the sluggish drifting, the sinking felt like a time lapse. The different colored hulls disappeared with frightening speed under the water.

I thought about the photos, the toys, the souvenirs, the beautifully varnished wood – all damaged, all gone. The time, the money, the tears to have to replace everything. Somewhere I still have a picture of all seven boats at various sunken points, their masts rocking against the gray sky.

The next morning everything was so still, the leaning masts seemingly frozen in a beautiful blue sky. What a difference a day makes. I have a picture of that, too.

The storm took a lot out of us. So before heading across the Sea of Cortez, we relaxed by spending a few days a little way up the coast. At Algondones Beach, we hung out with Joyce and Walter on *Just Do It*, and at Bahia San Pedro with *Tenacity, L'Escargot,* and *October.* For the first potluck we'd had in a long time, we made sushi and Mexican Lime pie. Dick on *L'Escargot* fixed lobster tacos.

Too hot to wear proper clothes, we were down to our skimpiest outfits when on the boat, and didn't have any company. Perhaps it was the heat, or maybe I was a little burned out from cruising, but I began to wonder what else we could do. *What about getting a nursing degree to supplement my Masters in Urban Affairs, or at least taking a correspondence course of some kind?*

When things didn't go right, Robb would say, "Don't blame the boat." Yet almost every woman I talked to found living on a boat unquestionably more difficult than life on land. Anyway, it was too hot to cook, let alone plan another life. And in any case, we had heavily invested in the life we were living. The adage, "Bloom where you're planted," streamed through my mind.

Robb got back to learning Morse code. He never reached 13 words per minute, the level required at that time for an amateur radio, or ham, license. Code, like languages, was something easy and fun for me, so I was the one with the ham license, which gave me a little cachet. Although I never had to use code, the license gave us access to a number of handy radio frequencies and ham nets not available to the general public. "Back in the day," Robb now says, "before cell phones and the

Internet, ham radio was the only practical way to contact the States, unless you wanted to go into town and find a *Larga Distancia.*" In Baja, that establishment sometimes amounted to – my favorite – no more than a few telephones under a thatched roof.

Return to Baja

On September 10, we left at 4 in the morning for a smooth sail across the Sea of Cortez to Bahia San Francisquito. During the passage, Annie asked me to read to her from a book about the ocean life cycle. Following her interest and questions, and my own, we skipped around in other books, and just when she asked to study whales, a pod of what are commonly called "pilot whales" appeared off the side of the boat. Our copy of *The Sierra Club Handbook of Whales and Dolphins* helped us identify them not as whales, but as dolphins, a sub-species of whales.

***

When Robb needed a hand from me, he often became impatient with my lack of sailing skills, and we sometimes snapped at each other. The one thing I did well was coastal navigation. Seeing an actual coastline from a boat differs considerably from looking at it on a chart. On that passage, I figured, correctly, San Francisquito to be farther north than we'd first thought. Robb didn't agree, and even wanted to bet on it. But guided by my certainty, a full moon and a red-and-white-banded lighthouse, we eventually pulled into the quiet, jasmine-scented bay – empty, except for us.

The first couple of days we explored the basin with its tremendous current. Robb caught a huge female lobster with eggs, and put her back, but an enormous male California sheepshead fish stayed for dinner. We saw lots of manta rays, a couple of seals, an octopus, a turtle.

On a hill overlooking the bay, an American woman, Debbie, lived with her handsome Mexican shark-fisherman husband and their children, Zimran, nine, and Shoshona, five. Deb invited us and Kaye and Bruce from *Antigua* for an evening potluck on the patio of their home. After dinner she brought out her guitar and sang a stirring rendition of "Delia," a mournful old Johnny Cash number, which roused us to clap and shout for an encore. After the second round, she passed the guitar to me. Her comment on my effort: "You're good, but you need to be more bold."

Deb made an effort to get the kids together often, either spending time on our boat, maybe watching a movie, or taking them all to the beach. On one occasion she and I walked with the children in the late afternoon to a small resort a couple of miles down the beach. As if coming back in the dark wasn't excitement enough for the kids, our flashlights scattered small, croaking frogs from the path up to the house. Before Annie and I went back to the boat, Deb and I packed in another hour of chatting.

***

The best adventure was the one Debbie organized for me and kids to spend a day visiting her friends on *ranchos*. Packed into her jeep, we bumped along washboard roads leading through stunning vistas – valleys thick with stately cordon cactus, distant mountains, billowing clouds, and blue skies. As we approached the first outpost, a few cattle and a windmill emerged from the desert, and soon a pack of ecstatic dogs raced to greet us. A veranda the length of the whitewashed one-story house teemed with outdoor beds, rocking chairs, benches, saddles, chaps, stirrups, bridles, birds in cages of all sizes, and hanging plants.

An amiable woman, wiping her hands on her apron, welcomed us. When she served coffee, I offered the homemade cookies I'd brought in a repurposed metal tin. As we were leaving, our hostess asked, "May I have that tin to store sugar?" Of course. The asking and the giving felt comfortable and familiar, a sharing of scarce resources among pioneers. My maternal grandmother, Charity, had bounced along in a Conestoga wagon all the way from Ohio to South Dakota to homestead in a sod house on a God-forsaken prairie. She's in my bones.

The next whitewashed home, a quintessential hacienda with its tasteful black-trimmed walls, red terracotta floors, and riotously colorful interior, looked to be straight out of *Baja Home and Garden*. After one more *rancho*, to stock up on olives, we headed home. Even though the long day had exhausted me, Deb and I continued talking over a glass of wine on her patio while the children played. Since she lived in a secluded place, and I was always on the move, we both savored the extra girlfriend time.

***

The afternoon *Samatas* arrived, we invited Mike, a Greek fellow, and Marie, a French Canadian, over for wine and snacks. We knew them from La Paz when Robb and the kids had helped crew *Samatas* during race week; and where Marie, Annie and I waited out the failed nautilus adventure. The next morning, Marie, Mike, and Robb took off to free dive for lobster from the dinghy. With four good-sized lobsters in tow, Robb returned to the dinghy to find Marie already there, sad and empty handed. He suggested they play a joke on Mike, and pretend she'd caught one of the lobsters. Mike hadn't caught any, so in a fit of apparent macho jealousy, he ranted and raved, growing red in the face and saying he didn't believe them. He was so furious they were afraid telling the truth would set him off even more. By dinnertime, he'd calmed down, and we ate our magnificent lobster dinner in peace.

Bringing a loaf of homemade bread, Mike and Marie came over one evening for a meal of sausages, new potatoes, *rancho* olives, and *scordalia*, a Greek potato and garlic dip I'd made. The following morning, Marie, Annie and I hiked up to the solar-powered lighthouse while the men went spearfishing. With the guys' catch we made fish cakes and shish kabobs. That evening we all ate together while watching *Star Wars*. Journal note, "Only two bottles left of case of French wine. Sigh."

The day *Samatas* planned to leave, Annie had gone to play with Zimran and Shoshona, but asked to be told when Mike and Marie came over so she could spend some time with them. I'd encouraged Marie to use her new red-enamel pressure cooker, and she brought over some of the beans she'd cooked. She also gave us wild rice, garlic, and lemons; I gave her a container of local olives. Those exchanges within the cruising family always left me feeling warm and strengthened. We rarely knew which goodbyes were final, so they were always softened with "See you down the road." That was the last time we saw *Samatas*.

Waiting for the Boys

With Alex back in San Diego staying with his grandparents, we had to figure out how to get him. Being closer to San Diego made sense, and after 10 gratifying days at San Francisquito, we headed north for Bahia de Los Angeles. For hours we motored through sloppy seas until a southerly came up, enabling us to sail downwind. As we jibed over, I tried to haul in the jib, but the sail wrapped around its roller furling pole. To my relief, Robb calmly sorted things out. The wind brought a little rain, and Annie, without being asked, closed the hatches, took down the wind scoop, and covered the generator.

Finally, we pulled into Puerto Don Juan, a small protected anchorage around the corner from spacious Bahia de Los Angeles, LA Bay. As we settled in, dolphins played around the boat, and a butterfly came aboard. Porous volcanic pumice stones, a few as big as our heads, floated in the water. Masses of shells and decaying carcasses of sharks and mantas left by fishermen cluttered the rocky shore. A yachtie we knew came by in his dinghy and collected all the mail *Shahrazad* had given us in San Francisquito for boats farther north. That first evening Kay and Tom from *Bastante* joined us for sushi, wine, and mail we had for them.

The very next day Robb found a ride, leaving in two days, to San Diego. We scurried around getting ready for the captain to be gone. He took down our roller-furled sail.

"Why?" I wanted to know.

"A heavy wind could unfurl it," he said. "Lots of boats don't bother to take it down, but you and Annie wouldn't be able to handle a massive loose sail."

We emptied the reserve water from the 30-gallon bladder into the tanks, created a what-to-do list, packed, and dealt with paperwork, including a revised crew list. Most importantly, Robb removed a dead and stinking fish that had gotten caught in the filter of the saltwater pump in the galley. *Antigua* dropped off mail for Robb to take to the States.

At 4 in the morning, we dinghied over to *Pablo* to catch a ride to the village in LA Bay. From there, Robb would travel to San Diego with another boater in his van. At a seafront palapa, Annie chose oatmeal, while Robb and I wolfed down a breakfast of exceptional *chilaquiles*: fried, softened tortilla chips mixed with scrambled eggs, and smothered with salsa and melted cheese.

We ran into Larry on *Ocean Angel* and Alan with his new mate, Susan, on *Carioca III*. Alan offered to take Annie and me back if we wanted to stay and shop. Our last chore in town was a stop at the clinic to get an antibiotic powder for Robb's skin, and something for Annie's plantar wart. The clinic didn't charge, but asked us to contribute what we wished. All I had left was 22,000 pesos, a little over $7. That seemed skimpy, though I had no idea of an appropriate amount. I hope it was okay.

⚓

The prospect of staying on the boat without Robb didn't worry me. I felt perfectly safe, and knew, if necessary, I could count on the cruising community to help out. At least 15 different boats, most of whom we knew, came and went from the snug little harbor. Without hovering, people took us under their wings.

The day Robb left, Tom and Lynn invited a few people to *Triumph* for a typical yachtie evening: a potluck and book exchange. I brought a huge bowl of Mexican *duros*, a popular snack made from dried pasta-like bits, which puff up when fried. Two good non-fiction books came home with me, one on inventors and inventions, and *God and Mr. Gomez*, a riotous account by a man building a house in Baja in the '50s.

In the course of the evening, Jo from *Silke* French-braided Annie's hair. Ken on *Occam's Razor* explained his boat name referred to a problem-solving principle that proposes, "Among competing hypotheses, the one with the fewest assumptions should be selected." Not a bad name for a boat – lots of fodder for discussion.

Four days after leaving, Robb sent a message via the Chubasco Net that he and Alex may have a ride down in a pickup in a week or so – the first of many false alarms. A few days later, John from *Silke* came knocking on the hull, "Come on! Robb's on the single sideband calling for you!" Robb's mother in Texas had been hospitalized, and he needed to go to her right away. At various times after that, I tried, but without any luck, to get through to him on the single sideband or via a two-way on *Carioca III*.

"See it? Right over there!"

My daughter and I settled into new routines. The kids' bunks, snug places in rough seas, were uncomfortable in hot weather. On most nights while her dad was gone, Annie slept with me in our bed under the big open hatch and a canopy of stars. Besides, we each felt a bit lonely. On the positive side, with just the two of us, not having to worry about meals freed up a lot of time and lifted my spirits. Each day I swam 10 laps around the boat, studied Spanish, read, and worked on our photo albums and other projects.

For example, if I could have found commodores from Seven Seas Cruising Association to sponsor us, we would be eligible for a 10 percent discount on boat insurance. At renewal time, our $1,800 premium would have doubled thanks to enormous payouts that year for Hurricane Andrew. That storm caused $26 billion in damage in Florida at the same time Lester struck Mexico. Even if we'd had a discount, the insurance would have been prohibitively expensive for us. So, from 1993 on, we traveled without any, a gamble that could have been ruinous, but we were lucky. We didn't have health or dental insurance either, but the sea goddess looked out for us in the form of inexpensive or socialized health care in every place we needed help.

***

Casual visits back and forth took up a good part of each day. Early one afternoon, Maggie from *Wirraway* and Jo from *Silke* stopped by for a lively, satisfying visit. I showed them my beloved miniature shell collection. The kids had vied for finding ever-smaller shells. Whenever they were lying on their stomachs, their faces a couple of inches from the sand, I knew what they were up to. Holding up sand-flecked palms cradling wee little shells, they'd say, "Mom! Lookit! Do you have one like this?" I almost never did, which pleased us all.

The next morning, Jo invited Annie and me over to *Silke* for waffles, a unique treat on a boat. She gave me a jar of seventy-year-old "friendship" sourdough starter from San Francisco, and a small bottle of lacquer to strengthen my shells and bring out their color. When our friends on *L'Escargot* came in, Annie raced over to visit Schwartz, the third boat-cat she befriended in the anchorage, along with *Carioca III's* Chelsea and *Lookfar's* cat. Dick and Mary fixed me one of their famous Bloody Marys.

On various days Alan and Susan stopped by for afternoon drinks, a yogurt-making lesson, to take Annie fishing, or to invite us for a potluck dinner. When a boat went "next door" to LA Bay to shop in the village, they often invited us along. The proprietor of little Isla Grocery drove to San Diego once a week to load up at the Price Club. Though local products were fine with me, getting stateside stuff was irresistible.

Mo and Ken from *Cheeky Hobson* taught Annie and me how to catch, kill, fillet, and cook the triggerfish that lounged on the rocky bottom, right under our boat. Because she and I'd been learning about the human body, we attempted to figure out which organ was the fish's liver. Comparing the encyclopedia drawing of a fish's anatomy to a real and different fish reminded me of trying to figure out a coastline from a chart. In the fish's case, we never did identify its liver.

Snagging eight of the flat, salad-plate-sized fish in short order, we fried them, and the four of us had a scrumptious lunch with pasta salad, a green bean salad, and French wine. The whole triggerfish process left Annie and me with an inflated sense of self-sufficiency.

"Something's Wrong ... I Need Help"

Maggie told about swimming with a 20-foot-long whale shark in LA Bay. Easily identified by a grid pattern of white spots covering its back, the filter feeder poses no danger to humans. *Triumph* had offered to take several of us to the bay the next day for a hike up to a gold mine. Anticipating the prospect of also getting to swim with a whale shark, Annie and I wore our bathing suits beneath our clothes, and took our snorkels and underwater camera.

The day ended after a long hike, most of it in the hot sun. On the way down from the mine, several people, worried about my extremely red face, asked if I was okay. I felt fine, just a little tired. By the time we got to the beach, I was sweating profusely and desperately thirsty. At the little restaurant, the busy wait staff, uncharacteristically for Mexico, wouldn't give me a glass of water for free, and I didn't have any money with me.

Light-headed and weak, I made my way outside and sat in the shade at a table next to Alan and others in our group. My skin became clammy and cool. Nausea, a headache, and weariness crept over on me. I couldn't think straight or understand what people were saying. Finally, I asked Alan to get Annie. "Something's wrong," I managed to say. "I need help."

Recognizing I was suffering from heat exhaustion, Alan plied me with several glasses of water and poured salt into my hand to lick. In a short time, I felt stabilized enough to strip down to my swimsuit, walk into the cool water, and dunk my head. Tom offered a ride out to *Triumph* to lie down. He found some Tylenol, and left me to rest. By the time everyone came on board to go home, I felt okay, and had already resolved in the future to take along more water than I thought necessary, to ask for help early on, and to be alert for anyone looking as if they may be in trouble.

Planning for Disaster

I'd read a lot about survival at sea. Robb said, "If you spent as much time learning how to sail as you do planning for disaster, our odds for surviving would improve."

Nevertheless, I wanted to do a man overboard drill, something of no interest to him. With him gone, the calm, warm anchorage provided a perfect setting for a drill. Jo from *Silke*, Maggie from *Wirraway*, Susan from *Monte Cristo*, and Adele from *Steeldiver* all enthusiastically supported the project. We agreed no men would be allowed because they tend to take over. A couple of male single handers begged to be included, but we remained firm, even when one man offered to be the dead body.

The women came toting the life preservers they'd use on their own boats. Before we'd figured out how to go about the drill, Annie leaped into the water with a big splash, "Help! Help! I'm drowning!"

We flocked to the lifeline. I tossed her a life ring and started to pull on the attached rope. The thin line felt as if it was cutting deep into my skin. I had very little strength, and simply couldn't lift my daughter from the water to the deck.

In a true emergency I could probably have counted on adrenaline to kick in, but the need to rethink the whole thing became obvious. The short-lived drill taught us three lessons. First, each boat is different, no single solution fits all. Second, you have to practice and probe the weaknesses in your plan. Third, taking the first step of something important to us felt empowering. Next step for me: get Robb involved.

When we weren't busy socializing, Annie did schoolwork, we burned trash, and explored the beach. Playing card games like Fish and watching movies filled the evenings. And, although the feminist in me opposed Barbie dolls, since there were no little girls around, I deigned to play Barbies with her. Neither of us maintained our best behavior during those weeks. I often returned her stubbornness or rudeness with shouting, lecturing, or the occasional swat on her derriere. Robb would say, "Well, we're not as good as some parents, but we're better than others. We love the kids, and we're doing our best." Thankfully, they turned out great.

I'd always thought that if the boys were gone, the boat would be tidy. In fact, the boat was a mess. The saltwater in the galley had turned foul-smelling again, like when that fish got caught in the filter. Neither of us could see how to get to the filter, so we took to washing dishes on deck.

How in the world I thought we could handle the boat in an emergency, if we couldn't figure out something as simple as where the water filter was, boggles my mind. And why we didn't ask another yachtie about the problem is a mystery. Chalk another one up to magical thinking. Later on, the smell in the galley disappeared, but then the saltwater pump sprang a leak. Rags huddled in wet piles on the galley floor, and dishes still traveled to the deck to get washed.

***

A few days into October, word came that Robb may be driving down. In anticipation, we bustled around, straightening and cleaning. Annie scoured the stovetop for over an hour, and did an admirable job cleaning the cockpit, including the cushions. After I'd talked to Robb three days in a row, I thought they'd show up any day. A week later the report came that they'd be back the next day, Sunday, October 11, in LA Bay. But, no surprise, no boys. In those days, sketchy communication was simply a matter of fact.

Wanting more information, I tried on the Chubasco Net to get a two-way to my mom, our friend Cat, or Downwind Marine, but only reached answering machines. Finally, I got in touch with Robin. He told me Robb and Alex were riding down in a pickup, had been delayed 24 hours, but were scheduled to leave at 3 a.m. the next day, Tuesday, arriving 10 to 12 hours later in LA Bay. On the strength of that information, I made yogurt, baked bread and a cake.

The next morning, I invited *Golly Gee* and *Cheeky Hobson* for tea, and we helped ourselves to the homecoming cake. Later that morning confirmation came on the net that Robb should be in LA Bay about 5 in the afternoon, so I baked another cake and put together a turkey tetrazzini. *Carioca III* and *Antigua* had both gone to LA Bay for the day, and I asked if one of them could bring the boys home.

Cheeky Hobson spotted Annie and me struggling with a tangle of signal flags on deck and came by to help dress up the boat with a line of flags running from the masthead to the bow. With the wind flapping everything about, we hoisted Annie up the 70-foot mast to shackle the line of flags to the top. The boat looked splendid. Proud as peacocks with our homecoming preparations, we were eager to see the boys.

Five o'clock came and went. About 11 p.m., way after we'd gone to bed, we heard them clamoring onto the boat. Alex wrote this about the homecoming:

We had to borrow a friend's dinghy and arrived soaking
wet. But we were cheered by the thought that we were
home, and that we could dry off. Mom and Annie had made
a big sign that said, Welcome Home Alex & Dad. They
made two cakes, but ate one before we got home.

Robb was the least happy of the bunch. He was indignant I hadn't
brought *Sorcery* around to LA Bay. What? I'd never once taken the boat
and anchored by myself, let alone to a new place, *nor* had doing so ever
been discussed, *nor* was I certain when they'd arrive. The idea that he
thought I should have stunned and incensed me. By morning we'd set
aside our pique and had a good day. We returned the borrowed dinghy,
bought groceries and beer at the village, and toured the little museum
before settling back into normal activities and chores. Robb repaired the
saltwater pump and broken ladder, replaced an antenna, and cleaned the
bottom of the boat.

One evening, Mary and Dick from *L'Escargot* came over for linguini
and the clams that Dick, Robb and the kids had dug up earlier in the
day. A hike one morning across the isthmus to Quemado Cove rewarded
us with far-reaching views of the land and sea.

A Birthday with Turtles

On the north side of LA Bay, a modest research station housed and
rehabilitated injured loggerhead turtles. Worldwide, nearly all species of
sea turtles were considered endangered, and the killing and trafficking in
them has been against Mexican law since 1990. Nevertheless, convincing
fishermen to bring in even the injured ones was a challenge, and
enforcing the law faced many problems despite the severe penalties.
Turtles commanded a high price, due in large part to a long tradition in
Baja of eating the reptiles. Even some authorities still wanted to serve
the meat on their own family's special occasions, notably Easter,
birthdays, and weddings.

On our first trip to Mexico while anchored, ironically, in Turtle Bay,
a couple of youngsters rowed up in a weather-beaten panga and offered
to sell us the huge, forlorn, barnacle-spotted turtle in the bottom of their
boat. Coming as we do from a world where turtles are pets, the idea that

the young salesmen assumed we'd want to eat the poor thing never crossed my mind. Nor did I think of buying and freeing it to live another day.

At the research station we watched the managers, husband and wife Antonio and Betty, feed shark meat to their charges living in a round concrete tank. Painted sky blue, the 15-feet-wide and 4-feet-high tank had a removable thatched roof and a grand view of the sea and islands beyond. After the feeding, the couple invited us to come back the following afternoon for the monthly weighing and measuring of the "bale" of turtles.

The next day will always be fondly remembered as the day Annie turned nine and the birthday we helped with the turtles. Alex jumped right in, assisting with transporting each turtle to the weigh station and onto a big square of net. Robb held the animal in place, while Antonio took measurements. Next, the men gathered the edges of the net, and caught it on a hook dangling from a scale. After Antonio noted the weight and the turtle was lowered, Robb and Alex held it down while Annie applied antibiotic salve to any wounds and painted a stripe of temporary blue vegetable dye on the back of its neck to mark completion of all the steps.

Working with the animals felt like an honor, and as the expedition photographer, I was right in the thick of the action. At least 20 turtles got processed, including four big ones – the largest tipping the scale at 175 pounds, according to Alex's notes. The following day we made one last visit so Robb could give Antonio a D-ring to make it easier to hold the net together when attaching it to the scale.

Recently asked if she remembered that day, Annie said, "Thinking back as a nine-year-old everything seemed hectic, the animals were scared and the humans yelled and dashed around. But overall, I had a great time. I loved touching and interacting with the turtles, and was happy the end goal was for them to be reintroduced into the wild."

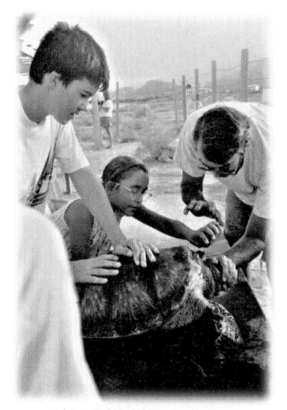

Helping at the turtle research station

Several days after Robb and Alex returned, I insisted on an overboard drill before leaving that anchorage. As we were doing it, Robb seemed to seriously consider what we'd really do if someone went overboard. On our first trip he'd used a magic marker to draw a face on an empty gallon milk jug, and then pitched the container overboard.

"Okay, that's me. You're in charge."

The sealed plastic jug would probably float forever, but in a matter of seconds it disappeared among the waves. I knew the boat had to be turned around, but had no idea what to do first. Especially with sails up, turning's not a simple matter. I didn't want to ruin a sail, lose a life ring, or even a cushion for a drill.

After less than a minute of watching my panic and paralysis, Robb said, "Well, I'm dead."

Rather than being prompted to plan for the possibility of one of us being the disappearing jug, we put more effort into not going overboard in the first place. We already had lifelines strung 3 feet high all around the edge of the boat. When we were underway and on deck, we all wore harnesses with a leash and shackle attached to the lifeline. Each harness had a water-activated light, a high-pitched whistle, and a small canister of dye which, when emptied, would change the color of the surrounding water for easier visibility. After Robb told me about a sailor who'd been hauled up to the side of his boat, only to slip out of his harness, never to be seen again, I sewed crotch straps into all four harnesses.

***

Back to the family drill. We practiced Plan No. 1, the halyard retrieval system. A halyard is a rope with a heavy clip on the end used to haul sails up the mast. If someone fell in the water, we would toss them a halyard, which they could clip to their harness, enabling the person to be reeled in. When Alex, the first volunteer, jumped in, Robb realized the halyards, set up to be attached at deck level, wouldn't reach down to the water without an adjustment. Taking a minute to lengthen a halyard, he cranked Alex up to the deck.

If we'd been underway, the boat would've been moving away from the victim. And what if the sea was a little rough? What if the person was injured or unconscious? In that case, someone else would have to swim out with the halyard, hook it to the person's harness, then both could get pulled back to the boat. What if the overboard person was Robb? Even a landlubber could see the halyard retrieval system bristled with difficulties.

Plan No. 2 was to lower the dinghy, the 13-foot boat always left inflated on deck, into the water. Before we tried that, we could see we'd lose valuable time deploying the dinghy, getting ourselves into it, starting up the outboard, then finding the person. If Robb were unconscious or injured in the water, I could never get his limp, wet 185 pounds into the dinghy. Meanwhile, two young children would be alone on deck. It was all too much.

***

You might think that would have been a good point to turn around and go home, or at least to sit down and fine tune our plan. But no, other activities beckoned. On our way to Smith Island a few days later, we were sailing along at a couple of knots when I said, "Looks like a good day for a man-overboard drill underway." Robb agreed by saying, "Well, if something goes wrong, you can swim to that island over there." *Was he kidding? The one shimmering in the distance?* I'd taken adult beginner swimming lessons at the Y, but still …. I jumped into the water and Annie threw me a floating cockpit cushion. The boat sailed off, literally leaving me in its wake.

Soon enough *Sorcery* circled around and, as she went by, I saw a halyard lowered to sea level. The boat was going so fast that if I'd managed to grab the line, it would have taken the skin right off my hands or jerked my arms out of their sockets. Next time around, the boat moved more slowly and closer to me, but not enough for me to grasp the line before moving on. By the last pass, Robb managed to maneuver so I was right at the ladder, which had been put over the side for the exercise.

Afterwards, he said the boat was too close for him to see me from the cockpit, something he'd never considered. I don't remember giving What to Do If Someone Goes Overboard much more thought. Maybe that's because I moved along to What to Do If the Boat is Sinking. But that was later.

To Go or Not To Go

We were feeling kind of down, undecided about where to go next, or when. Robb talked about staying in Mexico another year. Although I loved the country, after three tours I felt ready for new adventures, those alluring slides of French Polynesia I'd seen years ago still called to me. In any case, we needed to head south. At the end of October, we anchored around the corner at Quemado Cove, then sailed down to San Francisquito, where Annie and I had a several-day reunion with Deb and the kids.

After stopping at Santa Rosalia in mid-November, we moved on to Punta Chivata for Alex's thirteenth birthday, Robb took him fishing first thing, while Annie and I baked a cake, hung the multi-color Happy

Birthday letters, wrapped gifts, and fashioned a card. For breakfast, we had Alex's favorite: *huevos rancheros*. Later that afternoon, the half dozen folks on *Cruisin' Time* and *Crystal Wind* came over for a little party with a second cake. Chandler gave Alex the latest thing, a book on tape. We watched the short and thrilling documentary, *Around Cape Horn*. In 1929, Irving Johnson had filmed his trip during an A-No.1 storm as he crewed on the windjammer *Peking* around the treacherous tip of South America. A day or two later we moved on, first stopping at San Sebastian, then at Mulege.

Getting to San Juanico wasn't as scary as going around the Horn, but did involve our worst sailing in the Sea of Cortez up to that point. The sun was out, but the wind had created treacherous seas. Robb moved around the deck checking on gear and making decision after decision.

I manned the wheel and dealt with steep waves higher than eye level when the boat reached the bottom of a trough. Robb directed me to head down into each valley at an angle, then how best to immediately ride the wave back up. Once, when I headed up too steeply, two big waves rolled into the cockpit. I was scared. Maybe not to death, but scared enough.

Down below, poorly-stowed objects crashed around until the kids got things under control. During that passage Robb injured his ribs, and *Crystal Wind* broke a steering cable. After we made it to San Juanico and found a spot without surge, we were able to unwind.

First Cruising Thanksgiving

A few days later, *Crystal Wind*, *Cruisin' Time*, and *Perpetua* with Jack and his crew Norman joined us for Thanksgiving. Jack brought a luscious ham, while Chandler, Vicky, and I came up with traditional side dishes aplenty: yams, mashed potatoes and gravy, stuffing, creamed green beans, cranberry sauce, biscuits, pies, tarts, and a cran/apple punch. I liked my outfit, a long, tan skirt, purple top, belt of many colors, and dangly earrings. After our first trip, when I regretted not having any clothes for special occasions, I'd upped my wardrobe, though staying within the no-ironing requirement.

The next morning Robb and I woke up at 6 in a pitch-black cabin. Sliding open the hatch above our bed, we stood and saw the horizon glowing a fiery rust, outlining the magnificent pinnacles to the east. We'd lingered over two cups of coffee in bed, when Robb said, "I hate for this to end." I reached over and closed the curtain separating us from the rest of the boat.

Later, the family feasted on leftover pie for breakfast, and hiked to the cruisers' shrine at nearby La Ramada Cove. On the way, the kids picked up handfuls of Apache Tears, shiny black pebbles of obsidian. High winds, rough seas, and Robb's still-painful ribs kept us in the anchorage a few more days, along with *Crystal Wind* and *Alrisha*.

I was reading James Michener's *Rascals in Paradise*, true stories of adventurers in the South Pacific. The tales encouraged me, but we still weren't committed to going there. My hesitation partly concerned money. I'd calculated we'd spent about $37,000 on the boat since we bought it. "Will the expenses ever stop?" I wondered out loud.

"Well, there's really no alternative," Robb said. "There's so much money invested, we may as well continue." That exchange seemed to have been the one that turned the tide. We agreed to the South Pacific idea, if only by backing in.

We sailed on to Isla Coronados, Loreto, Chenque, and then Puerto Escondido, where lots of mail waited for us. At that last stop I suggested to Annie for a writing assignment that she interview Lynn on *Scout*. Annie loved the funny *Story of the Constellations* Lynn read each morning on the cruisers' net. It took some coaxing and my going with her, but Annie did the interview and wrote a nice little report. Years later in college she majored in journalism. Just sayin'.

By the time we'd reached La Paz the first week in December, we already had lengthy lists of things to do and buy, and began preparing for the 3,000-mile passage from Mexico to the Marquesas. Robb figured the best time to leave would be in early April.

Though it would mean the family being apart for Christmas, I decided to take Annie to San Diego to say goodbye to my mom, shop for supplies, and take care of other business. We needed, for instance, to arrange for paying the half a dozen bills we'd have while we were gone and get visas and charts for French Polynesia. Two possibilities for a ride to San Diego fizzled: one with Chris on a delivery boat and the other with Chandler in her car. How we actually got there and back, none of us remembers, though we must have taken a bus.

From early December through New Year's Eve, Annie and I stayed with my mom while I tackled paperwork and bought food, spare parts, math workbooks and other books, medical supplies, who-knows-what-all. Chris, by then back in San Diego, offered to take our supplies down to La Paz on *Rebecca,* the boat he was then captaining. After I'd dropped off nearly everything I'd bought, including several gallons of bottom paint, he announced the boat had been repossessed, and all our stuff had to go. Pronto.

Downwind Marine let me leave 20 boxes in the back of the store, amidst other items destined to be delivered to boats in Baja by yachties headed that way. Despite my best efforts and those of Susan on *Alcatraz* and Chuck on *Morasum,* we never did get the bottom paint, which we sorely needed and had cost a small fortune.

***

During the time we were gone, Robb and Alex had continued to be cruisers: snorkeling, fishing, and visiting other yachties on Isla Santa Catalina and Bahia Agua Verde. "After a month had gone by," Robb told me later, "people started to hint maybe you'd jumped ship. I kinda wondered myself."

Poor guy. Not coming back had never crossed my mind. Historically though, a few women, after coming all the way down Baja on a boat, decided cruising wasn't for them. Joan on *Dream Merchant* had been one of them. By our third trip, a woman named Luanne had become first mate on Jim's boat.

Luanne planned a round-trip to San Diego in her station wagon, and offered to buy and bring back anything we needed. Always concerned about having enough food, I gave her a wish list, with stars by the most important items. She returned with $650 worth of food, everything on the list and then some, none of it from the Canned Food Outlet.

For three months, while readying ourselves for the trip, we lived "on the hook," that is, anchored out, not tied up at the dock. We often ate out and got together with other yachties.

Our kids had several young people on other boats to spend time with when they weren't busy with homework, chores, or seeing a doctor in town for some ailment or inoculation. One morning we heard on the net that Annie had a fax waiting in the marina office – astonishing news since neither Robb nor I had ever received one. Following up on something they'd discussed, Chandler on *Crystal Wind* had sent the fax to Annie. How I wish we'd saved the Family's First Fax.

Good Deeds and Community Service

One day, our neighbor Margaret on *Galatea* radioed asking if we could come and get her and her dog that had just died. She wanted to bury him on Mogote, a short distance from where we were anchored. Neither Robb nor Alex would have the heart for the assignment; this was a job for the women. When Annie and I arrived, we could see Margaret was incapable of picking up her dead pet, a sweet, chocolate-colored dachshund she'd wrapped in a blanket. I didn't know if I could pick him up either, but wanted to be strong for the grieving woman and for my daughter.

Annie had spent many hours with the dog on her lap, its wet nose snuggled into the crook of her arm. Imagining the blanket held a pet of my own, I picked up the limp, warm lump and carried it to our dinghy. On Mogote we dug a pit and lowered the bundle into it. Not knowing what else to do or say, each of us mumbled, "Ashes to ashes and dust to dust," tossing in a handful of sandy dirt. Once the hole was filled, we placed a red flower with a long stem on the grave and, through her tears, Annie read a goodbye letter she'd written after we'd gotten the call.

Incidentally, we'd met Margaret and her husband, Archie, at a yachtie event where she gave us a copy of *The Boater's Weather Guide*, an impressive book she'd just published. I mention this because the "real" lives of cruisers always interested us. We ran into folks from all walks of life, from authors to zoologists, with perhaps a disproportionate number of lawyers, engineers, and doctors. Over the years, knowing a few of the latter came in handy.

***

In early March, Robb and Alex left at sunup to join about 50 volunteers of various ages and nationalities to pick up trash on Mogote, the 7-mile-long sand spit protecting La Paz from the open sea. A fleet of 15 dinghies joined the pangas and crew from Baja Expeditions, who'd organized the cleanup. For several hours the team scoured the eastern side of Mogote and filled 100 large trash bags and several barrels with human-generated trash.

***

Responding to an advertisement asking people to visit an old folks' home, Annie and I spent a couple of hours using what little Spanish we knew to communicate with residents. The quiet, the bleak décor, and lack of activity in the small facility compounded the overall sense of despair. One woman was only 48, leading me to believe the facility doubled as a home for people incapable of taking care of themselves for reasons other than age.

Mostly we busied ourselves preparing for our upcoming odyssey, making list after list, though I'm hard-pressed now to remember what all they entailed. One note mentions taking an inventory, another that we had gone through our survival equipment.

Keeping an eye on the weather, when April rolled around, we pulled up stakes from La Paz. Easing our way back south, we spent a night or two at Punta Bonanza, then Los Muertos, and finally Los Frailes. On the morning of April 12, 1993, ready and excited, we sailed off the edge of our known world.

THE SOUTH PACIFIC

Mexico to New Zealand
April to December 1993
Alex was thirteen, Annie nine

THE trip from Baja to the Marquesas, a group of islands in French Polynesia, the South Pacific, is a little farther than the distance as the crow flies from San Diego to the farthest point in Maine – approximately 3,000 miles. The difference: no stops in between.

The First Eighteen Days

The winds were disappointingly light all the way. If we'd had the winds Robb expected, he calculated we could have made the transit in 16 days. As it was, even though *Sorcery* was a good light air boat, the passage took 18 days – the longest we were continually at sea in our entire world cruise. Some boats took as many as 25 days for that same crossing, so we counted ourselves lucky.

The light winds not only slowed us down, but when there wasn't enough forward momentum, which was way too often, the boat rocked miserably from side to side. That motion also caused various unrelenting noises. The most irritating was the loud banging of the thick rope halyards with their heavy, metal fittings against the aluminum mast. This was especially punishing when we were trying to sleep. If we'd been at anchor, there are things we could have done to soften the banging, but underway, we pretty much had to tough it out.

Light winds or no, we sailed, rather than motored, the vast majority of the time. This was dictated in part because we only carried 100 gallons of fuel, and also because sailing was a source of pride for Robb. The boat was a sloop, meaning it had one main mast. Most of the time we used both the mainsail and a headsail. Variations in wind speed and direction required sail adjustments and, sometimes, sail changes.

When there was enough wind from behind to keep the sail full, we hoisted the spinnaker, a deep, colorful sail made of nylon, and therefore lighter than the sturdy canvas sails. When the winds picked up, the spinnaker had to be pulled down into a sleeve, called a "sock." This sounds easy enough, but there are numerous steps involved. One time something went wrong and the spinnaker ripped in two.

If the wind was coming directly from behind and wasn't too strong, we used a sail configuration poetically referred to as "wing on wing." That involved having two sails going out at 90 degrees, one from each side of the boat.

***

The satellite navigation system, or satnav, told us where we were, but we always had a backup by hand-plotting our course on a paper chart every hour or two. Robb knew celestial navigation, and I'd taken a class. But it's a time-consuming process, so we elected to resort to it only if the satnav failed. Unless we were on deck to keep our eyes out for any obstacles, our trusty timer went off every 10 minutes – even throughout the night when, of course, an adult was on watch. Robb and I took turns of four-hour night watches: 8 p.m. to midnight and midnight to 4 a.m.

We didn't have radar, partly because we didn't trust it. What if it malfunctioned? What if we couldn't distinguish a solid object from big waves? What if we went to sleep and didn't hear the alarm go off? Single handers obviously had fewer options, but we were always surprised when boats with two or more people blithely went to sleep with only the radar keeping watch.

The radio was on all the time. We listened for other boats, to weather reports, and had a scheduled call with our friend Susan from

Alcatraz, now at home in San Diego. Touching base made us feel connected, an important thing when you're but a tiny speck on a big ocean.

When we saw a ship, we called on the radio, "This is the sailing vessel *Sorcery.* You are a few miles off our port bow. Do you copy?" When big ships responded, which was rare, we asked if they could see us. "No. We can't," was the usual answer.

Even if we had the right of way, we changed course. The middle of the ocean, on a collision heading with a ship of any size, is no place to argue the law.

In addition to tankers and other huge ships, which we learned did not always stand watch or even use their radar, there were smaller ships, sleeping whales, and the rare but deadly floating container that had escaped from a cargo ship. We never saw a sleeping whale or a floating container, but we heard credible reports.

From time to time, smaller fishing boats didn't use lights at night until they saw another boat. Once I saw a light that was quite close and, I was certain, hadn't been there a few minutes before. No one responded to a radio call, so I woke up Robb.

The boat appeared to be stationary, and Robb said we had to get upwind of it as fast as possible. Within minutes, we passed it so closely we could see a man, backlit in a doorway, smoking a cigarette, watching us go by. We knew they were fishermen because pirates tended to have fast boats and came right up to vessels underway. We always avoided areas noted for plunderers.

We knew there was danger, but the ocean is immense, and the chance, especially if you're paying attention, of running into something was not high.

Life on the Open Ocean

First of all, our Fleming wind vane steered at least 90 percent of the time. Relief from having to be at the wheel around the clock gave us much more time for rest, work and play. Even so, Robb always had his antennae out, continually checking around for anything that might be going wrong or need adjustment. There's a lot to keep your eye on with any boat underway, but even more so with one the size of *Sorcery*.

Just like life on land, we had ordinary chores: cooking, dishwashing, clothes washing, homework, bathing. We bathed with the help of a heavy duty, five-gallon plastic bag called a Sun Shower. The saltwater-filled bag was left to warm in the sun, then hung either in the rigging or in the shower stall below deck. In cool weather we filled the bag with saltwater heated on the stove. A hose and shower head on the bag made it easy to manipulate the stream of water.

Since we rinsed off with only a couple of cups of fresh water, it was always a treat if it rained and we could take total fresh water showers on deck. We also took that opportunity to top off the water tanks. I don't remember ever being short of water.

Laundry was done in a bucket of soapy saltwater. The kids either stomped on the clothes with their bare feet or, when the weather was too cold, used a plunger. After a saltwater rinse we put everything through our hand wringer. That took out most of the salt, along with the water. Next we made a neat stack of the clothing; poured just enough fresh water with fabric softener over the pile to saturate the clothes; wrung them once more; then hung them on the lifelines to dry. The laundry came out soft and smelling sweet.

From a distance, a thunder shower was a treat to see. We always called each other up on deck to marvel at it: a mammoth, far away, gray cloud. You could see the rain, but couldn't hear it – a small incident, like a child's drawing of a raincloud, in a wide, wide expanse of sea and sky.

The effortless beauty of sunrises and sunsets was never taken for granted, even though we experienced it nearly every day. Under the vast dome of a pearly, pastel morning sky, Alex once said it was like being on the inside of a seashell.

Sometimes, when a big fish or dolphin blazed along beside the boat at night, their bodies acquired a coat of sparkling light as they set off the bioluminescent organisms in their path. The boat too, when disturbing those tiny animals, left a trail of zillions of fireflies caught up in the froth.

There's no warning for a moonrise. Especially if the moon is full, there's just a gigantic bright light growing larger and larger on the black horizon. This alarmed me the first time I saw it because it looked like a monster cruise ship or something heading straight towards us. When the weather was clear, the millions of stars were the best part of night watch. Hot ramen noodles in a warm cup came in a close second.

Crossing the Equator is traditionally a momentous occasion for sailors. Here's Annie's account of our first crossing:

> Sat. 4-24-93. Today We crossed The Equator at 11:30 AM P.S.T. We had shampane, corn, pepsi, cranberry juice, salam, Asperigis and good stuff. We took pictures told jokes, "you are exspeshally nutty today Annie" Alex said as we were celebrating. We teased Mom alot tickeld each other a lot (exspeshally me). And Dad yelled "We're in the southern ocean … yahoo!"

My own log entry was less colorful: "Beautiful, sunny day – just passed the Equator! Had champagne – even the kids. Robb noted that like in *Morgan's Passing*, someday Annie will not want to be silly with her dad." Even though Robb's contribution was teasing the kids by sending them up to the spreaders to see if they could find the line of the Equator, the crossing segued nicely into a geography lesson.

People always wonder about schooling for the children. The first time we took them out of school for a five-month trip to Mexico, I wondered myself. I envisioned a truant officer chasing us in a helicopter. Actually, after some initial hesitation, the kids' teachers were quite supportive. They suggested focusing on the three Rs, a term first used regarding education in 1818. The children would learn other subjects from "real life." An educational bookstore provided us with grade appropriate reading lists and math workbooks.

You can hardly stop a cruising kid from reading. When we were at anchor, they even had their own book exchanges with other boat kids. Most of their traded books were fiction, so after the first trip I picked out several non-fiction young adult books to take along. Alex was reading the last of the Tom Clancy series and re-reading *The Hunt for Red October*. For writing, we only required half an hour a day of a letter, journal entry, or essay. Alex tried to get ahead in homework so he'd have more time off when we got to the Marquesas.

Virtually any time a question of fact arose, we'd say, "Let's look it up!" And Alex would read the encyclopedia – I'm not kidding – simply for pleasure. Whenever we were in port for at least six months, one or both of them attended a local school.

The children always begged for family games, which we played at the galley table nearly every evening, sailing conditions permitting. We often chose Dominos, which for me had the added pleasure of the agreeable sound of the tiles clacking against the varnished table. We played board games like Pictionary, Scrabble, Chinese Checkers and Parcheesi, plus all manner of card games. Robb got a kick out of playing poker with the kids, claiming it was a math lesson.

When the boat wasn't heeling too much, we had afternoon tea in the cockpit with Robb asking, "May I play Mother and pour the tea?"

The Marquesas ~ May and June 1993

Hiva 'Oa

After 18 days of only sea and sky, the hilly, green island of Hiva 'Oa looked strange and inviting. Seeing smoke rising from the treetops, Annie remembered her recent history lesson on cannibalism. "Looks like the natives are roasting someone for lunch!"

A pod of melon-headed whales escorted us to the entrance of Atuona Bay. At first, we'd assumed they were dolphins; but our *Whales and Dolphins* book told us they were something even more unusual and wonderful. It seemed an auspicious start, except the whales left us at a small harbor already packed with boats.

Normally we would have moved on to find a less crowded anchorage, but we were tired and needed to be near the administrative center in the town of Atuona. Like most of the other boats, we anchored bow and stern to prevent swinging. This also enabled us to face into the increasing swell that was already quite substantial for inside an anchorage. High winds were predicted, and Robb said that if it got much worse, we almost certainly would have to leave.

Shortly after we got the anchors set, another boat came in. We watched closely as *Orion* proceeded to drop anchor right on top of us – that is, over our anchor and a mere boat length away. The captain wore a headband and had a long braid down his back, a hippie on a sailboat, heaven help us. Even though the boats were close, Robb felt we were okay for the time being. We dropped the dinghy into the water to visit our friends Dick and Mary on *L' Escargot*. They welcomed us with big smiles and two wonderful treats, a fresh baguette and our very first pamplemousse. The fruit resembled a grapefruit, the best one we'd ever eaten.

⚓

The high winds never came, so we stayed in the anchorage several days, resting and taking care of business. I had to get a reciprocal ham-operating license for the radio, but the first and most important thing was to obtain a bond from the bank. The government required yachties to post a cash bond, equivalent to the cost of airline tickets for everyone on the boat, to fly from Tahiti to a major city in their home country – in our case, to Los Angeles. Luckily, Robb had researched this so we had the cash. Apparently, in years gone by people arrived on boats, and then, understandably, didn't want to leave.

For reasons not clear to me at the time, I had to make three trips to the bank on three different days to get the bond. On the third trip I broke down and cried, and the bond materialized. I gave around $4,000 in exchange for a receipt in the equivalent in French francs. Weeks later we heard the banks were running out of dollars. So, when we got to Tahiti, we told them we were leaving and cashed in our bond. The dollar had fallen in value – usually a depressing turn of events. In this case though, we got back more money than we gave because after devaluation, it took more dollars to equal the francs stated on our receipt.

One of those days in Atuona, while sitting on a stone plaza waiting for the bank to open, I met Katherine, the wife of the hippie on *Orion*. We hit it off right away. Many weeks later in the Tuamotus, we finally met her husband, Rodney, and that was the beginning of a decades-long friendship.

Rodney and Katherine on *Orion*

To get to the small town of Atuona we walked 45 minutes uphill along a dirt road. The walk through the lush, exotic countryside was beautiful and good exercise. But on the return trip, when we were too hot and tired or when we'd bought a lot of groceries, we'd hitchhike, even if it meant a fast, bumpy ride in the back of a pickup. Traffic was light, and virtually any vehicle would stop if they had room for us. Small motor scooters with one or two family members clinging to the driver passed us up. Also, young Marquesan men whizzed by in sleeveless shirts, all the better to show off their muscular, tattooed arms.

Tattoos were still a novelty to us, so we marveled at the bold patterns that told the history of the family. Annie recently reminded me I'd seriously considered getting a tribal tattoo, but decided against it after learning from an American anthropologist working there how the tattoos were done: one common mixing pot for each color; sterilization nonexistent; the danger of contracting a blood-borne disease high. AIDS had already arrived in the Marquesas.

Alex had a tendency to be quiet and observant. Annie, on the other hand, was outgoing and had a knack for seeking out girls her age. Young

Myriam brought us strange, sweet fruit and an avocado that was so big – the size of a very large eggplant – at first we didn't know what it was. It didn't taste much like the Hass avocadoes we were accustomed to in California, but it was good, and one was plenty for the four of us. For an easy lunch I'd cut one into four sections and fill them with chicken or shrimp salad.

An outdoor clothes-washing station at the anchorage consisted of concrete tubs and cold running fresh water. It was basic, but decidedly a step up from our normal routine of small buckets of saltwater hauled up over the side of the boat. We were able to wash blankets and other big items that were all but impossible to do on the boat. It would have been more enjoyable if the mosquitos and no-see-ums hadn't tormented us relentlessly.

Mom's Isopods

We had a mission, a science project. I'd promised Dr. Brusca we'd collect isopods from as many different Marquesan islands as we could. It was the one island group in French Polynesia his team had not been able to get to for his research.

Isopods are crustaceans, distant relatives of shrimp and crabs. There are 4,500 species of marine isopods worldwide. Among these, I'm sure, are some perfectly fascinating giant isopods, which can grow up to 7 inches long. The ones he wanted were microscopic. He assured me, however, if we simply scraped the mossy debris from the bottom of rocks at the shore, we couldn't help but collect some of the minute creatures. At every single stop in the Marquesas, we faithfully scraped rocks into the thick plastic bags he provided and labeled the bags with location and date.

L'Escargot loaned us a microscope for our project, but we had no idea if what we saw were the isopods in question. Gary and Donna on First Light showed us a book with pictures of various isopods. Gary helped us build a trap because the isopods he knew about were big enough to catch. Just for fun, we punched holes in a quart-sized can, attached a handle, secured a fish head inside, and lowered the contraption into the water overnight.

The next morning, we found the can bashed and dented, the fish head gone and no isopods to show for it. We resumed rock scraping, and from the Tuamotus we sent the labeled bags back to San Diego. Dr. Brusca never responded. Much later I heard he'd left the museum. It would have been gratifying to learn how we'd done. Nevertheless, we had a blast with Mom's Isopods, as the project was known.

***

On an exploratory trip of the bay, we hit a manta ray, putting a 6-inch tear in the bottom of the dinghy. Water rushed in, but as Alex pointed out, the tear was not in the air tube. Annie noted that by the time we got home we were more worried about the ray than the dinghy. Another repair task for Robb.

Although we saw practically nothing of Hiva 'Oa, just being there seemed adventure enough. We were content to rest and regroup. I do regret not making the effort to visit the grave of Paul Gauguin, buried in Calvary Cemetery, overlooking the town. Not that I'm a particular fan of his art, but he had a remarkable life and is part of our Western cultural heritage. Besides, cemeteries always intrigue me. But off we went to the next island, less than a day sail away.

Tahuata

We were ready to be tourists. As if they'd read our minds, a local family of five paddled up in their outrigger and asked if they could come aboard. Roselyne, Sebastian, son Marc, daughter Gishlyn, and nephew Timau brought gifts of pamplemousse, bananas, mangoes, papayas and two handmade, carved wooden bracelets. We gave them a bottle of perfume, three or four baseball caps, a bag of Cheetos, a small American flag pin, and shared a modest snack of what we had on hand, ceviche and banana bread. I did try to explain that the two foods didn't really go together.

After some time, they paddled off to visit another bay, leaving Gishlyn to play with Annie. "I must say, it was pretty boring," Annie wrote. "She didn't speak English, and I spoke very little French."

The family invited us to visit them when we came ashore. The day of our visit they served an enjoyable, if unexpected, snack of popcorn and lemonade. The village of Hapatoni could have been a movie set. Lengths of cloth with brightly colored patterns festooned the island people and their homes and shops in every way you can imagine:

clothing, curtains, wall coverings, table and counter covers, bedspreads, awnings – you name it.

Set against a dense tropical background, a promenade stretched the length of the bay. It seemed like a Sunday because scores of families, well-dressed in Western clothes, strolled and visited. A few people asked for their pictures to be taken with Annie. With her light-tan skin, she looked like a little Polynesian and blended right in with the family portraits.

One of my most cherished souvenirs appeared when we were going up the river through town in our dinghy. An inch-thick bunch of yard-long straws, held together with orange yarn near the cut-off ends, floated by. I figured if we didn't rescue the broom, it would end up in the ocean. Having items people in other countries use in their everyday lives somehow connected me to them.

After just a few days, we were eager to get to the next island, another day sail away.

Fatu Hiva

Sailing into the Bay of Virgins transported us from the merely beautiful to the "hauntingly beautiful," as James Michener described the island in *Rascals in Paradise*. This bay is commonly acknowledged to be one of the most picturesque sites in the South Pacific. Cliffs plunged directly into the sea, dwarfing the dozen boats already there. Surrounding the bay, hefty pinnacles of dark basalt rose against a setting of velvety green peaks. Due to these towering basalt cones, the bay was originally called the Bay of Penises, but missionaries felt compelled to rename it.

Before we left San Diego, our friends Drew and Dennis gave us a fascinating book, *Fatu Hiva*, written by the Norwegian Thor Heyerdahl. In the 1930s he and his young bride went to Fatu Hiva to return to nature. Toward the end of their stay they moved to the eastern side of the island and lived with the very elderly Tei Tetua, the last survivor of the entire east-coast population. A former chief, he was also the last Polynesian known to have participated in cannibal ceremonies. Tei's only companion was his adopted daughter, Tahia-Momo, who, by the description and photos in the book, was a bubbly girl of about twelve.

A fellow cruiser met the mayor of one of the villages, who was a descendent of the old cannibal. There's more: The mayor had the address of the adopted daughter, who was alive and well and living in Papeete. The cruiser shared the address with us. Part of me wanted to leave that very day to try to find the woman. Robb, being on a different trip, failed to see what was so compelling.

***

One of our goals on this island was to buy a tapa. Tapa cloth and tapa paintings take many forms and appear in most societies in the Pacific, probably throughout the world. In French Polynesia the art had nearly disappeared at the time we were there, except for some villages in the Marquesas. Hana Vave, where we were, was one of these places, and we walked by several huts in the village where people made and sold tapas. Diane from *Kama Lua* insisted Antoinette made the best and showed Annie and me where she lived and worked.

Antoinette received us in a blue, patterned pareo worn in the standard fashion: the rectangular piece of fabric wound about her substantial body – rather like a wrap-around skirt pulled up to her armpits – with the top two corners tucked in at the middle of her chest. It's the perfect outfit for hot, humid weather, and I took to wearing a pareo that way myself, but only on the boat.

The tapa process involves painting a picture or design, usually in black, on paper made of bark. Antoinette showed us the basic steps of how she made and painted the paper, starting with stripping the bark from a small tree. While we trailed her around the shop, a breadfruit roasted quietly, nested in big green leaves on coals in a fire pit.

With her few words of French, Annie did most of the bargaining. Goods were in as much demand as money, with used clothing valued at approximately $2.50 per piece. For the biggest tapa, about 2-feet-square, Antoinette asked 6,000 francs or $65. We gave her $30 cash, an old dress with a jacket, and a sizable plastic container with a crack in the bottom. She surprised us by gifting Annie the last of the five tapas we picked out: a foot-square, stylized rendering of a turtle.

***

As we wandered through the village, people we met beamed at our one word of Marquesan, "kaoha," meaning hello. Here and in other villages throughout our travels, locals often stopped Robb and asked if he would have a look at one broken object or another. Cruising men had a justifiable reputation for being able to repair things. One day he and Karl from *Kama Lua* decided to spend the whole day helping as many people as they could. Each man in the traveling repair team carried a small tool kit. They labored with varying success on a VCR, a sewing machine, a couple of outboard motors, a satellite receiver, a generator, and something like a weed whacker.

Iris, the owner of the generator, fussed with two little girls and a baby in a living room infused with half-a-dozen smoking mosquito coils. Lines of ants investigated the ubiquitous breadfruit roasting in the smoldering coals. She served us pamplemousse juice from a bucket and, in French style, bowls of coffee. In exchange for oranges, bananas and coconuts, we gave her perfume, jewelry and used clothes. We'd heard perfume was something Polynesian women desired, so we'd stocked up with several bottles. We could have used at least three or four dozen.

***

The Heyerdahl book described a taboo cave on the coast with a subterranean lake that had been used by a medicine man. His skeleton was supposed to be in an inner chamber seated at a stone table. We heard about a cave with a lake near where we were, so we put on our wetsuits and took off in the dinghy to have a look. With the help of a small, wooden sign posted on a stick, we found the cave. It occurred to me how different it was in the States, where a similar place of interest would be occasion for all manner of advertising, cautioning, and money-making hoopla.

We anchored the dinghy and climbed over rocks to the cave. Cautiously stepping into the dark, shallow water, we worked our way to the back of the cave. We could make out at the waterline the tip of an entrance that continued underwater and up into an inner chamber, presumably with the skeleton. As much as we wanted to see it, none of us was willing to risk swimming underwater to find out if the skeleton was really there.

We settled for further exploration of the cave where we were. Robb stubbed his toe on something solid and pulled from the water a 6-foot-long, heavy, black pallet. The 2-foot-wide platform had faint decorative carvings. The slab looked as if it was capable of holding a body for who-knows-what purpose. After I took a photo of Robb with his prize, he let the platform slip back into the water.

Sitting on a rock looking out to sea, Annie reluctantly posed for a photo: a re-creation of one of Heyerdahl's wife sitting in what looked like the same spot. After that day, we moved on to the next island.

Nuka Hiva

A miserable, eight-hour sail through rain and big, sloppy seas brought us to Comptroller Bay while it was still light. The wind stayed outside the bay, and the rain settled down to a foggy mist. At first the hills appeared to be solid green; but closer inspection revealed as many verdant shades as there were varieties of trees and plants. We poked around in this beautiful setting until Robb decided on the best of the three possible places to drop anchor. A local man, Thomas Tata, and his young son, Lewis, came up in their small motorboat to welcome us and invite us to a Mother's Day celebration a few days away.

The evening of the Mother's Day fête, we stopped by the Tata home so we could all walk together. Thomas's wife, Marie, had made a flower lei for me, a flower hair ornament for Annie and, for herself, a tall, flower headdress that resembled a three-layer cake. The celebration took place outdoors at the community center. Three naked lightbulbs on an overhead wire did their best to illuminate a cement platform that was the stage. A few palm fronds and pots of flowering plants cheered things up. Thirty or 40 folding chairs for the audience had already started to fill – no other foreigners in sight.

Eight heavy-set women in long dresses and leis around their waists and heads took the stage. Four or five bare-chested men in pareos and headdresses joined them. The group performed a modest island hula to the encouragement of a small band with our new friend Thomas on the guitar. What we appreciated most about the evening was that it wasn't a tourist show. It was the real deal – one of the reasons we were traveling. On the way home, the flashlight fell apart over the water, and we lost four rechargeable batteries, something else to ask for in our next care package from the States.

***

We spent about three weeks in Nuka Hiva, mostly because Thomas had an activity lined up for us every few days. Early on he introduced us to his parents and took us on a tour of the family property with its orchards of fruit trees, including a grove of 70-foot-tall mango trees. They were loaded with fruit so ripe that fallen mangoes littered the ground, and their heavenly scent filled the air.

Thomas and Marie invited us to their home for a scrumptious meal of chicken stew, cucumber with a spicy-hot mustard dip, breadfruit, taro, rice, bread, and lemonade. Thomas's "killer hot sauce" so impressed Alex that he asked for and wrote down the recipe: four heaping teaspoons of mustard, a teaspoon of vinegar, a little salt, dash of catsup, and oil until the consistency is right. We reciprocated with a Mexican-themed lunch of tortillas, a rice ring with a meat-sauce center, yogurt, and mango chutney. Since Thomas did some cooking, I was pleased when he asked for my chutney recipe.

One day, Thomas took us on a trek through red mud and no-see-ums to find tikis. The ancient stone figures were still in the places where they had played such an important role in the lives of the local people. Annie posed for a photo with her head on a sacrificial chopping block as Thomas held a machete above her neck. It seemed funny at the time, but now I feel sad about the men and women who may have lost their lives in just that way. More benignly, Thomas used his machete to whack open two types of coconuts. The drinking ones were sweet and refreshing. The sprouted ones for eating had the taste and texture of mildly-sweet, mushy Styrofoam. Annie loved them.

***

Thomas drove us in his pickup to Taiohae, the main town of Nuka Hiva. We shopped in Maurice's exotic store – small, dark, and smelly, but brightened by a smiling young woman in a skimpy top and pareo skirt behind the counter. Robb remembers another young woman taking off her top to try on another. Don't know how I missed that. Sitting on stone steps at the wharf, we watched the offloading of provisions for the island. A forklift coaxed pallets from the hold of a longboat struggling with the heaving surge. Except for the plastic wrap and items such as toilet paper, it could have been a scene from the last century – lots of gunnysacks leaning against old barrels.

We visited Dick and Mary from *L'Escargot* at the Kaiho Inn. They had work there, applying their expertise in hotel management. Alex and Annie palled around, surfing and playing soccer with the *Alia* kids, Loren and Dylan, "some of the nicest kids we had met cruising," Annie wrote.

For lunch we feasted on a gallon of vanilla ice cream. This was not unique while we were in French Polynesia. A restaurant meal for the four of us was prohibitively expensive, so ice cream was our go-to lunch – not a great hardship. Without question or reservation, Robb and the kids loved it. I had to rationalize that all the calcium and protein made the "meal" somewhat wholesome. Bread was cheap, so we always supplemented the ice cream with a baguette or two. You would see the four of us sitting on a bench or even the curb, with chunks of baguette in one hand and eating out of the carton with the spoons we always carried in our backpacks. Thus, we did our part to perpetuate the French view that Americans really are uncivilized.

***

In addition to an endless supply of mangoes, Thomas brought us oranges, guavas, pamplemousse, breadfruit, Marquesan apples, cucumbers, hot peppers, and taro. Once he turned up with his boat loaded to the gunnels with three entire stalks of bananas. We hung one from the spreaders and gave the other two away, one to *Dream Merchant*, one to *Halcyon*. He gave us vanilla beans and homemade wine. Upon hearing our complaint about insect bites, he produced a bottle of flower-scented coconut oil for protection.

Although Robb helped Thomas fix his boat, and we gave him and his wife several things, they seemed to give us much more in terms of time and goods – not an uncommon theme in our travels.

***

After a final day or two in Comptroller Bay, we moved farther west along the coast to see the fabled waterfall at exquisite Taioa Bay, or Daniel's Bay as it's known to cruisers. Daniel himself came to greet us. He and his wife, Antoinette, lived in a house they'd built on the beach and had been welcoming cruisers since 1970.

When we bought *Sorcery*, the broker told us, "Wherever you go in the world, people will know the boat." Sure enough, Daniel remembered seeing her 15 years earlier. Robb confirmed the fact, knowing *Sorcery* had stopped there on her way back from a race to Tahiti. Before we left San Diego, a man with the Japanese entry into the America's Cup race told us he'd seen *Sorcery* in Japan 20 years ago. Over the years, a dozen people came up to the boat asking, "Is this the original *Sorcery?*" Most people said they'd crewed on her. One man, Robert Simms, got Robb's undivided attention by relating his experience of being on the boat when it rolled over and lost the mast in the north Pacific.

⚓

A delightful German couple, Klaus and Claudia on *Wadu Ryo,* joined us for the three-mile hike to the falls. Early in the morning we started up the single-file, rocky trail, which took us across many small streams. A lush and varied tropical forest gave way to a spooky landscape of moss-covered trees and tikis.

At last we reached our dazzling destination. The highest waterfall in the territories plummeted 1,000 feet into a cul-de-sac where a wide, deep pool had formed. Foot-high cairns, created out of smooth, black stones by previous visitors, studded a bright green meadow. Stripping down to our swimsuits, we threw our hot, tired bodies into the chilly water. The bravest of us swam through the stinging curtain where the waterfall ended, and then challenged the others – maybe it was only me – to join them on the other side. I did, but in the process lost one of my plastic sandals.

After a while, we sat drying in the sun, ate our picnic, then headed back. I put both socks on the shoeless foot. Predictably, the heels of both socks soon developed giant holes. Strange, but my bare heel made it the rest of the three miles without so much as a drop of blood.

During the entire round-trip we encountered only one other person. A roughly dressed fellow trudged toward us with a gunnysack slung over his shoulder and a butcher knife tucked into his thick belt. As we stepped aside to let him pass, we saw two pig's ears and the tip of a snout sticking out of the top of a bloody sack – not something you see every day.

One evening, Klaus and Claudia joined us for Spam & Marquesan-Apple Sushi. He brought his guitar and led us in exuberant renditions of American songs like "House of the Rising Sun." Another evening we had fried bananas with papaya/mango chutney, baguettes lathered with garlic mayonnaise, and baked breadfruit with mustard sauce.

Klaus was from Berlin. During the Berlin Wall era he and some friends dug a tunnel under the wall and helped several people escape from the East. The night of November 9, 1989, when he'd heard on the radio the wall was coming down, he rushed out to take part in that historic moment.

***

It was time to head to the next island group. So, the kids and I dug out our Flag Making Kit – scissors, glue, needle and thread, a ruler, a pencil, straight pins, permanent markers, little pots of paint and some brushes, and pieces of fabric in basic colors – to create a courtesy flag to fly while we were there. Some cruisers made quite elaborate banners. Ours were minimal in size and design and best viewed from a distance.

The Tuamotus ~ July 1993

Three nights of sailing brought us to the largest chain of coral atolls in the world. That archipelago of reefs surrounding lagoons spans an area roughly the size of Western Europe. We only visited one of the atolls, Manihi. My journal reports the trip this way, "Yet another passage where I wonder how I got here – utterly miserable rocking and rolling. Bed damp and musty smelling. Then some nicer days with pleasant, steady sailing. Delicious rendezvous with my husband between watches. Weather fine until we reached entrance to Manihi, then rain, dark clouds, choppy entrance."

The current at Manihi never reversed, but came out of the deep, narrow pass at greater or lesser speeds. Since we arrived at high tide – when the current was fastest – we had a couple of hours to kill until it slowed down. We motored in circles and talked to boats inside. It was lunchtime and the Fourth of July, so I set about making the closest thing I could to hot dogs – happy little Canned Vienna Sausage piglets in biscuit blankets.

When the time came to go through the pass, Robb climbed up to sit on the first spreaders to better see into the water. I was at the wheel.

Theoretically, our Audionics headsets enabled us to speak and hear each other without wires or shouting. As we motored slowly through the pass, he was gesturing while my eyes were glued straight ahead. I heard him say,

"Starboard ... Starboard." I made a slight adjustment to the right. Then heard a much louder

"Starboard! Starboard!" Steering a little farther to the right produced a loud crunch.

"The *other* starboard!!!" He'd meant port, but luckily the close encounter wasn't serious.

In spite of the rain, flies, and mosquitoes, we spent a relaxing, and mostly pleasant month in Manihi. Shortly after we anchored, someone we recognized motored up in his dinghy, the hippie from *Orion*. Rodney chatted and hung on the lifelines for some time before we invited him aboard. Robb offered him a beer. By the time he left that day, we'd all fallen under his spell. He was warm and funny and, we found out later, a genius at motor repair. Actually, he could fix nearly anything.

Annie became the first in our family to be invited to *Orion*, and after that she spent most of her Manihi time with Katherine and Rodney. "They're the best adult friends I have ever had," our girl wrote in her journal. They gave her their address, and 20 years later, in 2013, she visited them, still in Valdez, Alaska. In 2017 Robb and I visited them too.

Someone called for the first of many potlucks on the beach. *Dream Merchant, Orion, Alley Cat, Gannet, Mini-the-Mermaid*, the South African boat *Tshuza*, and others showed up. That was the day we first met *Sannyasi*, with Al and Lisa, who would become dear friends.

In addition to the food, the main attraction was Hermit Crab Races. Carefully selected entrants were positioned, then released all at once in the center of a 3-foot-wide circle drawn in the sand. The first crab to go outside the circle would win. The little fellows, dressed up in a variety of shells that had been abandoned, wobbled here and there, entertaining us for quite some time. The crabs didn't get the concept of the race, so the circle gradually got smaller and smaller until we had a winner. We took a couple of crabs – and a few larger, empty shells for them to move into – back to the boat as a science project. Like the circle game, they weren't on board with our plans, and after a couple of days we took them back to their home.

Alex and Robb snorkeling at Manihi

For a month time passed with regular chores and things to repair, reading and homework, snorkeling and windsurfing, watching videos, visiting with other boats, and lots and lots of really awful arguing among the four of us. I didn't record and don't remember the details, but I imagine the arguing was all fairly normal family stuff, compounded by the close quarters. Reading Irving Stone's *Darwin* and Paul Theroux's *Happy Isles of Oceania* helped keep me grounded.

Besides spending time with Katherine and Rodney, Annie made pasta from scratch with Joan on *Gannet*, and spent days with Justin from *Uwhilna* building a fort out of debris on the beach. Alex busied himself with some cooking and started delivering baguettes to other cruisers. That project lasted until the island ran out of flour and the bakery closed. Robb repaired our leaking dinghy, put the wind generator together, cleaned the VCR, fixed the fuel pump on the dinghy motor, and got banged up falling into an open locker.

Katherine from *Orion* and Trish from *Uwhilna* came over with their guitars for a memorable ladies' afternoon. Katherine with her splendid voice sang a moving song she'd written. We played and sang and talked women's issues – a welcome break from boating and cruising.

⚓

Manihi is where I turned fifty-one. Robb put out the word for an unheard-of, desserts-only potluck. But it rained the day of. So Alex, after searching through several cookbooks, made pancakes. Mine had a candle. And Robb fixed mimosas for me and himself. They were probably made with Tang, but there's an outside chance we had orange juice from the village store. In any case we had champagne, so it was fun.

The next day was sunny and bright with "potluck on the beach" written all over it. What started out as a birthday party for me had expanded to encompass all July birthdays. People from about 14 boats participated and produced a dazzling array of pies, cakes, cookies and candies. Alex and Annie contributed two Key Lime pies.

A young Italian couple, Babs and her husband on *Diario*, misunderstood and brought garlic bread, which was in fact very welcome. Babs entertained us with magic tricks, juggling, and fashioning balloon animals for the children. I wore a bikini with a sarong and sported a temporary tattoo of a lacey heart with streamers. Those were the days.

I'd been complaining my hormone replacement wasn't working, and the hot flashes killing me. At the party Robb learned Darryl on *Tshuza* was a gynecologist, and asked him if he could help me. Misery overcame embarrassment and the next day I went over to his boat to see what he had to say. He started off in a doctorly manner, "So, tell me about these hot flashes."

"Actually, I'm having one right now."

"Maybe it only happens when you see me?"

He was cute and half my age, and advanced his theory in a playful, innocent way. Then seriously, he recommended two different regimens, each to be tried for a month. I seem to remember the one where I took a pill each day worked better than the one that missed some days.

***

One Sunday we attended a service at the little Methodist church. Like many buildings on the atolls, heavy cables over the roof helped keep the structure from flying away during a hurricane. Barefoot girls of six or seven giggled and flirted with us in their Sunday best, Western dresses all frills and neon colors.

From the gallery, we looked down upon a garden of wide, flower-adorned straw hats. I'm sure there were a few men, but the women in their finery overshadowed them. We'd come for the singing. Magnificent a cappella voices filled the nave. Though I didn't understand the Tuvaluan words, the melodies stirred up pleasurable memories of childhood hymns.

⚓

We intentionally swam with sharks – it was the thing to do there. The bottom-dwelling lagoon sharks were not as aggressive as the pelagic sharks that patrolled outside the reef. Here's how it worked: Since the water was always flowing out of the atoll, someone dinghied you to the lagoon end of the 100-foot-long pass.

Dressed in your wetsuit, you lowered yourself into the water with your snorkeling gear and let the current carry you out. As you floated, you could easily see the sharks lounging on the bottom, several yards below. The dinghy driver waited to pick you up at the ocean end of the pass. Robb said some sharks were as long as 10 feet. That sounds about right, though typically the sharks I saw were at least twice as long as what everyone else saw.

Black Pearls

Manihi had a great number of pearl farms, and was the original home of the highly-prized Polynesian black pearls. A French couple owned a small island, a motu, and operated a business cultivating these gems. Annie and I visited their farm, and she was invited to help extract the precious balls from craggy, open-hand-sized oysters. She wrote at the time, "They have to buy little samplings which they put inside the oysters while there [sic] growing. The sampling gets caught in the tissue of the mallush, then gets layered by something called araamite or calcite."

The wife showed how the pearls got processed – which wasn't much. Loaded into small gunny sacks with handfuls of salt, the messy little balls endured rubbing and rolling around until they gleamed. Next, she separated them by quality. On her kitchen table she emptied two bags, hundreds of pearls, onto the blue and white checked tablecloth. A photo shows Annie and the couple's three-year-old girl, arms around each other, admiring the two black puddles of pearls.

"How much do they cost?" Annie asked.

"Why do you want to know?"

"I just wondered if they're in my budget."

The woman rummaged around and found two enchanting, if visibly imperfect, baubles and gave them to Annie. "It was really kind of her to let me have two 60-dollar pearls," Annie wrote at the time. We didn't let on that $60 was the price of a perfect specimen. At any rate, the ones she got are worth far more than that to us.

The Society Islands ~ August and September 1993

The Societies were every bit as stunning as pictured in the slides I'd seen years ago. Mammoth, cotton-ball clouds hovered above each small, green mountain that nestled between the blues of the sky and the dark ocean. Palms and other trees lined unspoiled sand beaches. A reef surrounding each island held a lagoon, where we anchored in shallow, bright-aqua water.

Tahiti

Rather than stay in the crowded, expensive harbor at the capital of Papeete, we ventured around to the southeast side of the island and found a delightful place to anchor next to a botanical garden. Some little boys in small, handmade boats paddled up with offerings of star fruit, lemons, bananas, and pamplemousse. From our collection of giveaways, we found some small American flag pins for those miniature ambassadors.

One day before we left the boat, I'd hung Robb's best and only good shirt, a black Ralph Lauren polo, on a hanger on deck in a whiff of breeze. When we returned, the shirt and hanger were gone. A big problem with losses when you're cruising is things can be devilishly difficult to replace. Probably in Papeete we could have bought a Ralph Lauren shirt. But back then, buying another new, designer shirt wasn't something we'd have considered doing.

***

A public bus, Le Truck, took us on a crowded ride into Papeete. For an hour and a half, bustling passengers kept us entertained. I was disappointed no one came on board carrying a clucking chicken. It was that kind of scene.

The trip ended in a strip mall parking lot cleared of cars. The space had been taken over by a couple of dozen teenage boys and girls milling around in native dancing costumes. Elaborate 2-foot-tall feather headdresses, loads of flowers, beads, shells, and raffia figured in the gorgeous ensembles. The young women wore tops made of coconut-shell halves lacquered shiny black and held in place with a minimal amount of black cord. The bare-chested young men were just as stunning.

A band of older men in straw hats provided rhythm with a huge red drum, big conch-shell horns, and various simple, wooden shapes that got teased and thumped with straw whisks and drumsticks. The directress was rather elegant in a flowery straw hat, a simple black dress with a yellow flounce, and black pumps. It's true she was a bit heavy and had a double chin; but you could guess from her proud bearing and the profile of her face that she had probably danced with the best of them.

When the program started, a luscious young lady pulled Robb out of the crowd to join her in an energetic hula. To the applause and amusement of everyone, he did a very credible job. Clearly this was a semi-professional troupe, and thus produced the sensuous island dance we'd been hoping to see.

Robb's dance lesson

The show was a promotion to get locals to attend a store opening, and they came in droves. Flower-bedecked men, women and children packed the sidewalks. A sprinkling of them, even the men, wore what looked like their everyday outfits of pareo skirts with T-shirts. Quite a few of the adults smoked. That seemed incongruous when, at the same time, they were adorned with fresh flowers. The audience was as colorful and entertaining in its own way as the performers were in theirs. The whole experience pleased me in a way no big show at a hotel could even touch.

⚓

When the dancing finished, we went on into town. At the post office we found three pounds of mail addressed to "S/V Sorcery, General Delivery, Papeete, Tahiti." In those days before cell phones or email, there was no waiting until we got back to the boat to open the trove of letters. Hearing from family and friends, even if the news was weeks or months old, renewed our spirits. After going through the mail during our customary curbside lunch, we strolled around.

Thousands and thousands of multicolored pareos hanging by one corner from revolving display racks filled street after street. I bought pareos for the whole family, one for a curtain for our cabin, and a few for friends back home. I bought a coconut shell bra for the one woman I thought would at least try it on, Gabrielle. The lively harbor with all the rocking boats, flapping flags, and human activity added to the shifting, swirling urban color.

The Old Cannibal's Adopted Daughter

Feeling confident about taking a bus to town, Annie and I took off on our own one day to find Tahia-Momo, the old cannibal's adopted daughter. The scrap of paper with the address, plus asking directions once or twice, led us straight to her home, a modest couple of rooms in a warren of connected apartments in the city center. Even though we arrived unannounced, a jolly, plump, seventy-something Tahia-Momo made us feel welcome. My rudimentary French wasn't getting very far since she spoke Marquesan. Before long her gracious, French-speaking granddaughter appeared. With her smattering of English and mine of French, the conversation moved along.

I opened my copy of *Fatu Hiva* to the photos. Tahia-Momo's eyes lit up and she jabbered with excitement as she pointed and leafed through the pages. The granddaughter translated as I asked questions about people and events in the book. When we came to the photo of the young Tahia-Momo taken in the 1930s, we could see the resemblance between the woman before us and the twelve-year-old with flowers in her hair and a face that was all smiles.

"Would you please sign the photo?" I asked in words and gestures. With a shaky hand, she wrote "Kamis Tahia mo mo." As we were saying our goodbyes, the granddaughter told us they once had a copy of the book, but didn't know what happened to it.

"May we have this one?" she asked. Oh, boy. Tough call.

"I love this one with the signature," I told her, "but I'll try to send you another copy when I get home." To my regret, in the ensuing years the address got lost. It feels like another example of us getting more than we gave, though Tahia-Momo seemed pleased to relive those years, if even for a little while. The book with her signature is one of the most cherished mementos of the trip.

***

Robb's and my wedding anniversary had come and gone the month before without much recognition, so we decided to splurge for dinner in a little French restaurant near where we were anchored. Dressed in the best evening-out attire we could muster – a skirt and black top for me, a sport shirt and his best shorts for Robb – we dinghied over to the modest, candle-lit place on the shore. Our budget allowed for a salad, a plate of cheeses, dessert and a bottle of Beaujolais. The ambiance and wine more than made up for not having money for an entrée. To end the romantic evening, we rowed to the middle of the moonlit bay and lingered there a while.

⚓

The morning we left Tahiti for the day sail to Moorea, seaweed clogged the intake hose. Robb unclogged it while I steered through the sizable waves. And Robb remembers a fish, "something really big," bit the hook on the line over the transom and spooled the reel. That is to say, the fish took the line and ran with it until the line was completely out and finally snapped off, "exploded," as Robb put it.

Moorea

We anchored on the north side of the island. *Uwhilna* stayed an extra day because we had come in; and that evening our two families played a hilarious game of Pictionary. We rarely "buddy boated," that is deliberately traveled with another boat. But many of us were on the same "milk run," a route most cruisers took, so we often ran into each other. Then, even if we'd met only once, we felt a kinship.

Moorea is where we first met a delightful French family, Soazic, Manou, and toddler Thomas on the catamaran *Diabolo*. Soazic had a good figure and wore a bikini most of the time. It was hard not to stare, not so much because of the scanty attire, but because the thick, frizzy, red hair she didn't shave from her armpits, bikini area, or legs. I thought a lot about American TV advertising and about how traveling expands your mind.

At one place we anchored in water so shallow only a few feet separated our keel from the rock–hard coral bottom. We were just off a resort, so we took a walk around. It was seductive to me: tidy thatched huts scattered over vast expanses of green lawn, a clubhouse, a restaurant. *How heavenly it would be,* I thought, *to stay here a night or two, with everything neat and clean, a vacation from the usual chores …*

Then Robb broke the spell. "Wouldn't you just hate to stay in a place like this?"

⚓

Our primary mission on this island was to deliver information we'd collected on marine mammals we'd seen since leaving Mexico. Before we left the States, I'd read in The Seven Seas Cruising Association Commodore's Bulletin that an American researcher in Moorea was asking people crossing the Pacific to record sightings of marine mammals. We had bought the reference book he'd recommended, the aforementioned *Handbook of Whales and Dolphins* by Leatherwood and Reeves.

From mid-April to mid-August the whole family enthusiastically participated in recording every sighting: weather and sea conditions, geographical coordinates, number and specific type of animal, behavior, and physical description. I'd prepared the notes on my portable manual Brother typewriter, and we took photos.

Dr. Michael Poole took our report seriously and studied it and the photos very carefully. We felt like real researchers when he told us our notes showed this was the first record of sighting common dolphins south of the equator. In the photo of a pod cavorting just underwater around our bow, he pointed to the smallest one, and thrilled us by saying, "That's a newborn. You can tell by the fetal folds."

We were shocked at how few animals we saw: seven sightings of dolphins in four months, no whales. Dr. Poole assured us that was normal. Marine mammals were disappearing from the Pacific Ocean.

Huahine

Maybe a school bus on a ferryboat was common throughout the islands, but this was the only place we saw one. I talked the kids into riding the bus/boat to visit a school for the day. The minute we arrived, friendly English-speaking students and teachers gathered around us. I checked in with the principal, who was nonplussed as to our purpose. Evidently this was her first encounter with foreign visitors who simply wanted to see what a local school was like. The teachers, on the other hand, understood and were eager to have their students interact with us, mostly, I believe, to practice their English.

Alex decided the visit wasn't for him, and after one class spent the day in town. Annie and I joined English and French classes and had lunch in the cafeteria. The girls drew pictures of her, gave her little gifts, and sat with us at lunch, so Annie had fun. Half a day would have been plenty for me.

A family walk to a village was more rewarding. A neat pyramid of dozens of cannonballs on the side of the dirt road turned out to be breadfruit for sale. I took photos of a woman's tattooed barefoot and of a tall, muscular transvestite who was posing and dressed all in hot pink: a wide-brimmed hat, a belly-revealing sleeveless top, and a short, tight skirt. Five dollars bought us an entire stalk of bananas still on a tree. The cost included cutting the stalk down and delivering it to our dinghy in a wheelbarrow.

On our way home from a trip into the main town of Fare, a hard rain overtook us in the dinghy. Etched in my memory is racing to take refuge under a bridge, but once in its shelter, we were in no hurry. Listening to the rhythms of the rain hammering overhead, we ate cheese sandwiches at leisure, watched the rain beat down on the water. Once the rain let up, we motored back to our boat, changed into dry clothes, and warmed ourselves with cups of hot butterscotch punch.

Each day two men maneuvered a raft loaded with mini watermelons around the bay to their customers on shore. The morning we left Huahine, the raft stopped at our boat to give each of us a personal-sized watermelon as a going-away gift. One of the men was the school bus driver, who'd remembered when we were leaving. That was the first of many times we received presents on the day we left – a heart-warming island tradition.

Raiatea & Tahaa

The small jewels of Raiatea and Tahaa, huddled within the same surrounding reef, seemed little more than stepping stones to our goal of Bora Bora. After the lushness of Tahiti, Moorea and Huahine, we'd become jaded. At Tahaa, we motored past a church with a red roof and a tall, tall steeple perched right at the water's edge. The spark of color against the pervasive greens and blues added a note of interest.

We anchored one night at each island, walked on shore and bought baguettes. The elongated baguette shape was convenient for home delivery. Throughout the Society Islands, nearly every mailbox on a post at the side of the road had a fresh, unwrapped baguette or two poking out of it each morning. The system seemed so trusting. We hoped it meant everyone could afford at least a loaf of bread.

A shy boy, coming up to our boat in his leaky, handmade canoe, got chased off by an older man. A little later, as we walked on shore, the same man came up to us with all the flip-flops we'd left in the dinghy. Apparently, the boy had taken them. So theft was not unknown. Were tourists fair game? Was he just being a little boy? Did his family need shoes? Except for small, uncertain incidents like that and the time we lost Robb's shirt, we didn't experience or even worry about thievery in all those years of cruising. On the other hand, we usually took common precautions, like not leaving valuables in plain sight, and always avoided places reported to be unsafe.

Bora Bora

We forgave the weather for raining every few days and for being hot and muggy most of the time, because the island was almost too beautiful. Using the same elements as the other Societies, this island managed to be even more breathtaking. In the center of a wide lagoon with a barrier reef, the remnants of an extinct volcano rose to two green peaks. We motored in from the dark purple-blue ocean to the bright aqua lagoon, and anchored in shallow water near the pass. White sand beaches and puffy white clouds accented the greens of the land and the blues of the sky and water. Luminous air lent a sharp, pure quality to the whole panorama.

At anchor, the nearly transparent water gave the impression our boat and dinghy were suspended. At low tide, less than 6 inches of water separated our keel from the sand, and the illusion became even more intense. On two nights, the full moon and the calm water made the boat's shadow on the white sand bottom ethereal, dreamlike.

***

Several boats we knew were already there: *Orion, Sannyasi, Uwhilna, Monte Cristo, Diabolo, Guinevere, Pollen Path,* and maybe some others. People from various boats got together for tea and snacks, sharing confidences and gossip, holding book and food exchanges, swapping and watching movies, sharing meals on the boats, and having drinks at the Bora Bora Yacht Club.

Before we'd left San Diego, someone suggested we join a yacht club in order to get reciprocal privileges in other countries. With so much money being poured into the boat, we didn't feel we could invest in a club membership. As things turned out, every foreign club we visited welcomed us to at least have drinks and sometimes even meals, which is all we really cared about. A free day or two at the dock would have been nice, but awfully pricy considering the cost of club membership.

In the daytime, Alex windsurfed and snorkeled with Olin from *Guinevere*. Annie hung out with Olin's sister Elaine, doing girl things like styling each other's hair, watching *The Little Mermaid* over and over, exchanging books, and the ultimate, staying up one night talking until 6 in the morning. At an evening potluck on the beach, we threw coconuts into the bonfire to roast them, and wrapped snakes of bread dough around sticks to cook some "shoosh." Katherine, Trish, and I strummed guitars and sang.

One morning, Robb and I and the four kids rented bicycles for $5 per person for the day. At that point in their lives, both of our kids had been living on a boat for years. Although at various times they'd owned bikes, neither of them had much experience. So toward the beginning of the trip, each took a couple of nasty spills on the gravelly, dirt road.

"Listen, we could turn back, get cleaned up, then decide what we want to do," Robb offered at the first spill as I pecked at the gravel imbedded in Annie's bloody knee. Someone had loaned us a small tire repair kit, but we didn't carry a semblance of a first aid kit, or even a bottle of water. "Nah, I'm fine," she said.

The six of us continued pedaling the 18 scenic miles around the edge of the island. From time to time we stopped to admire the view, wade in the lagoon, eat our lunch, and climb out on palm trees leaning low over the water. Sagging rainbows of pareos fluttered on clotheslines to dry. Sometimes the lines were strung between two palms. Who knew laundry hanging in public could be such a gift?

A day or two after that, we drove the dinghy around the island and stopped at a workshop we'd passed on the bike tour. Using bold colors, a man hand-painted abstracts on fabric to create lava-lavas, the Bora Bora word for pareos, in the way an artist would paint a picture, with the cloth tacked to a huge vertical canvas. The results were striking enough to hang on the wall as art and just as expensive.

Regarding lava-lavas as clothing, even though men weren't "required" to wear them on Bora Bora, that day Robb had worn a handsome black and gray one tied around his waist. He looked terrific, even though he didn't learn to tie it properly the way the locals did until we got to Fiji.

***

We explored a snorkeling spot advertised to be one of the best in the world. However, I couldn't help but compare the drab, gray or faintly colored coral and skimpy schools of pale fish to other snorkeling we'd done, and particularly what I'd seen in the Red Sea in the '70s. Back then, massive schools of tropical fish – each group with its own startling hues and designs – darted and swayed before vast colonies of richly colored, fantastically shaped coral. By the '90s, much of the world's marine life suffered from a variety of environmental impacts. I felt melancholy for the losses, and fortunate I'd had an outstanding experience and point of reference.

When we went into town to buy supplies and call home, Robb said, and did not mean it as a compliment, "This reminds me of Tijuana." Through my rose-colored glasses, the comparison seemed harsh. In any case, the energy and the potential for bargains in a busy, cluttered, tourist town always attracted me. We needed a smaller salad bowl, and one of frosted plastic caught my eye. Boaters don't use glass, an obvious hazard, so the plastic vessel with its textured, cabbage-leaf pattern was perfect. Now when we use the bowl, it brings back happy South Pacific memories.

⚓

Robb couldn't wait to get to the English-speaking Cook Islands, whereas I would have been happy to stay in Bora Bora. One, because I wanted to continue working on my French. I'd just learned how to ask, Where's the trash can? *Où est la poubelle?* And two, I nearly always advocated staying wherever we were.

Katherine and Rodney asked about buddy boating for the three- or four-day trip to the Rarotonga. His ulcers were acting up, and the chance they might begin hemorrhaging while underway was a concern. Robb devised a plan whereby *Orion*, the slower boat, would leave a day ahead of us. That way each boat could go at its own speed, but never be that far away from the other. About halfway to Rarotonga, we passed close to *Orion*. Katherine called over the radio,

"Hello there! *Sorcery* looks like the fine race horse she is, galloping by!"

The Cook Islands ~ October 1993

The crowded anchorage at Avatiu on the main island of Rarotonga required us to med-moor, which is to say, drop the bow anchor and back perpendicularly into the dock. The maneuver was tricky because *Sorcery* didn't willingly go straight back. I personally could not talk her into it, so backing up was yet another job for Robb. We tied up at the only place left, between an empty "no parking" zone and another boat a mere 3 or 4 feet away, leaving far less privacy than we liked.

In this case though, friendly New Zealanders Jenny and Wayne made perfect neighbors – helpful, but not intrusive. They lived on Rarotonga the year round and had a game fishing business with their boat *Te Manu Rere*. Being at the dock didn't cost anything, and we only had to dingy a few feet to shore. We stayed 36 days. "Every one of them was fun and interesting," Alex wrote in his journal. Three times he mentioned that things were cheap.

The first night a radio call summoned people from all the boats for a potluck in the park: *Gannet, Lady Ruth, Wadu Ryo, Brigadoon, Rapunzel, Malaguena, Guinevere, Ecstasy, Energetic, Cetacean,* and I'm sure others. That overall sense of inclusiveness, widening the circle, was one of the most endearing trademarks of the cruising life.

Everybody loved Rarotonga. Due to its historical association with England and New Zealand, the locals spoke English. Yet the island, settled in the 6th century by Polynesian people, retained a strong South Pacific flavor. Our money went much further than in the Society Islands, so we stocked up on food and other basics. The best souvenirs, handmade from wood and affordable, included fishhook pendants, bowls, serving forks and spoons inlaid with shell, mortar and pestle sets, and decorative flowers.

Cheese-bread-to-die-for replaced the baguettes we'd thought we couldn't live without. We bought a stalk of bananas from a truck. The first stalk we ever got, back in Mexico, ripened politely a few bananas at a time. By the second stalk, I understood why someone recommended that when you go cruising, you need a recipe for 150 bananas. We always managed to give away most of them, but still had oodles of plain bananas, fried bananas, bananas in fruit salad, not to mention banana bread, banana muffins, and banana pancakes. A few special occasions demanded the crowd-pleaser bananas flambé.

Guinevere had planned to leave the day after we arrived, but the weather looked too rough. That gave the four kids a few more days together. The boys surfed and played computer games. Taking a lunch along, the two girls and I rode horses one day through coffee and fruit tree plantations to a waterfall and back along the beach – all six of us snacking on those bananas.

After Elaine left, Annie spent a lot of time with Katherine and Rodney. Katherine would play Office and Hair Salon with her. A call came over the radio.

"Hello, this is Annie at the Orion Hair Salon. Would you care to make an appointment?"

"Oh, yes," I said, "I'm desperate to have my hair done. When may I come in?"

"You can come now. And Mom, please bring that rat-tail comb and those big clips."

Annie adored Rodney. He let her "style" his hair, which he wore in a long braid, and had her help him with easy sailor's chores around the boat. When we parted ways for the last time, Rodney cut off a lock of his hair for Annie, which she still has somewhere. Years later, Katherine and Rodney said their experience with Annie helped convince them to have a child of their own. Such a compliment parents don't get every day.

***

Marcello, a young man from another boat, and Alex both earned Junior Open-Water Scuba Diving certifications with Mark on *Cetacean*. Neighbor Wayne took Alex and Robb to their first-ever rugby match. He explained the history and the rules, and led Alex into being a rugby fan to this day. Alex often went into the village on his own, sometimes to call his mom. Locally purchased phone cards made calling easy. I'd forgotten how many calls we'd made while traveling until I ran across Annie's prized and colorful collection of dozens and dozens of phone cards from all over the world.

For Katherine's birthday, we had a small party and gave her long, dangling feather earrings. The next day Annie turned ten. After our traditional early morning cake with candles and singing, she and I went to town to have her ears re-pierced. The holes punctured in her earlobes in Mexico when she was six had long since closed up. After the new starter earrings were installed, we headed to the farmers market, a daily fixture with stalls offering food, drinks, crafts, and inexpensive ready-made fresh flower crowns and leis.

The crown for the birthday girl was not a simple row of flowers strung together like the ones worn by cashiers, both male and female, in the supermarket. No, we're talking about an artistic assembly of large and small flowers – reds, yellows, and whites with ample accents of green. Back on the boat she changed into her new yellow and white pareo, a gift from Jenny and Wayne. "Annie, Raro '93" appeared in a corner of the hand-dyed garment.

Annie's tenth birthday

A day or two earlier, Nancy Griffith, an American skipper and owner of the Cook Islands 200-ton freighter *Avatapu*, had invited us aboard for a tour and coffee. She and her late husband, Bob, had sailed around the world three times in the 1960s, and were well-known in cruising lore. Captain Nancy asked me to take photos of a competing freighter that was illegally overloaded. On Annie's birthday, I took a few shots of the offending freighter, then used up the rest of the film on the birthday girl in her finery.

Feeling way too conspicuous in the flower crown and pareo, she had to be coaxed out from behind a tree for the photo shoot. The best of those photos turned out to be her signature picture from the trip, and is still an all-time favorite of ours. Later in the day Katherine and Rodney joined us for a little party and gave her a bracelet and two pairs of earrings. A game of ancient origins, Knucklebones, this one made with real goat knuckles, came from Mark and Cindy on *Cetacean*.

***

Annie visited and got invited to boats even if they didn't have children. *Energetic* had a twenty-year-old girl and, better yet, a dog. Both of our kids would have loved having a pet, but Robb and I couldn't face the complications of having one on a boat, let alone while traveling. Most countries required pets be quarantined, and sometimes a substantial bond had to be posted as well. Without a pet of our own, Annie gravitated toward and bonded with any she met.

Many people who'd started out with pets ended up shipping them home at great expense, or even lost them, one way or another. Muffin, the *Brigadoon* cat, circumnavigated and became as famous as her owners, Catherine and Bill. Ten days after they landed back home in North Carolina and all the three of them had their picture in the local newspaper, Muffin sprang for freedom.

***

Fixing meals for Frances and Rod from *Lady Ruth* intimidated me a little because she'd had her own catering business. But we enjoyed their company and began having regular teas and dinners together. Her first afternoon tea featured rum-frosted carrot cake. Here's one difference between her and me: I could make a decent carrot cake, but wouldn't dream of adding frosting – the rum, maybe, but not all that sugar and butter.

She showed us the latest thing for music – CDs instead of tapes – introducing Annie to the soundtrack of *South Pacific*. Years after we returned from the trip, Frances, an adult Annie, and I met in San Francisco to see a stage performance of that musical. Getting together with a friend, with a theme from the cruising days, evoked sweet memories and nurtured a strong sense of continuity in our lives. Frances and Rod are still close friends.

Frances, a registered nurse, loaned me a book, *The Boy Who Couldn't Stop Washing*, on Obsessive Compulsive Disorder. In the back of the book, a 100-question test showed where you were on the Obsessive Compulsive Personality, not the Disorder, scale. Robb gave me the test, then announced with pride,

"Dianne! You got 100 percent!"

The information interested me, but it didn't go so far as to change my behavior. I often felt that, absent a direct order, no one in my family seemed capable of picking up, cleaning up, or straightening up a single thing.

***

A handbill advertising the movie *Jurassic Park,* directed people to the beer factory to buy tickets. We hadn't seen a movie in a theater for eons, and this promised to be great fun. Coincidentally, the film was showing on Halloween, not something the locals celebrated, but for us added to the excitement. Rod and Frances joined us at the 200-seat, packed and noisy theater. We all enjoyed the experience, although the show would have been scarier if the audience had not talked when they were supposed to be holding their breath, and not laughed when they were supposed to be terrified. In his journal, Alex compared the film to the book, and ended with this note, "The dinosaurs are very good actors."

The day after the movie, Rod and Frances, Nancy, and Klaus and Claudia from *Wado Ryu* all stopped to visit in the late afternoon. Rod and Frances were still new friends with much to talk about. Nancy told us loads of cruising stories and appeared to enjoy the break from what must have been a rather solitary life.

"Is there any place you didn't get to you wished you had?" I asked Nancy.

"Zanzibar. I always wanted to go to Zanzibar." I added that island on the east coast of Africa to my wish list, but we didn't make it there either.

The usually upbeat Klaus and Claudia were a bit out of sorts. They needed comfort and diversion because a line caught in the propeller as they were anchoring and something on the boat's shaft broke. Five hours later we'd worked our way through a multitude of stories and jokes, several large bowls of popcorn, a couple of pitchers of lemonade, a few bottles of wine, and stacks and stacks of warm, toasted-cheese sandwiches cut in fourths. If I'd known ahead of time five people would be joining us for the whole evening, I'd have spent way too much time and energy planning, buying, and preparing food. Since they just showed up, the pressure was off.

Commercial Fishing

One day, because Wayne's game fishing customers didn't show up, he invited Robb and Alex to go out. Alex got a fancy certificate for reeling in a 35-pound wahoo, while Robb hauled in the front half of what had only recently been a 30-pound tuna. Wayne pointed out you could tell by the clean cut that the back half of the tuna had been bitten off by a wahoo.

Another time when Wayne did have customers, he took Robb along as crew. Robb must have impressed Wayne with his fishing, boat handling, and people skills because Wayne, who was buying a second boat, offered Robb a job. Maybe he would have considered the opportunity if we'd been younger and childless. In any case, he was flattered to have been asked.

***

In the final days when we began to think about leaving, I came down with the flu, then Robb got sick enough to go to the doctor. Robb's ailment, a lung infection triggered by a severe reaction to the pollen of a certain tree in the November spring air, responded well to antibiotics. I told the kids we had to take good care of their dad because without him we were in deep kimchee.

"Mom," Annie said with conviction, "we can do this."

During preparations for the passage, Robb caught his arm between the spinnaker pole and the lifelines. The arm swelled up alarmingly, but settled down with the application of ice which we must have gotten from another boat.

"We should just go home," I complained. "This is too dangerous."

"It's not that bad and could happen anywhere," Robb reasoned. My silent, closing thought on the useless exchange: *Yes, my point exactly. We could have been out at sea and far from ice or help of any kind.*

When the day came to leave, Jenny and Wayne placed long necklaces of small shells around each of our necks. That simple Rarotongan tradition of a standard, tangible symbol to say goodbye and wish us a safe journey chocked me up and revived for me the joy of cruising.

Beveridge Reef ~ late October 1993

Two overnighters from Rarotonga took us 550 miles to a microscopic point on the globe. Apart from breaking waves, at high tide Beveridge Reef's two-mile-long and four-mile-wide rim wasn't visible above the water. A mere 14,000 years old, this young coral atoll hasn't yet emerged like a proper atoll.

I read with admitted smugness that recently some cruisers were stymied by two competing navigation systems that couldn't agree on the location of the reef's entrance. The thing is, landmarks must be charted precisely so the navigation guides can tell you where you are in relation to whatever it is you're trying to find. Many charts for that area, such as the one we were using, were made over 100 years ago, and were still the standard. In the end, those cruisers negotiated the entrance the old-fashioned way, by climbing up to a spreader and using their own eyes. The space where there were no breaking waves was the pass.

Being inside the unusual lagoon was awesome in the strictest sense. There we were, hundreds of miles from anywhere, anchored at high tide in 20 feet of clear blue water, with nothing but a fringe of distant white breakers surrounding us. At low tide, hundreds of giant Tridacna clams took turns creating a symphony of squirts by spouting water a foot or two into the air through their huge, wavy and velvety lips. By giant, I mean that the ones we saw averaged about 2 feet across. I wanted so much to photograph a water-spitting clam, but by the time I saw the spout and clicked, I'd missed the action. In those days before digital, I didn't dare waste film.

⚓

The only other boat there, the *Nicky Lou,* was a shipwreck, still intact and above water on the reef. The former fishing boat looked as if she'd been sitting there for years and begged to be investigated. The steep angle of the deck required us to climb, rather than walk, around the ruined boat, while rust and dangerous-looking broken parts enforced caution. We debated before taking a memento, *Nicky Lou's* small, faceted-glass anchor light, which Robb wired up to be a cockpit light for *Sorcery.*

That object fulfilled my requirements for the perfect souvenir: an authentic article, not made for tourists; something useful, not a mere dust collector; and, finally, a reminder of our experience. Some years after we left, a storm swept the *Nicky Lou* away, so I'm doubly glad we salvaged some piece of her.

***

Underwater views on the ocean side of a reef are unfailingly spectacular. The coral drops off sharply into an endless deep blue void. Pelagic sharks, fish and coral of the open ocean are quite different from the species inside the lagoon. On the day we decided to explore just outside the reef, we loaded up the dinghy with wetsuits, flippers, masks and snorkels before motoring toward the pass. After anchoring, we began suiting up. As usual, Robb and Alex were ready and in the water well ahead of Annie and me.

By the time she and I began paddling – heads down, snorkels up – toward them, they were maybe 150 feet away. As we got closer, we could hear them shouting and looked up to see them standing in ankle-deep water. They gestured excitedly toward the water near their feet, but their voices came from too far away to make out the words. We assumed they must have found something fascinating: maybe a turtle? As we picked up the pace, we thought we could make out Robb yelling, "Go! Back!"

"What?" we shouted, not believing our ears.

"Go! Back! Go! Back!" The words reminded me of that scene in one of our most-watched movies, *Young Frankenstein,* where Gene Wilder tells Teri Garr several times, "Put. The candle. Back!"

Then a new directive from Robb with a hint of alarm,

"Bring. Dinghy. Here!"

We scurried back to the dinghy. Annie pulled on the anchor chain. Something was caught. She splashed into the water. Finally, she freed the anchor by pulling it from under a rock. Within minutes the heavy anchor was loaded, and we were on our way to rescue the boys.

As they got into the dinghy, they told how a shark had been circling them in the shallow water, at times appearing to scrape its belly along the sandy bottom to get closer. Also, when Annie had gotten in the water to free the anchor, they were too far away to offer a warning and watched helplessly as the menace moved toward her. Luckily she was out of the water before the danger got close. They said the shark then followed the dinghy, but Annie and I never saw a thing. Sometimes we cheated death and didn't even know it.

The gray reef sharks of Beveridge Reef were the most aggressive sharks we encountered on our entire trip. Once when Annie was fooling around with an oar in the dinghy, which was tied to the boat, a small shark started biting the oar and tried to wrestle it away from her. In an attack there in 2003, a man received severe bites on his chest and buttocks and had to be airlifted out.

A couple of days before we left, *Lady Ruth* came in with Frances and Rod. The six of us did a little very cautious snorkeling, always close to the boat and with someone on shark watch. Afterward, we talked and laughed over warm butterscotch punch with a splash of rum or brandy for the adults. I memorialized the sharks by baking a plump loaf of French bread, cutting a slit for a mouth, inserting toothpicks for teeth on the inside of the gaping mouth, and finishing the edible shark with sinister black-olive eyes.

Early one morning, our two boats set sail for our next destination, only 150 miles to the northwest.

Niue ~ Mid November 1993

In utter contrast to Beveridge Reef, the island nation of Niue (<u>Noo</u> ay), about one and a half times the size of Washington, D.C., is one of the world's largest coral islands. Steep limestone cliffs support a central plateau rising at the highest point to almost 200 feet above sea level.

There are no bays or beaches, but on the west side of the island the town of Alofi installed a few moorings.

As planned, we reached Niue before dark to make it easier to hook up. However, we arrived to find no moorings available and would have had to anchor in 90 feet of water. That night winds of up to 25 miles per hour were predicted to blow straight into the anchorage, one of the least protected in the South Pacific.

To be on the safe side, Robb chose to heave to for the night, hoping for better conditions in the morning. Heaving to requires setting the sails so the boat makes very slow progress, at the same time steadying the boat for comfort. Alex described it this way: "We're under a double-reefed main and a handkerchief of a jib." Robb and I took our usual turns being on watch all night, making sure we didn't get in too close, drift out too far, or bump into *Lady Ruth,* who was out there doing the same thing.

The winds never came. So in the morning, using 350 of our 400 feet of chain, we lowered the anchor into water so clear we could see the chain, anchor, and little fish 90 feet below. In order to secure the anchor, the standard practice is to let out a length of chain roughly four times the depth. Getting to shore presented a bit of a complication because, apart from there being no actual shore, the heavy surge would have smashed to bits any dinghy left in the water next to the wharf. A crane, which we ourselves hand cranked, hoisted the dinghy onto the dock.

High on my list of activities for Niue was going to the farmers market, which only took place once a week. Since I wanted to be there at the recommended optimum time of 4 a.m., neither Robb nor Alex, and not even Frances, had any interest in going. On market morning, armed with a waterproof flashlight and some shopping bags, my sidekick Annie and I took off in the dark and motored through the choppy water. She and I hadn't lifted the dinghy with the crane by ourselves before, but the operation went off without a hitch.

Robb and the kids hoisting our dinghy

When we arrived, right on time, the market was already in full swing. Lights set up in and around a dozen colorful stall awnings lent a carnival atmosphere. People buzzed close to the popular urn of coffee and trays of fresh breads and pastries. Most tables displayed food for sale: loads of fresh fruits and vegetables, fish and live coconut crabs, along with traditional food that had been prepared at home. Other tables offered handicrafts, neat rows of flower leis, a few articles of clothing, and some small household and personal items.

A model for Gauguin stretched out on a low wall and supported herself on one elbow. The local woman, with long, black hair and dressed in a pareo, appeared to be simply lending atmosphere. Indeed, she was the very picture of the South Pacific. Most Niueans dressed in Western clothing, although flowers often figured somewhere on their person: in their hair, behind an ear, or in a lei around their neck.

For Alex's fourteenth birthday, we splurged by having brunch with *Lady Ruth* at the Niue Hotel. As the waitress brought out the surprise birthday cake, her husband started playing "Happy Birthday" on the piano, and we sang along. Perched on a 180-foot-high cliff, the hotel overlooks the ocean. Huge boulders on the lawn, one the size of a Volkswagen, had, incredibly, been transported up the cliff by a hurricane. Annie wrote Niue was her "favorite place of all time." I'd guessed the honor sprang from her getting to cuddle newborn kittens several times at the hotel, but she says now she felt safe in that pristine part of the world with its crystal-clear water.

***

The best deal for renting bicycles was to get them for 24 hours, but we didn't see how we were going to be able to keep them overnight to get full use, not to mention our money's worth. We explained to the fellow at the rental place the difficulty of getting four bikes out and onto the boat.

"You can just leave them on the dock," he said.

"Really?" We were astonished.

"Yes, no one will take them. The jail's been closed for two years because no one's committed a crime."

In the fine weather, we biked through green countryside with pleasing views of hills on one side and the ocean far below on the other. In the village of Mutalau, we came across the Niue Handicrafts Store managed by Mrs. Lapiti Paka, who sat making things. She showed Annie how to weave part of an oval straw mat, which we then bought for $2.50. We also invested in a set of four matching coasters for a dollar each. The next day we used the bikes for some shopping before turning them in.

Renting a small van with Rod and Frances, we packed a picnic and drove to one of Niue's massive limestone caves with its stalagmites and stalactites in all stages of formation. Farther along we stopped for a swim with harmless sea snakes in one of the many sheltered pools carved out of the limestone at sea level.

Rod and Frances from *Lady Ruth* with the *Sorcery* crew

Provisioning for our next long leg included a stop at the duty-free liquor store. The shop sold roadmaps, including one for New Zealand's North Island, where we were headed. On impulse I added the map to the order.

We weren't allowed to take our goods until the day we left. We assumed that either Robb or I would have to pick up the alcohol, and that presented some sort of coordinating problem. But the store owner said it would be okay for our ten-year-old daughter to pick up the alcohol, which she felt privileged to do.

North Minerva Reef ~ Thanksgiving 1993

Our plan had been to sail non-stop from Niue on our way south to New Zealand to be well away from the Equator during hurricane season. However, on Thanksgiving morning, as we were approaching North Minerva Reef, we made radio contact with *Orion*. They were anchored inside the reef and insisted we join them. They and eight or nine other boats, including *Uwhilna*, were planning to have Thanksgiving aboard *Ho'o'nanea*, a boat from Hawaii. Although we'd never met Kay, Bob and teenaged Sheldon, this was the cruising way, and we knew we'd be welcome. The kids and I got excited, but Robb didn't want to stop.

"We just got some wind!"

"This trip is not about sailing," I reminded him. "It's about adventure." He carried on halfheartedly for a bit about weather windows and such, but soon caved to our pleading.

That being solved, what could we bring to the potluck? Besides a foot-high fold-out paper turkey, we had a big can of pumpkin and the ingredients to make a pie – not much for the anticipated 23 people. While we were underway, I baked a rectangular pumpkin pie tart on a cookie sheet, so each person could have a small square. The kids helped make Spam Pigs in a Blanket. Hostess Kay prepared the token bird, a dear little chicken from her freezer. Katherine made a pumpkin soup served in its own shell, which they'd brought from Tonga. I don't remember any of the other dishes, but we had plenty of food, and everyone appeared to have a good time, even those from other countries who'd never been to an American Thanksgiving.

Taking advantage of the good weather, we left North Minerva Reef a day or two after Thanksgiving for the 900-mile passage to New Zealand.

When we got to within 25 miles, the captain yelled, "Land Ho!"

"The three of us leaped out of the hatch to see," Annie wrote. "There it was: a faint small black dot off in the far distance making its way toward us."

NEW ZEALAND

First Big Stop
December 1993 to May 1994

SAILING conditions remained good until we rounded the tip of
North Island. As we headed into the Bay of Islands a storm came
along, forcing us to lower the mainsail and put up the storm trysail.

"All hands on deck!" ordered the captain. We grabbed our foul-
weather gear and scrambled up to tether ourselves to the rail, me at the
wheel, the kids standing by to help. With the boat heeling dramatically,
Robb had to crawl on hands and knees to the foredeck in the intense
wind and rain to make the sail changes.

"I wish I was a farmer!" he bellowed. After things settled down, he
denied having said that. "Even if I did, I was just kidding."

Every storm reminded us how lucky we were to have *Sorcery*,
especially when it came to her speed. A boat, that had left North Minerva
when we did, told us later how they'd been in the same storm for three
days. We'd only caught the tail end of it for about three hours.

The Bay of Islands

Entering the shelter of the bay, we made an unhappy discovery: the
navigation chart ended shortly after the entrance. The scene before us

presented a maze of options. We had no idea which watery path would lead us to our destination, the town of Opua. The moment had come to triumphantly flourish the Bay of Islands roadmap I'd bought on a whim in Niue. As we motored deeper into the bay, landmarks became evident, and eventually we tied up at the Opua dock. The kids were thrilled to see *Guinevere* and quite a few other familiar boats: *Halcyon, L'Escargot, Ho'o'nanea, Lady Ruth, Uwhilna,* and *St. Leger.* We side-tied to *Windrose,* and after a few days, *Orion* came in.

Since this was our first stop in the country, we had to stay on board until Customs came and cleared the boat. Waiting wasn't easy, especially for the children. After a long sail, there's lots of nervous energy and a great urge to touch land again. To while away the time and congratulate ourselves on cheating death again, we opened a bottle of champagne for Robb and me, and juice or something for the kids. Before we'd polished off the bottle, the Customs officer appeared and, even though on duty, happily accepted a glass of bubbly.

Annie wrote in her journal that one of his questions was, "What is your boat worth?" When her dad didn't answer right away, the guy said, "I don't mean right now. I mean after you've rested and calmed down." Annie remembers us all having a good laugh over that.

***

That early hint of legal flexibility didn't carry over to the food we had brought into the country. Anticipating he would be faced with big-time rule-breakers, the fellow from the Ministry of Agriculture and Forestry came prepared with an industrial-size, black plastic trash bag. We'd read the food restrictions and thought our foodstuffs were in compliance, yet watched with growing dismay as what seemed like half of our provisions disappeared into the trash bag.

I don't remember now what all he took, but in went dozens of cans and packages, anything containing even a hint of animal product. Any and all the fresh foods had to go. If he didn't take the flour he should have, since occasionally it was home to weevils. We did appreciate the need to prevent pests and unwanted organisms from being imported, but we sensed some individual discretion going on in the process. We hoped all that suspect food did not simply get thrown out, but got used in some way, even if for his dinner that evening.

Within minutes of our getting off the boat, a local woman with a daughter Annie's age came up to greet us. The girls hit it off immediately, and before long Annie was invited to spend the night at their home. They lived on a farm, had a horse and a telephone. We'd heard nothing but good things about New Zealanders, so trusting our instincts, we let her go. She doesn't remember now what she did, which is the very reason I did everything in my power to try to get her and her brother to keep up with their journals.

Another Christmas with Tragic News

A few days later at the grocery store I heard some chilling and solemn news from three women I knew. A boat from California with a family of four headed to the Bay of Islands had been hit in the night by a freighter and sunk. The boy, down below at the time of the collision, never made it off the boat. The girl drifted away from the overturned dinghy, and her father went after her. Neither was seen again. Two days later the mother washed up on shore with the dinghy.

We struggled to process the ghastly information and to comfort ourselves by wondering if the cruisers had done everything right, like having someone on watch, and allowing the freighter the right of way. We told each other that harrowing things, like fires, car accidents, and drownings, happened at home as well. Still, it came down to this: "I feel like taking the kids and getting on a plane," one woman said. The rest of us echoed the same sentiment. With a heavy hollowness, we finished our shopping and went home to our boats and families. Even though we learned more details of the *Melinda Lee* disaster, none of them good, by Christmastime the unimaginable horror had drifted to the back of my mind.

To ease into the Christmas spirit, Katherine and Trish came over with their guitars. Playing and singing holiday songs inspired us to organize a potluck with caroling. Days later, the Opua Yacht Club came alive with yachties, food, wine, and song. Frances, who often came up with simple yet unusual dishes, brought a savory, whole baked cauliflower to that potluck. Using a challah bread recipe, I created a fat sun with a smiling face and sunbeams twisting out.

For six weeks we anchored alone at eponymous Twelve Pine Island. As small as the name implies, the island was a study in elegant simplicity: a pile of rocks, a bit of green shrubbery, a dozen trees. The quiet spot provided a perfect base for as joyous and peaceful a holiday season as I can remember.

On Christmas Eve, Randy and Laura hosted a grownups-only, dress-up party on *Pollen Path*. At first I resisted, but our family's tradition of opening presents on Christmas morning allowed me to give in to being apart the evening before. And once Robb and I had dressed in something nicer than what we wore every day and joined the lively crowd on *Pollen Path*, the evening warmed and energized me. No doubt champagne added to the euphoria.

Despite not being there, Annie remembers the evening vividly as the one time she ever saw me, let's say, tipsy when we returned home. She claims I had to lean on a doorway to get into my pj's, all the while laughing and telling her not to laugh.

In the late afternoon of Christmas Day, folks from *Lady Ruth* and *Diabolo* joined us for a potluck dinner. After dark the wind kicked up waves so nasty that returning to the other boats by dinghy seemed dangerous. Frances and Rod chose to brave it anyway, but we convinced Soazic and Manou not to take the chance with their two-year-old boy and to stay the night with us. Having a packed house on Christmas was cozy and cheery, like being snowed in at Grandma's. Cushions, beach towels and all spare bedding were pressed into service for pallets on the floor.

***

After Christmas, *Ho'o'nanea* invited Alex and Tim from *Hasty* to spend a few days in Auckland with Sheldon. The boys could hardly believe their good luck at being invited and allowed to bus the 240-mile round trip on their own. Annie felt a bit left out, and the crowd of kids had dwindled, so she turned to her adult friends on *Lady Ruth* and *Orion*.

On New Year's Eve, Soazic and Manou had a classy little party – they were French after all – aboard their catamaran *Diabolo*. Holiday festivities came to a close on New Year's day with Rodney taking Robb and the kids clamming on Twelve Pine Island. They collected a bucket of the country's famous Pipi surf clams, which we cooked up in Pipi Chowder, made with milk, potatoes, onion and parsley. Warm homemade bread and an agreeable local wine rounded out our meal. We missed Katherine, who'd flown back to the States to visit her ill mother.

A couple of women and I walked along a three-mile wooded trail with views of the bay to the town of Paihia. In a shop that specialized in things made from Kauri wood, a label on the bottom of a wooden plate certified, "Carbon dated at 26,000 years." *What? Wow!* Momentarily, I felt confused. *Did humans use plates back then?* A clerk explained the date referred to the Kauri wood, not the plate. Swamp Kauris are trees that fell into salt marshes thousands of years ago and have been preserved. Among the few regrets I have from the trip, not buying that plate is one.

Whangarei

In early January, we moved farther south to the bigger town of Whangarei (Fang ar <u>ay</u>), so the kids could start the spring semester of school. With Annie at the helm we cautiously snaked up the shallow estuary toward the town. In spite of the high tide, we ran aground because Annie didn't understand the urgency of her dad's directions about which path to follow. To get us free, Robb put the dinghy in the water, lowered the anchor and some chain into the dinghy, and motored out to drop the anchor in deeper water. Back on the boat, he set the anchor, then pulled *Sorcery* off using the electric windlass.

We proceeded to the rows of mooring posts, two forward and two aft for each boat. As we pulled in between our four posts, each of us, ready with a lasso and coiled line, stood at a "corner" of the 61-foot *Sorcery*. Robb also had a hand on the wheel. Mooring in this way was new to us and we were nervous as cats. Adding to our discomfort, people on the boat to starboard stood on deck watching us pull in. With their arms folded, they showed no sign of any willingness to help. Annie was closest to them, and when we got within shouting distance, she did so.

"Is it true there's a McDonald's here?"

"Yes, it's true!"

We'd read that the sign of a nation's economic health can be measured by the number of McDonald's in the country, and that New Zealand had a few. So, the kids had something fun and familiar to look forward to.

***

A day or two later, we moved to the dock at the Whangarei Marina near the center of town. This was much more convenient, especially since my mother came to visit. We installed her at the Grand Hotel, not all that grand, but still satisfactory in every way. Annie stayed with her Grandma for most of the 10 days. Robb and Alex worked on the boat while we ladies shopped, ate, and visited tourist spots. The Kiwi Museum featured a live Kiwi bird foraging in artificial darkness. Since the birds are nocturnal, we appreciated the luxury of seeing one without having to traipse out into the woods at night.

Speaking of wildlife, late one night, Rod and Frances returned to *Lady Ruth* to find a full-grown possum rummaging around inside their boat. They couldn't persuade the ugly thing to leave, but managed to trap it in a locker so they could get some sleep. The next morning they chased the beast off their boat, whereupon it ran along the dock, then jumped onto another boat. The marina manager, Lew Sabin, and Robb caught the possum, escorted it out of town, and set it free.

Sannyasi was side-tied to us at the crowded marina. As Al walked across our deck one day, he caught a whiff of the stew cooking on the stove. "Something smells good!" If I'd known he was a chef and owned a restaurant, I might have thought twice before blurting out, "Would you and Lisa like to come over for dinner?" Thank goodness for my innocence, because a lifelong friendship took hold that evening. I may have sealed the deal when I baked a rhubarb pie, Al's favorite.

Lisa and I signed up for an Ocean Medic Course. One lesson involved giving injections of water, first to a piece of pork, said to resemble human flesh, and then to each other. Giving and receiving these shots turned out to be surprisingly painless. The next day, hoping my injection had not in fact hurt her, I tapped her arm and asked, "How are you feeling?" As if she'd received an actual medicinal dose, she answered, "Oh, much better, thanks!"

Lisa and Al on *Sannyasi*

Until the year we arrived, cruising children had been welcomed into a school close to the marina. I asked Lew, the marina manager what we could do. His advice, "Find a school that wants them." He suggested I speak with Val and Peter on *El Gitano,* who had four school-age children and had already done quite a bit of investigating. Val graciously shared information, and our two children enrolled in a school in the 85 percent Maori suburb of Tikipunga.

The school bus schedule indicated a stop at the marina. However, getting the bus to stop took three days, a visit to the school office, several phone calls, and ultimately me holding up a big "TIKIPUNGA" sign, while the kids hid in mortification behind a tree. After they'd been in school for a while, someone asked Annie what she liked about the school, and she was pleased to tell them, "Riding the bus!" What appealed to Robb and me was the cultural experience, so there you have another case of the family being on different trips.

Although they both got good grades, the experience seemed to work out better for Alex. He liked his subjects. In wood shop he made a nifty breadbox with a roll-top-desk kind of opening. He invited a girl to a movie, and although she didn't accept, he got kudos for asking.

Annie was the second-youngest in her grade, and didn't make friends in her usual, easy way. One day during PE she was pantsed by her classmates and then reprimanded by the teacher for not getting over her embarrassment quickly enough. Nevertheless, when school was out, she invited a few classmates, along with some boat kids, over for a combination end-of-school and bon voyage pizza party.

Road Trip

Over spring vacation, we rented a car and drove to Auckland. For two nights we stayed in a youth hostel, where we slept in bunk beds and had to venture down the hall to the bathroom. But we had a big, sunny room just for our family. After dinner, the kids happily spent the evenings by themselves watching TV in the comfy lounge next door. Robb and I read in our room. In the daytime we toured the Maritime Museum at the waterfront and spent one leisurely afternoon at the city's famous Easter Show – a lively combination of fair and circus.

On the way back to Whangarei, we stopped at a museum entirely devoted to the mighty Kauri tree. Some of these beloved trees are given names, like The Great Ghost, The Father of the Forests, and Kairaru. Not quite as tall or as big around as the Sequoias, the giant Kauris contain more timber than their rivals because the trunks are cylindrical, rather than tapering. The vast and intriguing museum had wall-sized photos of the trees, antique tree-cutting machinery, examples of everything from bread knives to a log cabin made from the wood, even a mammoth log mounted on a railway flatcar.

At the Northland Museum's Live Day, we saw an exhibition that really said New Zealand to me: a sheep-shearing competition. Men wearing special shoes, something like ballet slippers, used electric clippers hanging on cords suspended from overhead to shear full-grown sheep. Each fleecing took less than a minute, but any sign of blood counted as a demerit.

In the afternoon, we took a break for tea and scones at a little roadside restaurant overlooking a valley. North Island is as green as can be with lots of trees, and where you don't see cows you see sheep.

It didn't come out of the blue, but one day Robb said, "It's no fun cruising with you."

That brings to mind the saying, "Happiness is never experienced, only remembered." My family doesn't think of me as enjoying those years on the boat. They say I complained about everything: the physical discomforts, the hard work, the fear. That sounds true enough, yet isn't how I feel now. As the wonder of the adventure settles in around me, the unpleasant aspects recede.

When Robb made his announcement, my first thought was, *Likewise, I'm sure*, followed quickly by, *I think I'll get a job*. After a few phone calls, investigation of employment offices, and applying for a position at a city planning department, the realization came to me: I didn't want to work. Having seriously considered that option, the lifestyle in front of me became more appealing. I became a dynamo, tackling any number of undone projects.

Here's one: *Sorcery's* old, formerly-white cockpit cushions were in sad shape. Jim and Joan on *Gannet* offered the use of their industrial sewing machine to make new covers. I wasn't enthusiastic about the task until I ran across a marine fabric I loved, a pastel breadfruit-leaf pattern, very South Pacific. I laid out and cut the fabric on the dock. Kay on *Ho'o'nanea* showed me how to make piping around the cushion edges, which lent a professional finish. Modesty aside, they turned out beautifully.

***

We had a lovely ladies' event, a belated baby shower for Candia on *Moonshadow* for her infant daughter, Lana, born in French Polynesia. We knew we were still cruising when she told us the thing she needed most was Ziploc bags. Luckily, Catherine on *Brigadoon* had a huge supply and gave her quite a few.

Orion got the news the stork was on its way to their boat next, so Katherine and Rodney stayed in Whangarei to wait for Flora Ann to be born. We've kept in touch over the years, but didn't see them again until they came through San Diego one Christmas when Flora was twelve.

Bicycles and Friends

We bought two used bikes at a bicycle shop and another two at the police auction. Bill, on *Brigadoon*, a professional bike racer, helped us adjust each bike for our arm and leg lengths and gave us a few tips and riding lessons. For a while we rode each weekend on family adventures to nearby villages and through a towering Kauri forest.

Tony from the bike shop, his wife Carolyn, and children Stewart and Stephanie, belonged to a family-oriented biking club. One weekend they drove us and the bikes out in the country to a little clubhouse for a 15K ride with 30 or so people. Winded before the clubhouse was out of sight, I had the good sense to turn back. I spent the time chatting with other people who'd stayed behind and helped set up the barbeque.

Riders started returning. At first fairly crowded together, they began to thin out, and then a long break, and still no Annie. Neither Robb nor Alex had seen her, but of course they were way ahead. Before I had a chance to advance from pre-worry to panic, in she came to a round of applause, and accompanied by two adults who'd stayed behind with her.

Another weekend Tony's family took us to a banked track in an empty stadium to do timed trials on our bikes. The immense black oval track with its green grass center and the bright blue sky created a striking still life on that calm, warm day.

***

The night we forgot to put the bikes on deck, three of them disappeared. Annie loved her bike, and felt a little insulted hers hadn't been considered worthy of stealing. I knew the feeling. When burglars ransacked my apartment in New York City, they dumped my jewelry out on the bed, but didn't take a single thing. Anyway, two of the bikes turned up at the police station. Since we'd be leaving the country before long, we didn't replace the third.

While watching a small-sailboat race, we'd befriended another local family. Hans, Lillian, Michael and Teresa invited us for an afternoon at their farm and loaded us down with kiwis and avocados, garlic and potatoes, teas of lemon verbena and mint, and bread and honey. One evening we invited the family to our boat for dinner or "tea" as they called it. Having just a cup of tea was having a "cuppa." Their boy Michael invited Alex for boat racing and sailing, a weekend at the farm, and to Scout camp for a couple of days. We planned to travel north to Fiji for six months, after which Robb wanted to return to New Zealand to wait out the next hurricane season. So, we accepted Hans and Lillian's offer to store our bicycles.

Our biking friend Tony came to the marina every day for five or six days to see us off. Whenever we were ready to go and waiting for a good weather window, I thought about a boat we'd met in Mexico with the whimsical and enviable name, *Maybe Tuesday*, and its dinghy, *Maybe Not*. On Wednesday, May 18, the perfect, beautiful day arrived and Tony's whole family came down to say goodbye.

Along with *Sannyasi* we set out, exhilarated to be heading to South Minerva Reef 800 miles away, the one stop on our 1,200-mile journey to Fiji. A pod of dolphins joined us. They love to travel with boats, so nothing special about us. Nevertheless, we always interpreted their company as a good omen. If I add a rainbow to the picture, some might think I'm making that up, but there it was.

FROM WHERE WE SAIL

SOUTH PACIFIC TO CENTRAL PACIFIC

New Zealand to the Marshall Islands
Mid May to Late December 1994

T 2 a.m. and 2 p.m. every day, we had a radio schedule with *Sannyasi*. Lisa mentioned she usually felt nervous and unproductive while underway. Although sailing seemed a high price to pay for the adventure, as long as the weather wasn't bad I felt centered and managed to accomplish quite a few tasks while we were making our way from A to B.

For instance, we always made an effort to prepare for our next stop by learning a few words in the local language, at the very least *Hello, Goodbye, Please, Thank you,* and *Where's the bathroom?* So, we practiced Fijian from a short vocabulary we'd received from another cruiser. By the end of our second stop there we had pages and pages of delightful words and phrases, like the musical *senga na lenga,* meaning "no worries."

Before we left Whangarei, Alex, with the help of Jim on *Gannet,* had built a modem that enabled us to print out pictures from our weather fax using our laptop computer. Some minor glitches surfaced, but what a relief not having to worry about replacing the hard-to-get, not to mention expensive, rolls of silver fax paper. Alex was fourteen at that time, and the depth and range of his knowledge amazed me. He resembled his father in that way.

⚓

Somewhere along the way, Robb got serious about preparing for abandoning ship in case of an emergency. I always wondered if the sinking of that boat going into the Bay of Islands affected him more than he let on. He suggested we have a drill. Emergency meant the boat sinking, theoretically the only time we would abandon ship.

In lieu of a dedicated life raft, we kept the sturdy dinghy, now painted High Visibility Green, inflated and tied on deck forward of the mast at all times. Our first practice drill taught us volumes in a few minutes, and we created an Abandon Ship page in big print with detailed assignments for each person. After putting on our harnesses – we didn't usually sleep in them our jobs were these:

Dianne – Turn on the deck lights and put out a Mayday call on the VHF Channel 16, range of 10 to 20 miles, and on the Single Side Band ham radio, range of up to 10,000 miles. [I love the word Mayday. Coined in 1927, it's from the French, *m'aidez*, meaning "help me."]

Annie – Get into the dinghy and attach your lanyard to its lifelines. Grab the rigging knife with its sheath from its place on the mast and secure knife to dinghy. [That knife would be used to cut the dinghy loose if the boat were sinking out from under us]. Tie everything to the dinghy we bring to you, using the individual looped lanyard already attached to each item.

Robb – Take to the dinghy: Green backpack with documents, money and the emergency signaling equipment: EPIRB [Emergency Position-Indicating Radio Beacon], rocket flares, handheld flares, flare gun, signal mirror, dye packets, and signal flag. Ditch bags already filled with basic medical supplies, nutrition bars, sunscreen, hats, long-sleeved shirts, Mylar blankets and Mylar "body bags" for warmth.

Alex - Help others as needed, and take as many of the following items as possible to the dinghy: four gallons of drinking water, windsurfing sail and red poles [so we could sail the dinghy], throw-rope and man-overboard pole, fish net, spear gun, strobe light, extra food, knives, flashlights, cameras, and binoculars.

Everything that absolutely could not get wet had already been packed in its own watertight container. We practiced a few times, and could be in the dinghy with all the basics secured in just over a minute. If we included all the items on Alex's list, we needed another three or four minutes. Having a plan of what we would try to do in an emergency comforted me to no end.

South Minerva Reef

In late May, five days after leaving Whangarei, we reached South Minerva Reef at night, so we hove to outside the entrance of a three-mile-wide circle of barely submerged rocks. I'd stayed on watch and let Robb sleep until 3:30 a.m. At 8:30 I woke up to see him stripped down to his skivvies to clean a nice, fat yellowfin tuna. As we motored through the entrance, we counted 12 boats already bobbing at anchor. In the afternoon *Brigadoon* stopped by for beer, tea, and homemade bread. *Sannyasi* came in around dinnertime and joined us for barbequed yellowfin.

South Minerva was the lobster capital of all our sailing days. On one foray alone, Robb caught 15 of the spiny fellows as they peeked out from their ledges of pinkish coral in the clear, shallow water. If he couldn't reach in and grab the body, he tugged gently on the antennae until the curious and trusting animal crept out. Catherine on *Brigadoon* and Al on *Sannyasi* went along on one of Robb's excursions but didn't have any luck catching dinner for themselves.

The kids were older now and decided to give lobster another try. We had lobster every which way to Sunday. Luckily for me, the easiest, the old standby lemon and butter, ranked No. 1 with the family. We laugh about it now, but after a while the kids hinted broadly to their dad not to bring home any more lobster. Alex caught and cleaned an ugly grouper that we transformed into tasty fish tacos, a welcome change for supper.

Most days were more pleasing than exciting. We explored the reef, snorkeled, took showers on deck, made beer bread and yogurt, played family games, exchanged teas and meals with *Sannyasi* and *Brigadoon*, and once had them all over to see our slides of the South Pacific. Robb read a lot, sometimes technical manuals, and always, always worked on the boat. The kids had homework. Alex read, wrote, edited, and rewrote. Annie did math and read non-fiction. I cooked, organized our medical information, and read Alex de Jonge's *Stalin*.

Sannyasi planned to leave at the end of May or in the first few days of June because weather conditions seemed almost ideal; but we convinced them to stay at least through Lisa's birthday, May 30. The celebratory spaghetti dinner ended with, if I do say so, my best-ever eggless chocolate cake. The candles included two or three that relit after being blown out – a silly but amusing family tradition. Annie made a card and enclosed a dainty pressed-flower bookmark from New Zealand.

The Queen's Birthday Storm

At 4 in the afternoon on June 3, Arnold the Weatherman, who broadcast out of Rarotonga, announced that an unusual low with very high winds was headed our way. Preparing to leave, Robb went on deck, while I stayed on the radio. "What do you recommend we do?" I asked, knowing full well the answer.

"Leave!" Arnold said. "Get out of the reef as soon as you can."

On a boat, being at sea during a storm is usually safer than being near rocks or anything else you might crash into. *Sannyasi* decided to bail out too. Since we hadn't planned to go for another few days, we faced a big job preparing for heavy-weather sailing. Although we were ready in record time, way under an hour, we weren't fast enough. The sun had just started to set when we upped anchor. As we motored out, visibility deteriorated rapidly. Due to the curvature of the earth and being near the equator, there's not much twilight in the tropics.

Since we couldn't see well enough to safely go through the pass, we turned around along with *Sannyasi*. By then, darkness had swallowed up all the boats still in the anchorage. When I radioed that we were coming back in, a dozen masthead lights popped on. People we didn't know on the New Zealand boat *Whia* got on the radio. "We have a clear spot, no coral heads, right next to us, big enough for both boats. We'll have the spreader lights on so you'll know which boat is ours."

For two wild days we were on 24-hour anchor watch, re-anchoring three times as the 40-50 mph winds clocked around the reef. Sometimes we motored into the wind. At high tide, with the reef completely submerged, more fetch, or bigger waves, added to the maelstrom.

The first night the young German mother on *Talofa* became hysterical, begging over the radio for someone to come and get her two small children. She was even ready to put them in a dinghy alone and send them off to one of our boats. Fear had pushed the woman over the edge. People responded to calm her, and to say the children were far safer with her and her husband inside their steel-hulled boat. Any one of us would have been putting our own life in jeopardy if we had attempted to retrieve the children.

On the third day, when the winds calmed and the sun came out, we found most boats hadn't experienced any problems. A German boat, *Patuky*, lost an anchor when the chain snapped, but they rode out the storm on their second anchor. Her captain had an infected eardrum, so he asked Robb if he'd get their anchor. Just to see if he could, Robb went down more than 60 feet in a free dive – without an air tank – and retrieved the anchor.

Feisty Lady lost all three of its anchors when the three rope lines attached to them chafed through. The boat hit the reef, but escaped with only minor damage. That captain didn't have any chain, basic equipment for anchoring in coral. On *Sorcery*, to prevent chafing on the length of rope that passed from the anchor chain through the rollers on our bow, we slid a 4-foot length of practically indestructible used fire hose over the rope. I gave the man a piece of some of our spare fire hose. He accepted, but didn't seem to understand how it could be used. At that point I almost wished I hadn't parted with the hose segment, but hoped he would figure it out.

Over the next few days, we learned with growing dismay and sadness how 75-100 mph winds and 30-foot seas had devastated several boats. The storm was by many accounts the most severe in New Zealand's recorded history and the worst yachting disaster in recent memory. At great risk to themselves, five ships rescued 21 people from seven boats. An eighth boat, *Quartermaster*, disappeared with all three crew.

That sudden, unusual and violent storm was an example of genuine bad luck. On June 2, conditions seemed almost ideal for traveling north from New Zealand. What happened next is explained in great detail in an article by Mike Harris in Pangolin magazine. Here's a summary: "…a small area of low pressure between Fiji and Vanuatu unexpectedly began moving south and rapidly deepened. 'A worst-case scenario,' said Auckland meteorologist Bob Macdavit. The system moved too fast for boats to take evasive action and expanded, bringing gale and storm-force winds over a 900-mile radius."

Recently, as I was reviewing my journal and researching the storm on the Internet, I suggested to Robb that perhaps, by chance, we'd cheated death by staying at Minerva, where the winds turned out to be not as fierce as in other places. But he shrugged that off. "We'd have been okay."

"Really? How so?"

He pointed out that the vast majority of the estimated 150 boats in the storm's path had managed in spite of some personal injuries, rollovers, de-mastings, and other damage. Of the three boats we knew, the home-built *Pollen Path* suffered a roll-over, but the masts remained standing, and eventually the boat arrived safely in northern Tonga. *Mary-T* made it to Fiji even though her rudder had bent the propeller, putting both parts out of action, and at one point, water came in from an unidentified leak. *Jacaranda,* in Captain Chuck's words, *"came through like a champ."*

"The likelihood of our boat being rolled over was very slim," Robb said. "The rule of thumb is a wave height equal to the length of the boat is needed to roll it over. So it would have taken a 60-foot wave to roll *Sorcery*." In one of her previous lives as a race boat, *Sorcery* did get rolled by a 70-foot rogue wave and lost the mast, but that's another story.

Robb went on, "Since the boat was unlikely to have rolled, it was also unlikely she would have lost the mast. Masts can also come down due to mechanical failure, but our mast was in top condition. Both the mast and rigging were brand new when we bought *Sorcery* in 1989. Before we left San Diego, John Krase, who's a world-renowned rigger, performed a thorough inspection, and I continually checked on the mast and all the rigging before, during and after passages."

Of the seven boats from which people were evacuated, one was scuttled – deliberately sunk – by the rescuing vessel at the owner's insistence, so as not to be a danger to other boats. All six of the other abandoned boats were later found, one a thousand miles away. The storm only sank one boat. Robb's moral was, and is, to stay with the boat until she sinks.

"The biggest problem people face is fear," he said. "And remember, rescues have their own inherent dangers. If our boat had been sinking and we'd have needed to get in the dinghy, it would have floated like a cork."

"Maybe the lanyards attached to us and everything else wouldn't have held in such force."

"I thought of that," he said, "and made all the lanyards with high-test, hollow-core nylon webbing that would stretch but wouldn't break."

We always tied the life jackets with all their rescue paraphernalia into the dinghy before a long passage, so even if the dinghy had gotten punctured, we would have had an alternative. Robb liked to tease that we'd probably sink with all that stuff. But really, the safety devices only weighed a few ounces, and having them made me feel more secure.

The kids and I entrusted our lives to Robb's intelligence, knowledge, strength, and skill. Annie told me she's often been asked whether she'd go sailing around the world again. She answers, "I'd have to find someone as responsible and skilled as my dad. He checked the weather reports every time before we left. He knew how to fix things. He knew how to make sure things wouldn't break in the first place. When people ask if I was ever scared in storms or at sea, I say no. Maybe that's because I was a kid and stupid, but honestly, I just knew there was always a solution with Dad there."

Shortly after we bought *Sorcery*, my own confidence in Robb received an extra boost. Two boat friends advised me that Robb should do something I didn't understand about the mast. Apparently, they had mentioned the idea to Robb, but he didn't agree. I asked a third friend, an experienced boat delivery captain, what he thought about the men's suggestion. His answer:

"Robb knows more about boats than the two of them put together."

Fiji ~ Mid June through September 1994

On June 12, the actual birthday of Queen Elizabeth for whom the recent storm had been named, we arrived at Lautoka on the west side of the island of Viti Levu. Checking in on that national holiday would have incurred overtime fees, so we hove to outside the harbor for the night.

The next morning, after checking in, we headed into town. If I'd known beforehand about the significant Indian influence in the country, I may not have been so delighted to see the evidence everywhere we turned. Small dark women, gleaming with gold jewelry and adrift in exquisite saris, mingled in the streets with people in Western clothing.

Every other business seemed to be identified by the Indian surname Patel. In the morning, Indian shops put a fresh hibiscus or frangipani flower in the corner of the doorstep to welcome God. The custom resonated with the spiritual part of me, and to this day I place a fresh flower, whenever one's available, by the front door of our home.

At lunchtime we made a real find, an inexpensive Fijian noodle restaurant, which became our go-to place to eat. Annie remembers it like this:

They had the best pasta dish ever, a scrumptious pile of seasoned noodles and chopped vegetables that filled the entire plate. We wouldn't eat all morning, and then would go there for lunch. We'd leave stuffed to the gills, and not have to worry about dinner, except for Alex. He'd be forced to find something to eat on his own that night, and would go to bed asking, "What's for breakfast?"

Little chores and shopping became adventures. Sandals need fixing? Leave them at the bike repair shop. With too many batik patterns to choose from at Patel's Fabrics, I finally settled on an intricate paisley design in creams, tans, and browns. The soft cotton became a tablecloth and napkins to use on the boat.

Always on the lookout for practical souvenirs, I had a special weakness for things the locals used. I came home with bowls made of coconut shell halves, handmade greeting cards, party toothpicks with small shells pasted on the ends, some tapa cloth, and three "eyeball pluckers" for serving olives. These curious-looking wooden utensils are narrow forks with four long, pointed prongs arranged like the legs of a chair. I recognized this cannibal tableware from seeing one in a museum.

***

Another item on our shopping list was kava, historically important in Fijian culture. The dried roots of the plant are ground and added to water to produce a drink with mild sedative and anesthetic properties. When given as a gift, you may generally offer the ground version in a plastic packet. However, if making sevu-sevu – presenting kava to a chief – a half-kilo bundle is required. In preparation for visits to the outer islands, we purchased several regulation-size bundles of dried kava roots. Wrapped in newspaper and tied with string, the lumpy parcels each brought to mind a baby in a blanket.

My first experience with the national drink took place in an open-air market while shopping with another woman. "Would you like to try some kava?" a vegetable seller asked as we inspected her wares. My friend and I looked at each other with a smile and a shrug. "Sure!"

We each had a sip. Even if the gray drink hadn't been scooped from an enamel dishpan sitting on the floor, the brew would have looked and tasted like dirty dishwater. Our lips were numb for some time, so we relished the adventure. At least we hadn't tasted dirty dishwater for nothing.

⚓

Checking out of Lautoka temporarily, we motorsailed west and north through a magical chain of hilly, green islands. At Navandra Island we shared tea on *Khamsin* with Gillian and her crew and with Sandy and Heather from *Gjoa*. A nasty sail – choppy seas, lots of tacking, rainy but warm – delivered us to a pleasant anchorage on the south side of Waya Island. Mike and Tristan from *Stormy Weather* brought over some powdered kava, which we prepared and drank from our new coconut-shell bowls. Every day we had a radio chat with *Sannyasi* and sometimes with *Brigadoon* and *L'Escargot*.

***

At last we went into our first Fijian village. Several children and a young woman named Saylee helped pull the dinghy up on shore. She asked if we wanted her to take us to the chief. Our family and all the children trailed along behind her to a cinderblock house, conspicuous among the thatch huts. Everyone else was barefoot, so we left our shoes outside. The high-ceilinged room had portraits and framed documents on the wall, but no furniture.

Seated cross-legged on the linoleum floor, the thin and toothless chief indicated our contingent should do the same. Robb had forgotten to memorize the words used for presenting kava, but he did remember to put the newspaper-wrapped bundle on the floor in front of the chief, and not hand it directly to him. Acknowledging the gift with a hint of a bow, the dignified old leader let his eyes close and began to chant in Fijian as he rocked ever so slightly back and forth. From time to time he and the others clapped once. Sometimes the children mumbled the words too.

Suddenly the chief stopped, opened his eyes, and asked in a manner that suggested the answer might make a difference, "What state are you from?"

"California," we said, hoping he wouldn't hold that fact against us in any way.

He nodded, closed his eyes and resumed, inserting the word California a time or two in the chant. In a few minutes, the ceremony came to an end. He thanked us as we stood and followed Saylee out the door. We sensed the ceremony held meaning for the chief, a custom from ancient times, and not simply, *Thanks for the kava, goodbye.* We'd read that the blessing included the guarantee of our safety in the village and surrounding waters.

One of our cutest helpers

Later that afternoon, Saylee paddled out to our boat in her little corrugated-tin canoe. Like that of most people in the village, her clothing seemed an after-thought, evidently hand-me-downs. She had a Baby Wipes box full of shells for sale. As we looked through them, she shyly mentioned her grandfather sent her to ask for kava. We explained we needed to keep the kava for the chiefs of other islands, but we bought a few shells and gave her some lemonade and granola bars. How I wish we'd had a packet of powdered kava for her grandfather.

The next day she showed up with a papaya, priced at $3.50, a turtle shell, and two sad little fans made of turkey feathers, wire and a bit of wood. I bought a fan, and she ended up giving us the papaya, which made a nice chutney. Saylee invited us to come to her home for tea the following day.

Heating water for our tea

We sat in a circle on the mat-covered floor of a traditional thatch *bure*, the kitchen and eating hut. A wood fire in the room heated a big kettle of tea, which was poured into chipped enamel bowls. Baked cassava, something like potato, and a dish of rice cooked in coconut milk completed the snack. We bought some produce, including half a stalk of green bananas for $10. We didn't mind what we knew was a markup in price because we wanted the bananas, and her family clearly could use the money. Saylee gave Annie some pretty shells. Annie reciprocated with a necklace and a pillow.

At that island, or maybe a different one, Annie and I visited a kindergarten located in a one-room cinderblock structure with a sand floor and openings for doors and windows. As we walked in, 15 dear little faces turned and beamed at us, further lighting up the already sunny room. No desks or chairs, but a scratched-up old blackboard established the room as a place of learning. The teacher sat with the children in the sand while they sang "Ten Little Fijian Boys and Girls" in English to the tune of "Ten Little Indians."

Annie, the teacher

When we gave the teacher the paper and crayons we'd brought, she turned and spoke to the students. They fished around in the sand and produced little slates. As the children wiped off the sand the best they could, Annie, looking the part of a local teacher in her sarong, wrote a few simple words in English on the blackboard. Both of us helped the youngsters write the words on their papers, using the slates for support. The eagerness of people to learn under difficult circumstances always gripped our hearts.

***

At the mid-morning break, the teacher, Sovaya, invited us to her home for tea with her mother and uncle. As we walked through the village, we passed women squatting on the ground, tending small fires, stirring big caldrons of food, and washing clothes. In her thatch-roofed house, woven mats covered the floor. The worn furniture consisted of a bed, a dresser and a cupboard. Brightly-colored, happily-patterned fabrics covering the bed, the windows and parts of the walls softened the look of the room.

Joined by three or four children, we all sat quietly in a circle, sipping tea and eating rice from faded-pink, plastic saucers. Peacefulness and the soothing scent of wood fires filled the air. If I'd been a cat, I'd have curled up and drifted off to sleep.

To show respect when visiting small villages, the four of us usually wore lava-lavas, Fijian sarongs. Most often the people who greeted us wore western clothing. But one time a man about Robb's age, walked down to the water's edge to help pull the dinghy up onto the sand. Robb and Alex fidgeted to keep their Fijian "skirts" in place over their swim trunks. Without formally asking, and in the most gentle, brotherly way, the fellow showed my boys how to secure the material around their waists without having to tie it. He himself wore shorts.

Farther along the beach, several men hovered around a local trade boat hauled up on shore. Obviously, something was wrong. Robb went closer to have a look. The men showed him where the old, wooden boat leaked around the screws holding the propeller in place. A sense of urgency hung over the project because the vessel was the only one that brought in supplies and took goods to markets on other islands.

Robb worked on the boat for a day and a half, seeking advice from our friend Bill, who owned the wooden boat, *Brigadoon*. Robb had planned to use some high-powered epoxy, but Bill said, "You need to use traditional materials on a traditional boat."

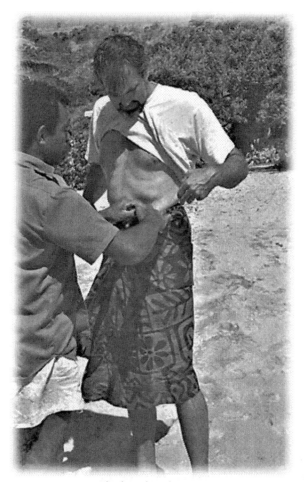

The lava-lava lesson.

Robb described his repair like this:

I got some longer lag bolts [big screws] from our spares kit, cleaned out the old screw holes, and packed slivers of new wood in the original part of the hole. Thus, when I installed the new lag bolts, the slivers filled in the spaces in the old holes, and the extra length meant the lag bolts were in virgin wood. It was actually more complicated than that, involving the cutlass bearing, but that's the gist of it.

To thank Robb, the family wove a sturdy basket from fresh, green palm fronds and filled it with three hands of bananas, several paw paws (papayas), and five shiny cowrie shells, each considerably bigger than a jumbo chicken egg. They invited us to their home that evening. Robb made an enormous batch of popcorn and I took pencils and paper, clothes, and a few *National Geographics*. As soon as we arrived, Robb and Alex were hustled off to have kava with the men.

Three children led Annie and me into the house where we all sat on the floor with only a lantern for light. Within a few minutes two women ushered us outside to sit on a mat where several women and children had already assembled. We shared tea, fried bread, and the popcorn we'd brought. After nearly an hour filled with easy laughter and touching hands playing a game we showed them, Button, Button, Who's Got the Button, the party wound down, and a woman asked in the nicest way, "When are you going back to your boat?" Taking the hint, we thanked them, collected Robb and Alex, and called it an evening.

***

In another village, Robb and Alex watched in fascination most of the afternoon as a dozen men labored with hand tools and local materials to build a house. At the end of the day, the men invited all four of us to join them for their after-work bowl of kava. We sat in a room in a circle of chairs and followed this ritual:

- Clap twice as the empty bilo, half a coconut shell, is placed in front of you.
- Take the bilo in one hand and say, "Noqu sevu-sevu gor."
- Dip the bilo into the bowl of kava and drink the cup in one swallow.
- Place the empty bilo on the ground in front of the next person.
- Keep the bilo going around until the kava bowl is empty.

When ten-year-old Annie emptied the bilo, the men laughed good-naturedly and clapped. Once again, the cruising gods were looking after us: none of us got sick from the unfamiliar potion or from using a community cup.

When we made sevu-sevu with a female chief, we were given a "bum's rush" in comparison with that first satisfying ceremony. From there, the sevu-sevu experiences had gone downhill. At one island, we approached a man who'd been lying on the deserted beach, and asked if he could direct us to the village and the chief. Of course, our newspaper-wrapped bundle made our mission obvious. He stood, squared his shoulders, and declared, "I am the chief." Not knowing what else to do, we gave him the kava. Later on, we weren't surprised to find ourselves empty-handed for the real chief. No one made an issue of the *faux pas*, so we figured one bundle per village was plenty.

***

In early July we motorsailed north to Naviti Island to join Al and Lisa on *Sannyasi*. That evening I prepared a rice dish made with a packet of yummy Fijian Instant Coconut Cream to go with the fish we'd caught on the way.

The day before my birthday, the fridge went on the fritz, again. So the champagne wasn't cold for our Tang mimosas or the water even cool for the kids' plain Tang, but no complaints from any of us. As customary for birthdays, before dawn we opened presents in our bed. Annie had spent hours making a paper-leaf necklace, a card, and wrapping the gifts. Robb surprised me with something I'd coveted in New Zealand, a palm-size wooden dish filled with seven dear little eggs, each carved from a different type of wood. He fixed us coffee while the kids started making a cake.

That evening Al and Lisa threw a little party for me, having us and Lynn, Tom, and Tim from *Hasty* for chili and salad, and chocolate cake with lots of candles. Lisa gave me a sparkling bead bracelet she'd made, like the one I'd admired of hers. We caught up on each other's recent adventures, and talked about the big one we planned for the next day.

Another Road Less Traveled

During World War II, an American Airacobra ditched in a nearby lagoon and came to rest on the sandy bottom. Jerry, a personable and good-looking young man from the village, offered to guide us there. Early in the already-hot morning, 10 of us lugged gear, including snorkels and wet suits, up a hill leading to the other side of the island.

From a small rise, we marveled at the extraordinary sight of an entire airplane, fuzzy with a thick green layer of algae, just a few feet under the clear water, and close to shore. The absence of other tourists and of any signs telling us about the plane, or even warning us to be careful, confirmed we were on the road less traveled. Everyone snorkeled to their heart's content.

Back at the anchorage, sitting on the beach, I asked Jerry how we could repay him. He grinned and only hesitated a few seconds.

"A book," he said. "I'd love to have a book."

Sometimes our luck is a little uncanny. In our stash of *National Geographics,* I found one with an article on sunken WWII planes in the South Pacific. The picture on the cover could very well have been the plane we'd just seen. Our group gave him several magazines, books, as well as some money.

Further north at Yasawa Island, we spent a couple of days with a local family, Isoa, Josie, and their three small children. They took us on excursions, to cathedral-like caves with pools of cool, still water and to a little market where I bought musk-scented coconut oil. For most of one day, we joined the family in their normal activities, starting with sitting on a mat for a hearty breakfast of dumplings, plain boiled fish, and tea with lots of powdered milk.

The men and boys cleared, tilled, and leveled a small plot of land for planting sweet potatoes. In neat rows, the farmers used their hands to shape the rich, dark earth into mounds a few inches high, then made an opening down the middle of each little pile. An entire sweet potato was placed in every hole, and then covered with soil.

We women and girls spent a leisurely day washing both families' clothes in a stream, then draping them over bushes to dry in the sun. Josie served yellow cassava and tea for lunch. The next day, Robb and Alex took Isoa fishing. On our last evening, the family came for a potluck dinner. Josie brought Indian roti bread and curried meat. I made two big pizzas, a chickpea salad, a platter of fresh papaya, and banana-bread cupcakes. We gave the family cooking oil, sugar, clothes, toys, and a couple of *National Geographics.*

Isoa's brother asked for medicine for his leg. With the help of photos in our medical reference book, *Where There is No Doctor,* I diagnosed pellagra, a skin condition due to malnutrition, particularly a niacin deficiency. The book recommended eating beans and other high-protein foods every day. I explained all that as well as I could, cooked a pot of beans, and gave him a supply of five kinds of dry beans. Even if the diagnosis was incorrect, I figured the beans wouldn't hurt.

⚓

Winds of 25 to 30 knots swept *Sorcery* along to the next island. As we got close to Yadua, we needed to keep a sharp eye out for coral heads. Alex enlisted, and wrote in his journal, "I put on my wet suit and harness and went up to the bow and secured my lanyard to the head stay. It was like surfing on a large board." We kept a close eye on him. We never asked or let the kids do anything they were afraid of doing, or that we felt was too dangerous.

As we came in to Yadua, *Sannyasi* welcomed us with loud, traditional horn blowing, a grand and uplifting sound. Getting to know Al and Lisa had been wonderful for our whole family. With friends old and new, the days sped by with potlucks, book exchanges, tea and cookies, snorkeling, and picnics on the beach.

A local man named Peeta led a few of us on a two-hour walk to a village where his sister flew toward us waving both arms and shouting, "Welcome! Welcome, everybody!" We'd brought kava for the chief and watched a bucket brigade clear mud out of a well. On the way back, we met a young woman coming toward us on the dirt footpath. In lilting English, she asked, "Where are you going?" The question wasn't an interrogation, just a charming pleasantry.

***

Time to make our way back to Lautoka. As we inched into a narrow and shallow anchoring spot where we planned to rest for the night, Alex again stood on the bow watching for coral heads. Here's his report:

> The water was cloudy and the sky was overcast. All the sudden I saw the reef and just then Dad put the motor in reverse, but too late, we were stuck hard and fast. We unrolled the jib in order to blow the bow around. Dad rowed

out an anchor, but it still didn't work. We set the main. After a few more minutes work the boat started to move. We dropped the main to keep the boat from turning back into the wind.

Some locals came by in their boats, took two more anchors out, took a line from the mast head, and powered out in an attempt to pull the boat over. We set the main again. Alas, this all failed. *Sula II* happened by and took a spinnaker halyard to the stern cleat of their boat, and motored out. Eventually, the boat heeled far enough to come off.

Thank yous were said all around. We gave a bundle of kava to each boatload of Fijians and a tour of the boat to a few who asked. Then we set about the task of cleaning up on deck and below as the mess was horrendous. At one point our starboard rail was a foot underwater, but nothing fell overboard. We collected our anchors and had some food then we motored back to our previous anchorage where I inspected the bottom of the boat. There was a lot of missing paint.

Come to the Front of the Line!

Commercial ships and private vessels checked in and out of the port of Lautoka at the same noisy and crowded office. The last time I'd checked out, hot, sticky, motionless air pushed the room's grumpiness level even higher. Finally getting to the front of the line, I'd commiserated with the fellow behind the desk about his tough job.

When we returned a week or so later, I waited behind a couple of dozen men. A burly man at the head of the line shook his fist and yelled at the same official who'd checked me out. As the harried government employee looked up, he spotted me, then grinned and waved me forward as if I were an old friend.

"Mrs. Dianne! Come! Come to the front of the line!"

***

Because of the number of children on other cruising boats, we stayed in Fiji, especially Lautoka, longer than we might have otherwise. When we first arrived, a windfall of youngsters ranging in ages from eight to eighteen hung out together. At one time or another, besides our two, Tim from *Hasty*, Megan from *Fat Cat*, Anna from *Mary T*, Dannielle and Kevin on *Spirit of Kalahari*, Olin and Elaine on *Guinevere*, Chris and Robin on *Our Way*, Heather on *Tiaka*, and Sheldon on *Ho'o'nanea* filled the ranks.

Naturally, having lots of other kids around was fun for all of them, and a relief for the parents. We adults observed the camaraderie and how the children looked out for one another, so we let them organize their own activities, including going into town by themselves. They didn't find much to do there besides walk around, window-shop, and have lunch. But as Annie said, "Just being on our own was exhilarating enough."

I swear I don't know what Robb and I were thinking, but one time, Annie talked us into letting her stay overnight with the two kids from *Our Way* on a half-sunken ship in the harbor. Robb declared the wreck a "safe enough" place to camp for a night. We gave her a hand-held VHF radio so she could call us, and we were only 100 feet or so away. Here's Annie's memory:

> We were dropped off pretty close to sunset. We didn't really do much as there was nothing really to do. I remember the wind blowing and the sounds of the water. The boat was rusty and creaky and a little scary at night, so we didn't move around that much. We talked, ate the food we'd brought, and then went to sleep. We slept on the slanted deck so that our heads were up. The sunrise was beautiful, and we got picked up early.

To see fire walking, a bunch of us, including Al and Lisa, took taxis to the Mocombo Hotel a few miles out of town. Costumed men hot-footing it over the coals impressed us, even after we learned the act is based on physics, and doesn't require any special talent or state of mind. I wouldn't try this at home, but apparently the fierce-looking coals aren't hot enough to burn your skin as long as you keep moving.

While waiting for taxis for the return trip, a fellow in a Fiji Radio van offered us a ride, so we all squeezed in. As a bonus, he delighted the kids by inviting them and all their friends to tour the radio station the next day. At last, something interesting to do in town.

***

At one of our frequent haunts, Gopal's Indian restaurant, bright yellow fliers appeared one day: "Come to the famous Hare Krishna Sunday Feast." Lisa and Al and the four of us found ourselves at noon *puja*, or prayer, the following Sunday. A young woman in a saffron robe greeted us. Somewhat disappointingly, she was from California, but most of the other Krishnas looked to be locals.

With the men on one side of the room and the women on the other, we sat on the bare floor for over an hour and shifted from one of our aching haunches to the other and back again. The chanting, soft beating of drums, and tinkle of small hand cymbals, which transported the Krishnas to bliss, distracted us only a little. Never thought I'd miss the wooden pews of the Methodists.

At the end of the service four children threaded their way through the congregation bearing brass trays, each about 2 feet in diameter with three short, white, burning candles. When a tray came to me, I added a donation, and copying what I'd seen others do, circled my palms over the flames, and then held my cupped hands close to my face. The warmth transferred from the flames was the spiritual moment for me. That unexpected pleasure brought a welcome, soothing physical sensation after sitting uncomfortably for so long.

The men took off, but we gals stayed for the simple vegetarian lunch following the service. Dozens of people sat at long picnic tables, almost everyone eating with their hands. Since the food was fairly messy, we three used forks. We'd barely started eating when a woman came up to us. "Please excuse me, but we only use our right hands to eat." Annie the Lefty quickly shifted her fork. Seeing the apologetic, but bewildered looks on our faces, the woman added, "That's because we use our left hand…." Words failed her, as she made a vague hand motion behind herself.

***

One day while Robb and Alex were off somewhere, Annie and I lounged in our cockpit with Catherine from *Brigadoon*. As we chatted, a fish made a great leap out of the water and landed on our deck. Annie rushed forward.

"Oh! Let's rescue it! I'll throw it back in the water!"

Catherine followed right behind her with a counterproposal. "Let's kill it and eat it! Do you have any coconut milk? Limes? We can make *kokoda*, Fijian-style ceviche!"

Annie caved to Catherine's enthusiasm. The only thing I could see handy to kill the foot-long fish was an equally-long piece of sugarcane. Using that stalk required a little negotiation, because technically it belonged to Annie. Promising to buy her more sugarcane, I dispatched the fish. Catherine had the *kokoda* ready in minutes. We were still in the cockpit savoring the treat with crackers and a glass of wine when the boys came back. They sampled a little, complimented us, then Robb began scrutinizing the bit of fish on the end of his fork.

"Where'd you get the fish?"

Ah, the rare pleasure of a *Believe It or Not* moment.

***

By August, all of us were looking for something new and entertaining to do, when lo and behold The Magic Circus of Samoa came to town. Thirteen of us, folks from *Mary T*, *Hasty*, *Sannyasi*, *Fat Cat*, and the *Sorcery* crew, jostled with the crowd to find seats under the small Big Top of faded red and yellow striped canvas. An astonishing number of skilled and colorful clowns, acrobats, jugglers, high-wire artists, and fire dancers dazzled the audience. But the show wasn't named The Magic Circus for nothing. The best parts for me were the perfect and pleasing acts of illusion, the kind that really did look like magic.

Back in the real world, on a side street in town, a sign in English, Lautoka Women's Crisis Center, hung over the porch of what looked like a private home: The establishment provided counseling along with legal, medical, and practical support to women and children who were victims of violence. A secret safe house somewhere else protected extreme cases.

Without government support, the group relied on private donations. Wanting to do more than simply give money, I helped set up a tamarind chutney sale with all proceeds going to the center, put a labeled box in the marina office for donations of clothing for the women and children, and collected $120 by going from boat to boat. Being able to help the center was reward enough, but a dozen or so of the volunteers, made up equally of Fijian and Indian women, insisted on having a tea party to thank me.

***

Of our three months in Fiji, not all of our time focused on learning about the culture. I started sorting and varnishing my shell collection. On some days Robb and the kids played Game Boy for most of their waking hours, or so it seemed to me. We all read a lot. Sometimes we were able to exchange videos with other boats, but most often we watched movies from our own collection. While Robb fired up the generator on deck, I'd make a huge bowl of popcorn sprinkled with parmesan cheese and/or taco seasoning. Then we'd all settle down to an evening with a much-loved movie.

During those cruising years, we always kept up with basic preventative healthcare, like getting routine inoculations at local health centers. An enterprising American dentist, Kurt on *Whitecap,* had a teeth-cleaning business on his 34-foot boat. So there we were, taking turns sitting on the floor of the small cockpit with our feet propped up on the seat on one side, and our head on the opposite seat, while Kurt buzzed away with his dental tools plugged into a generator. He'd quoted a cost of $30 each, but with his family discount, the bill only came to $100.

Robb is Exhausted

With hurricane season coming, we could no longer put off deciding where we were going to travel next. Robb wanted to go back down to New Zealand, but I had in mind somewhere new and more exotic. I'd heard both of us could work and make good money in the Marshall Islands. But the idea of traveling over 2,000 miles up to the Central Pacific didn't appeal to him, in large part because we'd be deviating from the route most cruisers took. At one point he said, "I'm exhausted from being responsible for so much and for the hard work. Sometimes I just want to go home."

Overhearing the conversation, Annie interrupted. "I want to keep cruising," she said, and started sweeping the floor to demonstrate her willingness to help.

Later, Robb mellowed. He said he was glad we'd made the trip, but was tired of being in charge. He liked just being crew, like the time he was racing to Hawaii on *Scottish Fantasy,* and the only thing he had to think about was doing his part to make the boat go fast. "Now I'm responsible for all of our lives."

As we heard stories from others who'd been to the Marshall Islands, Robb warmed to the idea of going. Bill and Anne on *Sendaya*, friends we'd known from Mission Bay Marina, told us the Asian Development Bank was doing a lot of work there and paying big bucks. We started gathering information about going up through the Central Pacific. To get visas for our respective next stops, Lisa and I took a taxi to Suva, the capital of Fiji on the other side of the island. Instead of our everyday pants and T-shirts, we dressed up in skirts and earrings and made a day of it, lunching in style at the Suva Yacht Club.

The time came to part ways with *Sannyasi*, as Al and Lisa headed for Vanuatu, New Caledonia, Australia, and home for Christmas. Not knowing when we'd meet up again brought on sadness and hugs and vows all around to make every effort to get together.

Tuvalu Islands 1994

Funafuti

After three overnights heading north from Fiji, we pulled into the atoll of Funafuti, the capital of the island nation of Tuvalu. The passage had been smooth except for the wind and rain squalls that came along in the dark hours just before we made landfall. The captain called for all hands on deck to help set the storm jib, so everyone was pretty tired. Robb had strep throat and felt awful enough to use my line, "I never want to leave this place."

As we were anchoring, Jane and John, an American couple from *Hawah*, the only other cruising boat in the lagoon, pulled up in their dinghy and welcomed us.

"How long are you staying?"

"Oh, just a couple of days," Robb said, the threat of never leaving already forgotten.

"You'll stay longer," they prophesied as they pushed off.

While Robb finished anchoring, I prepared lunch, a skillet lasagna, which we ate while listening to a tape of the soundtrack from *Evita* before venturing ashore. As we dinghied to the jetty to tie up, a scattering of two dozen public buildings and businesses – a modest settlement in a lush setting – spread out before us. The first structure we came to, the Vaiaku Lagi Hotel, introduced us to the wonderful contrasts that characterized Funafuti. The hotel was modern enough, and the bellboy delightfully local. He wore flip-flops, a red "Licensed to Hit and Run" T-shirt, shorts, and wrap-around reflective sunglasses. A fresh flower crown sat on his young head.

People dressed cheerfully – never mindful of matching colors or patterns. More men wore sulus, their word for lava-lavas or sarongs, than anywhere we'd been. As we wandered along the dirt road to town, we passed traditional raised, wooden lounging and eating platforms with thatched roofs, alongside haphazard homes of cinderblock and corrugated tin.

Getting off the boat after the passage was a relief, but walking in the stifling heat and humidity aggravated my hot flashes. Within a day or two, using the recipe from *Where There is No Doctor*, I concocted a poor woman's Gatorade: water, sugar, salt, and baking soda. Jumping into the water helped too, if only for a few minutes. Wind scoops in the overhead hatches coaxed any hint of air down into the boat. But when the daily downpour arrived, we closed the hatches and went topside to sit in the cockpit under the awning. We watched the rain, read, ate or worked on some project until the rain stopped. By early evening, things did cool down.

***

The weather was too hot for cooking, or even thinking about what to cook, but I knew I'd better figure out something before we ate our way through all our snacks and reserves. Buying food presented challenges. Boats or planes from Fiji brought in fresh produce only intermittently. Canned food came in a limited variety of fruits, vegetables, and meats. The corned beef was okay, the duck horrid, and we didn't even attempt the corned tongue. Frozen chickens and turkey legs were inedible, but sausage wasn't bad. Chinese rice noodles and Top Ramen provided starch.

We caught fish, and Jennie, a young Jehovah's Witness, sold us cheese, pickles, dried peas, and minced meat of some kind. From that unpromising selection and our own stores, many acceptable meals emerged. No matter how marginal the outcome, Robb always said, "Thank you for this meal."

The one redeeming local food was *laulu*, the tender, curled young shoot of a particular fern. That first week, Jane took me to the edge of town to gather some in the thick undergrowth of the palm trees. I'd gone picking for the adventure, but returned a devotee. The drawback to that source was fighting the mosquitoes, so I kept a sharp eye out for packets of *laulu* being sold on the street across from FUSI, the grocery store. With its pale-green color, crunchiness, and fanciful shape, the mild-tasting vegetable added a fanciful touch to stir-fries and salads, and was even scrumptious on its own.

One day led to the next. Too physically and mentally exhausted to think about moving on, Robb would still not fully commit to the Marshall Islands. For one thing, we had to start thinking about high school for Alex. Robb had written this reasoning in a letter home:

> If we kept going west, it could be a while before we got to a "real" school. If Alex decided to go to college, having a high school diploma and all the things that go with a traditional educational system would be a big advantage. On the other hand, a trip through the Mediterranean with all of its history and changing political climate would be a living classroom beyond compare.

Two sizable factors held us back from the Med, the expense and the sailing/motoring conditions. Not only were prices high in the various countries, most of them would not let boats anchor out, so we'd have to pay to stay at a dock or marina. The winds were notoriously too much or too little. And even back then, the amount of trash in the water was hazardous for boats' propellers.

The Dead Body and the Pig

Ten days after we arrived in Funafuti, John stopped by in the morning, and asked if we'd like to make some money. No, not really.

"It's $500 American."

"What do we have to do?"

A local man had been killed in a motorcycle accident a couple of days before, and the tradition was for the body to be taken back to the island on which he was born. Transportation required the use of an inter-island trade boat, an arrangement that was not usually a problem. Now, however, both the trade boat and the refrigeration system in the morgue had broken down. The plan was for us to travel overnight to Vaitupu Island that very day, taking the coffin and some family members. The next morning, we would leave the coffin, pick up some goods, and return to Funafuti.

My first thought was these people would need to eat on the way, and I asked what we could feed them. "Oh," John said, "they just eat canned corned beef and rice." Okay, I had that.

Before we could pick up the body, we had to wait for permission from the Minister of Health. It was already late afternoon, and we had to make it through the pass well before dark. Because we didn't have a minute to waste, we picked up the anchor, kept the engine running, and drove in circles near the wharf.

When the go-ahead came over the radio, and we pulled up to the commercial wharf, we saw the top of it loomed above us by some 15 feet. A makeshift pulley system lowered the simple wooden box by one nerve wracking arm's length at a time. A large, black piece of fabric was draped like a tablecloth over the length of the coffin. The cloth, only stapled around the top, fluttered as the coffin eased and bumped its way down. For a short time, the coffin went vertical, tilting the poor man inside Heaven only knows which way.

With the coffin secured with ropes on deck, we were ready for the family. Seven heavy people, each juggling two or three big, open, overstuffed bags, made their way down the ladder onto the boat. A pregnant woman had to be lowered by her arms until someone on deck could grab her.

By then it was seriously dusk and we could barely see the pass. A small open boat, like a Mexican panga, was leading us out. We felt fairly confident until the driver slowed down, came alongside, and pointed in the direction of the pass before speeding back toward shore. Robb was a little unnerved, but two of the older men on board had no such concern. They indicated with much gesturing to Robb and talking between themselves that they could see well enough. With their guidance, we motored through the pass without incident, thus reaffirming the Polynesian reputation for remarkable eyesight and navigation skills.

***

My attention turned to food. We had plenty of rice, but I realized our four little cans of corned beef would not be anything like enough. Our interpreter, Sam, a man of about twenty, spoke excellent English. He assured me if I could just make a lot of rice that would be fine; so I set about cooking while the group unpacked some food.

They produced whole, cooked, root vegetables, probably taro or cassava, which resembled big yams. Next came the biggest can, maybe five pounds, of corned beef we'd ever seen. Two industrial-sized bread pans contained loaves that rose up and over so much they looked like cartoons of bread. How was I going to serve all this? Sam suggested putting the cooked rice in the largest bowl I had and the corned beef could go on top of the rice.

I carried the cooked rice up in the big aluminum bowl we used for bread making, then went below to get forks and spoons. When I returned, the group was seated in a circle around the bowl. They were already eating the rice, corned beef and chunks of taro using their fingers and chunks of bread as utensils. Reading the hint of surprise on my face, Sam shrugged and said in a low, somewhat apologetic voice, "That's how we like to eat."

Our family had some dinner of our own, but we accepted the offer to share a little of our guests' food, which we found quite tasty. After dinner we all sat around with tea while the group sang and played my guitar. This was truly a treat because they had lovely voices and easily drifted into harmony.

Later in the evening, Sam approached us with a proposal to which we agreed. They would pay an additional $500 if, rather than come back in the morning, we would stay in Vaitupu most of the day and make the return trip overnight. Robb actually preferred that because entering the Funafuti pass at dusk, as originally planned, would be worrisome to him, even with our trusty guides.

Now I wondered about sleeping arrangements. Sam said they would sleep on deck, so we brought out our extra blankets. It was a calm warm night and we would motor the whole way – in fact an ideal night to sleep out on deck. Having a coffin in plain sight was odd, but not as eerie, at least for me, as you might think. The night went well, except perhaps for the unfortunate pregnant woman who had to throw up, mostly over the side of the boat, every so often.

⚓

The next morning at dawn, Robb used his expensive Furuno binoculars to scan the horizon in search of the island. Although he knew where it was supposed to be, he couldn't detect even the faintest smudge. But the men pointed and assured us they could. Just as the bit of land began to take shape through the binoculars, the men started reporting specific landmarks, like the big rock just off the island.

We already knew there was no dock, not even a place to anchor. We hove to – drifted and motored – as close to land as we could safely do, and a panga roared out to meet us. Robb's an excellent sailor and managed to steady our boat enough for the coffin to be lowered into the smaller boat.

Sam invited us to spend the day on shore. Robb and I would have liked to, but we had to stay with the boat, so just Alex and Annie went. Sometimes I wonder about the things we let the children do. In this case we believed we were far enough away in time and space from the New Guinea of the early 1960s, where cannibalism and headhunting were still practiced in some areas. Michael Rockefeller, of The Rockefellers, disappeared there in those days, and – some researchers believe – was killed and eaten. We were proud the children wanted to go, and we were eager for them to have this unique opportunity to experience relatively untouched island life. For their part, I believe they may have just wanted to get off the boat and be on their own, away from us for a while.

***

A small rain squall headed our way, so I gathered up shampoo, soap and a towel. The line of the squall, however, stopped just feet from *Sorcery*, and we didn't get a drop. About 4 in the afternoon, the panga came out to the boat with what we hoped would be our children. Instead, we were given 299 – we counted them – coconuts to take back. We tied them with their own peeled-back husks to various places on deck. On its next trip the panga dropped off four enormous edible tubers, each about 2 feet tall and half as wide. They had to go into the dinghy to contain the dirt, since lots of dark, moist earth still clung to the masses of roots that covered the skins of the vegetables.

The panga's third trip brought the *pièce de résistance*: a live pig, which had to be at least 100 pounds. It came with a rope tied to one of its front legs. We secured the other end of the rope to the base of the roller furling at the bow. Thinking that was that, we began to ready the boat for passage, Robb on deck and me below. Minutes later Robb shouted, "Dianne! Get out here! PIG OVERBOARD!"

I raced up to find Robb at the bow, holding onto the rope to the pig, which had jumped ship. Somehow, we managed to get the terrified animal back up on deck. The experience caused the poor thing to lose control at both ends.

***

Our sunburned children returned, along with six of the seven original passengers, and it was time to head back. The only information we could extract from our kids about how they spent the time was they got to ride bikes. So much for untouched island life. Annie spent much of the return trip comforting the pig. She sat with her for hours, talking to her, petting her, and giving her water. One of the youngest island men and Alex joined Annie, and the three passed the time discussing the latest music. A man played my guitar and sang.

The next morning, we arrived in Funafuti and unloaded the people and the goods. Without a word from us, four of the men got busy cleaning out the dinghy and scrubbing the deck – a welcome and unexpected gesture.

The Funeral Feast

The family invited us to a feast held a few nights later. Near the community hall where the ceremony was held, we passed a truck with a flatbed covered with big, green leaves that served as plates. The 200 leaf-plates were heaped with food including a loaf of bread, a small frozen chicken still in its plastic bag, and a roast fish. We learned one of the men who'd been on our trip had caught all the fish. The food was destined for villagers not invited to the feast.

Although we were not told in so many words, we seemed to be the guests of honor. No doubt this was due to our recent service to the family, and also because we were foreigners. We sat cross-legged on straw mats that covered the floor of a spacious, low-ceilinged room built of cinderblocks. Tired lace curtains covered the windows. Room-long lengths of colorful, patterned fabric served as rows of tablecloths. Everyone else had a leaf for a plate, which we coveted; but our special status required we use plastic ones. A pitcher of what looked like Kool-Aid sat near us. Robb advised against drinking any. Fortunately, no one insisted, as sometimes happens. Other people appeared to be drinking tea. But for whatever reason, they didn't offer any to us.

Food was a show of wealth in their culture, and women carried in dozens of huge platters, each heaped high with food, and placed them on the cloth on the floor. All the food looked good, but only a fraction of it looked familiar. After rice, breadfruit chips, fruit, mashed coconut with toddy (a sweet coconut juice), fish, and spiced meat bits and chunks, we gave up trying to figure it out. Last, but most significantly, the women paraded in with four whole roast pigs; one of which was placed directly in front of us. Alex told Annie it was "her" pig, but she was surprisingly philosophical about it – no tears.

Other Work and School

John steered Robb to other employment. The first job entailed repairing the guy wires holding up the antenna of the island's 100-foot civil aviation tower. Who better to fix them than a man on a sailboat with all those stays holding up the 70-foot mast? Nevertheless, he had to produce a resume, fill out an application, and give references. Alex was a big help with the hard, hot outdoor work.

At the Amatuku Maritime School, Robb did some electrical repair inside the building. He fixed the fiberglass water-catchment system at the new Australian government residence. *Thunder*, an aptly named 15-foot boat with a 40-horse outboard motor, roared up each morning to pick him up and brought him back each afternoon.

One weekend *Thunder* carried all of us to a big house-warming picnic held at the residence on its wide, long porch facing the ocean. The food, including *laulu*, was all recognizable, appetizing, and served on plate-sized leaves. Some of the offerings were clearly from Fiji: carrots, cabbage, fancy bread, and butter. Latecomers heated their food in a microwave oven.

When Alex wasn't helping his dad, he stayed aboard most days working on the boat, reading, doing some math and English, and playing *F19* on the computer. Occasionally he and Sam windsurfed and snorkeled. He and Annie were getting along well, but we all missed the great kid brigade at Lautoka.

***

Since we were in no hurry to leave Funafuti, we decided to have Annie attend the last month of school before the break. Overnight, a seamstress whipped up a Smurfette-blue uniform for her. The classroom had rough, split logs for desks. I thought about Abraham Lincoln and how successful he'd been. She was ahead of the other students, so easily did well. At least once, students applauded her for getting the best score on a test.

One day after the teacher shouted in Tuvaluan, Annie stood in a line because everyone else did. As each student got to the front, the teacher rapped their knuckles with a ruler. After her punishment, Annie discovered the line was for kids who hadn't done their homework, although she'd done hers. Happy with school, she often stayed late to play tag and swim.

Before long Annie became good friends with Alifo, a sweet girl her age, and would spend two or three hours a day playing with her and her younger brother, Abner. Sometimes the kids played in the water around our boat, using the spinnaker halyard to swing out over the water, then drop in. Annie spent a lot of time at their home. Once or twice when she stayed overnight I baked a chocolate cake for the family.

The last week of school the teacher reminded everyone they'd need a flower crown for the graduation ceremony. Annie raised her hand. "My mom doesn't know how to make them."

"My mom will make one for her," Alifo offered.

On graduation day, a sea of blue uniforms filled a vast, open-air maneapa. At least 200 girls and boys, each with a flower crown, sat closely packed on mats. A third of the island's population was under fifteen years old. Prizes of dinners at the hotel were awarded for good scholarship. Afterward, families picnicked on the required "traditional foods only." Alifo's family had brought enough for us too: fish, coconut soup, and bananas.

Big toe helps make a flower crown

Not every island in the South Pacific had a high school, so it was customary for families on islands that had one to take in students from other islands for the school year. Alifo's neighborhood gave a huge block party one evening as a farewell to some of those students. More than a party, the event was an organized show. Strings of lights, balloons, and loud speakers hung above the packed-earth courtyards of half a dozen adjacent homes. Especially selected recorded music accompanied each rehearsed act. Annie and Alifo, in their bare feet and everyday shorts and T-shirts, surprised us by doing a choreographed dance to ABBA's "Dancing Queen." Traditionally- costumed youngsters performed indigenous dances. Adorable four- and five-year-old boys in their little sulus, miniature garlands, and crowns of flowers stole the show.

Annie and Alifo on graduation day

Our time in Funafuti was not all fun and games. Equipment problems plagued us, though that was not uncommon. The dinghy needed patching way too often. The options for replacing it were all fraught with difficulties. If we ordered a new Avon from West Marine or a used New Zealand lifeguard boat, we'd have had to wait either who-knows-how-long to have it delivered to Funafuti or to the Marshall Islands, which we would not want to do until we got there. We heard we could buy a new dinghy at the next island group more or less on the way to the Marshalls, but for various reasons we didn't want to stop there on the way up. No solution seemed suitable, so we continued to patch, and after Robb injected some dinghy repair foam, the dinghy held air remarkably well.

Robb found the Freon leak that accounted for the fridge not working, but by then we were out of Freon, and none could be found in town. He had to take the generator apart because the starter cord broke and got sucked up inside. All the flashlight batteries were low, a worrisome situation. Batteries were hard to come by, either because the locals didn't use the sizes we needed or because the ones available were old or of poor quality, or both. Mold started showing up on our beloved VHS tapes, causing "snow" when viewed. We became experts at removing the white mold with Q-tips and alcohol.

On a daily basis, Robb worried about westerly winds. He repeated he wasn't cut out for cruising, that he hated sailing where there were reefs. He didn't want to go back to San Diego, but he would like to cruise again in the Sea of Cortez while fixing up the boat to sell. We talked about looking at the East Coast as a place to live, exploring the inland waterway. Of course, the immediate question was: Where to go next? We were a long way from anywhere, and hurricane season was closing in.

***

On October 21, Annie's eleventh birthday, the $1,000 payment for transporting the dead man to his home island came through. We went a little crazy, celebrating the money and her day, by going out for both lunch and dinner. But first, tradition. The Happy Birthday song, a pyramid of cupcakes with plenty of candles, and assorted little gifts from us and others started the day. Later on, Al and Lisa sang "Happy Birthday" over the radio. And, a big treat, Annie got to telephone her best friend, Hallie, in San Diego. At the hotel lunch, the waiter placed a fresh flower crown on Annie's head.

We wanted to do something for Jane and John for all the help they'd given us; and since Annie liked both of them, we included them in her birthday dinner. They suggested Su's Place, an Asian restaurant. An exotic meal, presented family-style from a lazy susan in the middle of a big round table, consisted of six or seven dishes, including a whole baked grouper. John and Jane gave her a pretty hair ornament made of shells, and had ordered a big pink cake with a touching inscription written in green, "Happy 11th Birthday, Annie. Love, John and Jane." Slices of cake, ice cream, chopped dates, and a little sauce were served in banana-split dishes.

Working for the University of the South Pacific

By late October, I found two jobs at the University of the South Pacific. I tutored English in a classroom with huge windows opening onto banana trees. The pay was good, $14 an hour, though I only worked an hour a day, four days a week for the final month of the semester. And one class got cancelled on the day of a big food shipment. The other job didn't pay much, $3.50 an hour, but I loved the work: helping coordinate the adult continuing education program. The course, Learn to Read Music, was to start the first week in November, only days away. We needed students. I met with the instructor, a white-haired gentleman sitting in his sulu on a thatch-roofed, raised platform. From his description of the class, I designed a flyer and handed out 100 of them myself. Twelve students signed up, though only four remained at the end. The follow-up interviews I'd developed revealed the class to be too fast and complicated for beginners. Throughout November I worked on the courses for January.

The university director, who'd written me a long offer letter in flawless English, showed up one day with a leaf attached to his ankle to cure an infection from scratching mosquito bites. I may have missed a bet by not trying that local remedy when both Robb and Annie got infections causing their whole foot to swell up. We applied hot packs, soaked the feet, kept the wounds dry, used antibiotic powder, and applied black drawing salve until something worked.

***

On the subject of health, New Zealand had recently held a conference in Funafuti on cervical cancer, and nurses trained a few local women to do Pap smear tests. In full preventative healthcare mode, I presented myself for the procedure at the women's clinic, which looked like a small home. Inside, a woman escorted me through a door with a hand-lettered cardboard sign reading, unpromisingly, "Gynecology and Store Room." But the neat and clean room, and the shiny, new instruments reassured me. A massive yet gentle woman, with a noticeable mustache and a tight "I survived Hurricane Kina" T-shirt, took the smear. She was startled I had on underpants and, when she did the breast exam, a bra. I hadn't realized what novelties they were.

I asked Jane if Funafuti had a women's shelter. She gave me three contacts. Mileta at the local International Planned Parenthood office said they "definitely needed" a shelter. The Ministry of Health Community Affairs officer, Ms. Manuella, flatly stated a shelter was not necessary. And, at a meeting with the wife of the prime minister and three other women, they concluded a shelter might be useful, but "wouldn't work here." However, all did not seem to be lost. The wife entrusted me with a large, handmade, wooden mortar and pestle, a gift for the mayor of Majuro in the Marshall Islands. She told me the mayor, a female, had expressed interest in a shelter for women.

***

Two other cruising boats came for a week, *Fair Rover* with Chris, Cindy, and their kids Celeste and Jeff; and *Thesis* with Jim and Rhea. The kids all got along well, though after three days, Annie went back to playing with her island friends, and Alex was off listening to music and windsurfing with Sam. We all watched movies and had several pot lucks. One outstanding meal featured barbequed wahoo, potato salad, and beer bread. Before they left, *Fair Rover* sold us some canned goods, onions, potatoes, and paper towels.

The Wedding

Annie had come home from school with a wedding invitation from the relative of a classmate. "Miss Annie and Family" were cordially invited to attend the celebration, which turned out to be as exuberant as it was long, 9 in the morning until 4:30 in the afternoon.

At 9 sharp on the day of the wedding, the bride in a bright white gown and net veil arrived at the church under a small canopy held aloft by four women in sulus. Around the edges of the canopy, balloons of all colors bobbed gaily, and empty Twistie Chips foil bags sparkled in the sun. A dozen women, paid performers dressed in flowery sulus and white T-shirts, sang and clapped as they skipped along beside the bride. Every shirt had something to say. One advised, "Act now. Prevent AIDS." Deftly avoiding the café au lait puddles in the dirt path, the procession made its way around the outside of the building.

A stray dog accompanied the bride into the Methodist church, a vast, tin-roofed, open-air building with a view to the sea. Handwoven mats covered the entire floor, where a couple hundred guests sat facing the bridal party. Since fresh flowers were everyday fare, this upscale wedding featured blossoms and leaves of plastic and yarn. Six bridesmaids and two flower girls wore dayglow-lime taffeta dresses with belts of fresh, green ferns.

The groom and his six attendants wore flip-flops and Western suits, except instead of pants, skirts made of suit fabric came down to their knees. The barefoot minister dressed in the same way. In addition, the groom wore traditional grass and tapa skirts around his waist and shoulders. Like most other male guests, Robb and Alex wore their everyday, all-purpose sulu. The minister didn't speak long, and plenty of heavenly, harmonious singing helped pass the time. Finally, the moment came for the groom to lift the bride's veil and … shake her hand.

Singing, clapping, smiling performers led everyone out through the puddles to the hotel for a reception line where we were introduced to the bride, who seemed extremely pleased we were there. For the feast, we all traipsed to the meeting house decorated with garlands of real ferns and palm branches wound around each of the two dozen pillars.

The master of ceremonies sat us in the front row. Soon, the whole wedding party reappeared in fantastic, traditional wedding regalia: floor-length muumuus, skirts of grass and tapa cloth circling their waists and shoulders, bracelets and anklets of flowers, and fresh flower crowns perching at rakish angles on their heads. One young man simply could not bring himself to remove the last vestige of the 20th century, his cool sunglasses.

Along one side of the room, a substantial roast pig presided over each end of a 40-foot-long table heaped with food. Whole oranges studded one porker made fierce with two banana fangs. The other pig had a bouquet of artificial flowers stuck in its neck. We ate without utensils from plates made of woven palm fronds lined with breadfruit leaves. At the end of the meal, two "nubile maidens" knelt in front of Robb, one to remove his empty plate, the other to offer a finger bowl and towel. I guess the kids and I just licked our fingers.

Before our eyes, two white wedding cakes were assembled on the floor in front of the bride and groom. Inverted wine glasses separated the four precarious levels of each cake. Not wasting a moment once the cake towers were complete, slices from the three top layers were distributed to the family and relatives. The rest of us received an inch-square cube, which we weren't supposed to eat until after we'd all shouted in unison something like "*L'chaim!*" I'd missed that directive and had nothing to eat when the moment came.

The music that had been going on all day long began to kick up. A group of seven sat on the floor pounding a short, 4-foot-square drum. Older women wearing muumuus and flowers danced as the spirit moved them to the enjoyment of the wildly clapping and singing crowd, all of whom were also bedecked with flowers and leaves. *This is terrific!* I thought, *Just like a hundred years ago!* Then the bride started spritzing dancers with a spray bottle of perfume. She did that pretty often, and every time a roar went up from the crowd.

Great kettles of tea with sugar and milk, and dozens of platters of imported pastries and fruit appeared on the banquet table. From that point, people Twisted their hearts out to the live and loud music of the Funafuti Island Power band. We eased out a little before the party ended.

Alex's fifteenth birthday in mid-November was more or less a repeat of Annie's, except we had ice cream with his requested poppy-seed cake at breakfast. We lunched at Su's Place, then had dinner with friends at the hotel, where Alex, Annie and I each received a flower crown. The word must have gotten around we were moving on, because all four of us were given shell necklaces, something usually bestowed before a journey. We happened to be there on Island Night, and though we were only an audience of seven, 30 performers – who were one and the same as the hotel staff – danced and sang. We shared an immense chocolate birthday cake with everybody. Alex wrote, "That birthday was the best yet, but I say that every year."

***

Shortly after Annie became friends with Alifo and Abner, they'd given her a puppy. "My island puppy," Annie wrote later, "was white with brown and black spots and cuter than the dickens. I named him Buddy and was really sad when the time came to sail onward." That time was the first Saturday in December.

Nanumea

We almost didn't stop at the island that turned out to be the most exotic place of our entire trip. Most cruisers didn't even attempt the narrow, shallow entrance to the four-square-mile atoll, 300 miles and three nights north of Funafuti. A Swedish boat just ahead of us, *Jennifer* with Lars and Johanna, declared the pass "too scary" when they saw it, and kept on going. But we'd read that a man in Nanumea made beautiful water-tight wooden boxes for fishermen to carry fish hooks and cigarettes. Also, Jane and John had given us a carton of eggs to take to a woman there. Nothing like having a project and a mission for me to hope Robb would decide we could safely make it through the pass.

Without a detailed nautical chart of the island, but having a sort of street map, we used the church steeple to help us locate the entrance to the lagoon. The width of the pass looked to be about 60 feet, adequate for *Sorcery*'s 15-foot beam. However, the pass was only 9 feet deep, and *Sorcery* drew 8½. As we circled indecisively outside the entrance, a man in a small fishing boat came up and asked if he could help.

"8½-foot keel? No problem!" He yelled.

"Are you sure?" Robb yelled back.

"Sure! Follow me!"

As we motored slowly through the pass in his wake, several people dressed in sulus came to the shore, waving and shouting, "Hello! Hello! Welcome! Welcome!"

The chief of police and wife checking our papers

As soon as we'd anchored in the quiet, palm-fringed lagoon, the police chief and his wife, both dressed in sulus, paddled up in their outrigger. They climbed aboard and exchanged pleasantries before asking to see the ship's papers. Holding the port-clearance document upside down, the chief hesitated. We held our breath. But a big, official-looking stamp apparently satisfied him. Most people in these islands didn't read English, but spoke it quite well. We threw in our one or two words of Tuvaluan, pantomiming did the rest. The couple exited dramatically by jumping into the water, then lifting themselves gracefully onto their outrigger.

Our permit only allowed us to stay four days, so we grabbed our sulus and went ashore to track down the maker of the wooden boxes. The first person we asked understood what we wanted. She snagged a passing child and he led us to the man's home, a traditional raised platform with a thatched roof and crisscrossed stick walls.

We found him and his wife in their sulus, her seated on the ground making a new roof for the house, him sitting on the platform surveying his kingdom. He invited us up to join him. But before negotiations, he directed his son to fetch some drinking coconuts. The youth shimmied up one of the tall palms in the yard and kicked down half a dozen coconuts. Each scruffy ball got slammed onto a pointed waist-high stake, cracking open the husk, leaving the nut. The "eyes" were poked out so we could drink the refreshing water inside.

Yes, he could make us a *tuluma*. The work would take two days and cost $5. At that price we decided we needed three boxes if he could finish them within the week. Yes, again. That accomplished, and feeling confident we could get an extension on our permit, we resumed our walk, stopping at the only store, which was also the bakery.

The baker shook his head. "So sorry, the bread won't be ready until after 5 o'clock."

"That's okay, we'll come back then."

No sooner had we returned to the boat than the roaring screech of an electric power-tool ripped through the stillness. My eyes grew big. "What in the world?"

"It's a chain saw," Robb said. "He's getting wood for our boxes."

Toward dusk, we heard a knock on the hull. The baker and his wife stood in their outrigger, clinging to the side of our boat, holding aloft a warm loaf of bread wrapped in newspaper. We tried to pay, but they insisted with huge smiles that the bread was a gift.

All that on the first day.

⚓

The woman to whom we were to deliver the eggs worked in the hospital. We found her there and she invited us to her home for lunch the following day. What I remember about the meal is we drank from Mason jars, something now quite shabby-chic in the States.

Having seen the run-down hospital, we were reluctant to take Annie there when she developed a bad earache and a fever. Over a couple of days, we doctored first with decongestant and steam, then with antibiotic ear drops and a painkiller, and finally with erythromycin. She vomited, which may have been due to not taking enough food with the medicine. "Kinda scary," my journal reported, and, if she hadn't improved by the next morning, we planned to get on the radio to try to hook up with a doctor. Thankfully, the earache went away.

A day or so after we arrived, rain poured down solidly for two days. When the sun burst through, a red catamaran overflowing with singing and clapping revelers circled around *Sorcery*, simply for the pleasure of it. A fellow in an outrigger came alongside us to chat, then returned later with his wife and another loaf of hot bread. "A Christmas gift," they said, and happily accepted the deck of cards we gave them in return.

Wind and rain kept us in Nanumea longer than we intended. The weather, of course, was worse in the open ocean, so we used that as the reason for asking for a week's extension on our permit. We all welcomed the chance to rest, and I, especially, enjoyed the cultural experiences we were having. Lots of visitors stopped by, most of whom brought fruit: coconuts, bananas, papayas, and one time, two eggs.

Every sunny day, children swam out or came to the boat by outrigger. Annie played with them in the water, or sometimes invited them on board. The kids were adorable; the drunk men, not so much. They weren't really obnoxious, but talking with them was difficult, and they just didn't know when to leave. That only happened twice that I remember, but Annie started asking me to stay on deck as a lookout whenever she was dressing, because she feared a drunk man might be on the boat.

The next week a second storm kept us inside for another couple of days. We set another anchor and started double-tying the dinghy, which had gotten a small rip by swinging into the wind vane. We tried putting the awning up so we could sit outside, but the wind was much too powerful. The cover for the back hatch blew overboard and was lost. After that storm we saw several banana and papaya trees had been knocked down, and many of them propped up again.

The man and our watertight boxes

Before the promised time, our boxes were ready. They were perfect, except the wife confronted us with a new price, $15 each. We settled on $8 apiece and still considered the cost a bargain. In the village we watched an artisan sitting on a mat in his sulu making a model outrigger. We bought three of his exquisitely detailed miniatures.

John had recommended we look up his friend Namea at the weather office. He turned out to be a sweet old fellow who showed us around the office and came to visit.

"Do many boats come through Nanumea?" Robb asked him.

"Sure! Plenty! There was one here last August!"

Upon further questioning, we calculated maybe 12 cruisers stopped there each year.

One day, out for a walk, we got caught in the rain and happened upon a woman holding a huge umbrella while she fried dumplings in a pan of oil over a fire. She called to one of her four young sons to lead us into the shelter of her hut. Alex ran back to close up the boat. The clean and tidy two-story platform house accommodated only a few possessions. On the top floor we sat on decorated mats and saw only fluffy, embroidered pillows, suitcases for their clothing, a backpack, and Mason jars.

As the rain let up, Alex returned and the little boys walked on with us. We came across the *maneapa*, the meeting house for the Council of Elders, which had tables with documents and recording equipment, but no chairs. A caretaker explained that when the elders met, they sat on the floor.

***

Jim on *Loke Lani* put out a radio call asking if someone in Nanumea could please give a message to a local woman named Karlalisa. After we delivered the message to her on the other side of the lagoon, she invited us to return for a visit the following day. The next day, Robb and Alex weren't interested, and I was too exhausted to go, but the following morning Annie and I went over. Our hostess had prepared a tray of attractively arranged fruit, and the children gave us special little shells, a tiny abalone and a pink topshell.

We brought corned beef, canned fish, a length of patterned fabric, a blouse for the girl, a hat for the boy, and glass jars. Karlalisa braided small, multicolored beads into a narrow length of Annie's long, dark hair, and gave her a black, fringed top and a pair of black-and-white striped pants. Later, while Annie played with the kids, Karlalisa needed to get back to her chores, and I helped hang her tattered, sun-bleached laundry on a clothesline.

When Karlalisa visited us, she never stayed long. On the first occasion, she asked matter-of-factly for a towel to sit on because she was having her period. Apparently, the towel was merely a precaution, because it didn't get soiled at all. But the incident made me think about how much I take for granted the multitude of conveniences of the industrialized world. Years later I read that lack of disposable sanitary supplies is a big impediment to the education of young women in third world countries. On "those days" the girls stay home.

Karlalisa talked about her husband, who'd graduated from the Amatuku Maritime School in Funafuti and worked on German ships. Early on, she revealed he drank. Her coping tactics included these: running away to her home island, but her husband brought her back; staying on a "far island" and not sending the children to school; staying with a policeman for three weeks; and most recently she'd become a Baha'i to "straighten him out." I didn't pursue that plan with her, but I do know the religion forbids alcohol and has a prayer specifically for assistance with the challenges inherent in changing our expectations for those around us.

***

The woman I got to know best was Sineeva, who lived on a platform, slept on a mat, and used a traditional carved wooden block for a pillow. She took Annie and me to the second night of the Women's Festival, advertised as a three-day-long gathering for "singing, talking, and putting on plays." We observed women hanging out, talking, even sleeping, but that's about all. We thought maybe the main purpose of the festival was an opportunity for women to get away from men and housework for a while.

Sineeva invited us to the third day as well. Annie declined, but I showed up early at Sineeva's to help with her contribution to breakfast for the festival. I watched while she grated coconut and told me about her life. Her first husband was killed in a brawl in Nauru, a tiny island state, hundreds of miles away, where many Tuvaluan men went to work the dreadful guano mines. After his death, following custom, she married one of his male relatives.

Two daughters had died, one at six years and one at four days. In a photo, the lifeless six-year-old looked to be asleep, tucked in a blanket, surrounded with flowers.

"What happened to her?" I asked.

"She had a fever," was all Sineeva knew.

An eighteen-year-old daughter worked in Funafuti, where Sineeva would like to live, but she had to stay and look after her property. Her new husband worked on the inter-island ship and was rarely home.

One afternoon while visiting us, Sineeva gave me the lowdown on Karlalisa. Her husband beat her, that's what was wrong with her eyes. She was poor and lived across the lagoon, clearly meaning "across the tracks," where there was no electricity, and a pig lived under her house. I wondered to myself if other women avoided her. And if so, that might explain why, when she and I were hanging her washing, she seemed less interested in the help than in having the company.

***

Annie and I took Solepa, the police chief's wife, to another part of the island to pick the lovely green *laulu*, which can't grow where pigs can get to it. We hiked quite a way through the overgrown vegetation in the steamy jungle until the mosquitoes drove Annie and me back. Solepa persevered, filling two bags, one for us. We gave her perfume in exchange.

***

On one of our many walks out of town, we met Taasiu, a man wearing a sulu and collecting coconut sap to make an alcoholic toddy. His container was a coconut shell with a twine handle. Caving to my weakness for souvenirs of things people made and used, I offered to buy the container. He insisted we follow him home where he had another, better, one for me. At the head of our single file, he slashed right and left with his machete, causing us to wonder how long since he'd been home.

Once there, he handed me a coconut shell with a red plastic handle. The thing was, in town I'd watched a tattooed man sitting on the ground, employing his big toe to help twist some kind of fiber into twine. Taasiu was surprised I didn't prefer the plastic handle, but with a big smile, handed me the twine-handled shell. He insisted he didn't want any payment, but later we gave him something, probably a deck of cards.

One afternoon he turned up drunk at our boat with a plastic bucket of the evil-smelling toddy to share with us. To be polite Robb had the smallest of sips. Taasiu also had trained at Amatuku.

"I go to sea for 13 months, then drink sour toddy for six," he told us without any hint of either bragging or shame.

Whenever we walked outside the village we saw debris from WWII, much of it transformed into something useful: runway mats had become animal enclosures, shell casings as long as your arm served as bells, fuselages made strong storage huts and rain catchment systems. Taasiu took Robb and Alex on an excursion to see more wreckage. Among other things, he showed them a banged-up, corroded, but mostly intact, small airplane, and they brought home a few old bottles and bullets.

Another man offered to take Robb fishing and diving outside the reef, but Robb didn't take him up on it. "Why?" I asked.

"They're so much better than me. Anyway, I'm afraid of sharks on the outside."

⚓

Sometimes Alex and his dad stayed on the boat reading and playing computer games when Annie and I visited with the women, or she played with the kids. The heat and confinement took its toll on our dispositions. One night a quarrel erupted when we brought out the dominos. Although we'd played contentedly for years, Alex asked, "Do I have to play?

The day before Annie had asked the same thing. Petty accusations and complaints each of us had been harboring for who-knows-how-long flew around the table. Later, tempers cooled and Robb played poker with the kids.

By the end of a week or so, Annie wanted to leave because some boys called her "sweetheart," Robb and Alex because they were getting bored. But learning about these people whose lives were so different from my own brought out the Margaret Meade in me. The isolation and small size of the island with only a few hundred inhabitants – 644 in 2002 – fostered more and closer interactions with the local people than we'd experienced before or since. That we didn't have any other cruising boats to distract us was undoubtedly another factor.

***

Knowing we could count on listening to heavenly singing, we went to church on Sunday. The Tuvaluan words in the hymnal were beyond us, but Robb and I recognized many of the melodies from our Protestant upbringings. Virtually every person had a fan put to good use fending off the oppressive heat.

"Don't you have fans?" The woman sitting next to us asked.

After the service we were invited to the parsonage, where it transpired they were hoping for a donation to the church. Later, Annie and I sat in on choir practice.

***

During a heavy rain, a day or two before we left, the woodworker, his wife, and five of their nine children showed up at our boat. The wife said they'd stay for an hour and that's what they did. They brought handmade gifts: a conical fisherman's hat for Alex, a small handbag made from pandanus leaves for Annie, a flower crown for me, and some delicious cooked fish, cassava, and breadfruit.

Our gifts to them were three hats, a waist pack, dinosaur stickers, and sheets of sandpaper. Robb had learned the woodworker was down to his last 2-inch square. Although it was raining and the closed boat was quite hot, the visit went wonderfully. The couple sang while the man played my guitar, and the wife performed a sensual dance, similar to hula, in our narrow main cabin. She brought to the dance a confidence and inner beauty that shined past her gray hair, missing teeth, extra weight, and faded clothing.

⚓

Days before we left, people started asking when we were leaving. Finally, we let them know, "Tomorrow's the day." In the morning children came dressed in leaves and flowers, and had fresh flower crowns and leis for all four of us. Later in the morning, Annie and I went to church. The woman, who'd asked us the previous week about us not having fans, brought us gifts of three handwoven ones worthy of hanging on the wall. Sineeva sat with us. And even though I was the one leaving, and she the one staying, I passed on to her the traveler's protective shell necklace given to me in Funafuti by the wife of Tuvalu's prime minister.

At the last minute, the police chief's wife came to give Annie a shell crown and two hand-painted pillowcases with embroidered edges. I gave the woman a few small gifts and some of our boat cards with our address for people who said they'd like to write to us. Sadly, no one ever did, but then, we didn't stay in touch either.

Dressed to say farewell

Robb planned to leave at the height of the incoming tide at 5 p.m. The fisherman who'd led us in went to check on the pass, and then swam to *Sorcery* with the report that everything looked good. Fortunately, Robb had decided to start leaving at 4:15, which gave us some extra time when the anchor refused to budge, and he had to strap on his air tank and dive for it.

The minute he surfaced and everything was secured, he wrapped a towel around his waist, stepped behind the wheel, and off we went to the waving and shouted goodbyes from several people along the shore. The depth sounder showed 8 feet. The breakers on either side of the pass appeared to be only 10 feet apart, but we knew that was only an illusion. We easily powered through, and motored into the fast-approaching night.

Christmas at Sea ~ 1994

After leaving Nanumea a week before Christmas, we motored half the first night, then sailed slowly, averaging a little more than three miles per hour through huge rolling swells. The boat was stifling, and everybody except me felt "off." Annie made herself throw up. Alex felt ill, but not enough to resort to that cure, and Robb had hurt his ribs.

We set the staysail and took a reef in the main in an attempt to steady the boat a little in the windless, sloppy seas. During one wretched stretch of 10 hours we'd only made about 10 miles, and were pretty discouraged. It got worse. One night, due to the lack of wind and a contrary current, we drifted backward 50 miles. Robb was a nervous wreck, in no small part because even talking pained his bruised ribs. He decided we should bypass Tarawa in the Kiribati Islands and keep moving. Our destination, Majuro in the Marshall Islands, still lay over 600 miles north.

Numerous lesser problems added to our misery: Water came into the galley through the small overhead hatch; painful chafe marks rose on my skin from the heat and sweat; lice eggs appeared in Annie's hair. I'd watched island mothers picking nits off their kids' heads. So during a lull in the weather, Annie and I sat on deck "for a lifetime," as she remembers it, while I plucked dozens of tiny white eggs from individual strands of her hair. After a shampoo and a rinse, we never saw another egg or nit.

Robb and I revisited the conversation about how we could get out of the whole adventure, but came to the usual conclusion: there was no turning back. I wondered what we'd wish for years from then. Since we lived to tell the tale, I can say, without qualification, we're eternally thankful for the journey of a lifetime. In calmer moments, we made plans for after the Marshall Islands. We'd come back down through Kiribati, Tuvalu and Fiji, and then head west for New Caledonia and Australia for the next big stop.

We talked about what we needed to do to make traveling more comfortable and safe. Much of that involved spending money, which I was always reluctant to do, though I agreed with most items. Robb's list included a water heater for showers below deck, a feathering Max Prop propeller to improve motoring performance, an upgraded EPIRB (ours only talked to airplanes, not satellites), new chain, a new generator, a new dinghy. Before leaving Nanumea, our ailing yellow inflatable retired as a life raft, and was replaced on deck with our spare – an older, smaller, gray inflatable.

On the next radio call with Susan, I sank into envying her comfortable life. "My kingdom for a bubble bath and clean sheets," I whined. "Where the boat isn't rusted or corroded, it's being overtaken by black mold. We're low on staples like sugar, powdered milk, toilet paper. Worst of all, tomorrow's Christmas."

"What fun!" she bubbled.

Bless you for that, Susan, because my attitude instantly adjusted. Alone on night watch, I had to do a 30-second, 360-degree visual check on deck every 10 minutes. That left plenty of time to find most of the little gifts I'd stowed away, invent some more, wrap each one neatly in newspaper, and tie it with a red ribbon. I made a list of all the holiday things we could do, and dug out art supplies and decorations, so the kids could dress up the boat and make a program for the day. Using a little box of condensed mincemeat, I baked a pie.

When everyone got up, they were jubilant to find Christmas had arrived on *Sorcery*. The weather that had been overcast and rainy cooperated by being sunny and reasonably calm. We gathered outside in the cockpit with our coffee and hot chocolate, ate our pie, opened the gifts, and sang Christmas songs. A rainbow appeared, and dolphins played around the boat. The wind came up later in the morning; so we spent the rest of the day down below decorating, baking cookies, singing some more, reading Christmas stories – I don't remember what all. And to think I'd been ready to sulk the day away.

MARSHALL ISLANDS

Second Big Stop
Late December 1994 to Mid June 1995

FIVE days after leaving Nanumea and two days before the New Year, we arrived at the atoll of Majuro, the capital of the Marshalls and our home for the next six months. From the start, we knew we weren't in Nanumea anymore. Rather than a welcoming committee, the first person we met begrudgingly tilted her head in the direction of the town center when we asked directions. But we understood a bigger place was more accustomed to tourists, and we found most locals were friendly in their own way.

No more sulus for either men or women. Plump women, wearing loose muumuus that reached mid-calf or skirts with oversized T-shirts, shuffled along in plastic flip-flops. The tough-looking men were actually warm and polite. Occasional intricate flower crowns harked back to simpler days.

Majuro was a safe place. The kids could walk or take a 30-cent taxi anywhere by themselves. The subcompact taxis carried five passengers, more if some were children. Robb said the cars were mostly new, but they looked old to me. Nine out of 10 inside door handles were lengths of string. Poorer people took the big taxi vans for 25 cents.

Some traditional platform-type homes still existed in the outskirts, but in the town center insubstantial, unattractive houses, yards littered with garbage and junk were the norm. We were never invited to a local's home, and there was never any exchange of gifts. The convenience of disposables I'd remembered to appreciate in Nanumea displayed one of its darkest sides in Majuro. Trash everywhere. The few trash cans in evidence overflowed with empty cans and bottles, paper of all descriptions, used diapers, cardboard and plastic packaging, broken plastic toys. Items too big for trash cans – typewriters, desks, the proverbial kitchen sink, even vehicles – got dumped into the clear, blue lagoon.

It's hard not to implicate the United States in the sad condition of Majuro. Since 1946, with the nuclear bomb testing at nearby Bikini Atoll, we've been a huge presence, bringing with us some of the worst aspects of a materialistic, throw-away culture. In exchange for all the damage and displacement of people during those testing years, the Marshallese became heavily dependent on the subsidies and reparations offered by the U.S.

The country uses the U.S. dollar as its currency. And so, it was with American dollars we made our first purchases: root beer and vanilla ice cream to make floats. They were a little bit of heaven, so Majuro wasn't all bad. At the huge American-style grocery store, we stocked up with just about every stateside product on our list and then some: Pringles, Charmin, you name it. At the end of one aisle we spotted a girl.

"She looks about my age," Annie calculated and trotted off to introduce herself. Nikki turned out to be American and the girls got along like lost sisters throughout our time there. They are still friends to this day.

Annie and Nikki with floating lunches

The local high school wouldn't have been at all challenging for Alex. So, in January he flew back to stay with his mother in Chicago and go to school for a semester with the assumption he would return before we left in June. A couple from New York City ran a small, inexpensive, private grade school, which was perfect for Annie. Testing showed her academic level to be right on target for fourth grade. She liked school, and told us she wanted to attend school in Australia too.

When Annie wasn't hanging out with other kids, she devoted her spare time to reading *Teen Beat* magazine and listening to tapes on acting to prepare herself for her dream of going to Hollywood. To her delight, her dad read along with her as they made their way through her prized and growing collection of R.L. Stine's teen horror Fear Street series. Like the deteriorating un-chewed gumball that circumnavigated the world in her possession, each and every book made it back to the States.

When I met the mayor, Amatlain Kabua, I presented her with the mortar and pestle, or "pounder," I'd brought as a gift from the wife of the prime minister of Tuvalu. Kabua said she'd use it to make *iu*, a delicacy concocted from the pounded meat of sprouted coconut with added vanilla and other flavorings.

Ann and Bill on *Sendaya* had told me the mayor wanted to establish a women's center and shelter. They were personal friends of hers and wrote a recommendation for me. I'd been in contact with a friend in San Diego who'd established a women's center there, and she was eager to come to the Marshalls to help. But when I spoke with the mayor, she talked vaguely about the unavailability of funding and didn't invite further discussion.

***

Sometimes conversations struck us as comical. Here's a phone call I made to the library:

Him: Hello.
Me: Hello? Is this the library?
Him: Library?
Me: Yes, the library.
Him: Yes.
Me: Can you please tell me the library hours?
Him: What do you mean?
Me: When are you open?
Him We're open all the time!
Me: Okay, well, what time do you open in the morning?
Him: Eight o'clock.
Me: What time do you close?
Him: Five o'clock.
Me: You don't close for lunch?
Him: Sure we close for lunch!
Me: So you close from 12 to 1?
Him: We do.
Me: Then you're open 8 to 12 and 1 to 5?
Him: Right.
Me: Every day?
Him: Yes, every day except Thursday.
Me: What happens Thursday?
Him: We close at 6.

A few more exchanges revealed the library closed all day on Sunday.

The Best Job of My Life

For me, the highlight of being in Majuro was working as a reporter and photographer for *The Marshall Islands Journal*. In fact, now that I'm retired, I can say my stint at the *Journal* was the most fun and fulfilling job of all my working life. The 24-page weekly had been started years before, and was still published by Joe Murphy, a former Peace Corp volunteer who'd stayed on and married a local.

Every week I wrote half a dozen articles, almost 80 during my four-month career. I loved working on the stories, taking photographs, and that creative feeling of an article coming together. On Thursday mornings neither rain, nor heat, nor feeling ill could stay me from making my way to the office to see the newly printed newspaper with my articles, photos, and above all, the thrilling bylines.

My first article was nothing more than a long paragraph about the recent electrical blackout. Remembering those silly tourist postcards in the States, I asked the graphics and layout guy to print a solid black square with the caption "Majuro during blackout."

The second week, Joe asked me to do interviews and report on a government investigation into an allegedly fraudulent $9 million medical insurance scheme. I mailed a copy of the paper with my front-page article and byline to our Italian friend, Sam, in San Diego. Genuinely concerned, he called on the radio, warning me to be extremely careful.

"Where I come from in New Jersey, I've known of people who were killed for less." I shared Sam's concern with my boss, who laughed it off.

Joe fed me most of the leads on the civic, political, business, educational, religious, and human-interest goings on, but often I found stories myself. One day in line at the post office, I met three men who'd just arrived on a flying boat that had last been seen delivering mail to the Marshalls in the 1950s.

My photo of the 28-seater, Grumman G-111 Albatross didn't turn out, and I didn't have a chance to retake the picture. Meanwhile, the crew had discovered some rare postage stamps featuring the Albatross in the Alele Museum. I arranged with the curator to have a photo of the stamps taken to go with my article. She made quite a fuss about security.

Yet when the crew asked if they could have one of the two identical sets of stamps, she gave it to them.

Fellow cruisers made entertaining topics for articles. An enterprising French family on *Myste* was more than cruisers, for they had chosen a life at sea. The four children, born in France, Spain, Djibouti, and Costa Rica, ranged in age from twenty-one months to seventeen years.

A wide variety of ventures – from underwater diamond mining in South Africa, commercial fishing and chartering, to fancy sailor's knot display boards selling for as much as $1,700 – financed their lifestyle. We bought a small, yawning shark jaw with its fearsome rows of teeth. Their son macraméd a string holder for the basketball-sized, glass fishing float I'd gotten in exchange for an apple in Majuro. I still wear a fine pair of earrings fashioned from beads and seashore objects the girls gave me.

A month before we left, Annie and I were the subjects of my article "Detective Saves Day." After a routine trip to the laundromat, we couldn't get the dinghy outboard started. Rowing wasn't an option since we had a heavy load and only one oar. For over an hour we tried swimming and towing the dinghy, but a light breeze pushed us farther and farther from *Sorcery*. Fortunately, we were headed to an opposite, though faraway, shore and not out to sea. No other boats were within shouting distance. At last an alert off-duty detective in a skiff spotted us, and buzzed over to see what was going on. My photo showing our dinghy's bow, the tow rope, and the rescuing boat came in handy for the article.

***

Over spring break, Annie had a job at the *Journal* putting telephone books together for $1.25 an hour. She punched a time clock and received her first-ever paycheck.

"I'll take it to her," I told Joe when he said her check was ready.

"No," Joe, the father of 12, shook his head. "Have her come in. Sometimes parents keep the money."

***

Robb didn't have as much fun working as I did. He got paid for some electrical work at the Marshall Islands Club and sometimes helped another cruiser who had a boat repair business. Our own boat kept him busy repairing, supervising someone else who made repairs, and getting new parts and equipment. He purchased some boat and fishing gear in Majuro, but most items were ordered from the States.

For the two largest purchases, a dinghy and 400 feet of chain, we had to arrange transportation on two different container ships. Five offices in Majuro required separate clearance for each shipment before we picked up the goods. The 600-pound chain came in a barrel, but the dinghy arrived in three boxes. The box with the new oars mysteriously turned up in the office at the container yard.

Ordering a new generator from the States became a nightmare. Our credit card had already been charged about $300, and after waiting weeks, we received a frame saw. We returned it at our own expense, then, unbelievably, the saw showed up a second time, having to be returned, again at our expense. Extensive yelling and cursing over many expensive long-distance phone calls eventually produced the generator.

Majuro has U.S. zip code 96960, so we assumed the post office would be run efficiently like the ones back home. However, depending on who was behind the counter, I learned to ask to have a look around myself, since often enough I'd spot something for us the employee had overlooked. I'd made such a pest of myself while we waited for the generator that, when the box finally arrived, it had been stamped 67 times with the date of receipt.

***

Most cruisers worked while in Majuro. Terri and Rob on *Querida*, Lisa and Gary on *Almitra*, and Ron and Joe on *Panacea* all had jobs, so that curtailed the usual potlucks and other get-togethers. We did spend a little time with Jim and Rhea on their power boat, *Thesis*. They gave us a copy of *The Crest of the Wave*, a fascinating book by Willard Bascom, who relates his experiences as a young wave expert at the bomb testing in the 1940s. Our biggest social event was a mutual birthday party for Robb and Jacqueline, the woman on *Myste*. After a potluck supper, the teenage girls, Sarah and Anise, dressed up in South Seas costumes and danced to recorded music.

A Major Blow

In April, Alex called to say he'd decided to stay in the States and finish high school, two more years. We'd been warned that cruising kids in their mid-teens often no longer want to stay on the boat. He'd been restless for months, and a web of tensions involving him had grown among us. Even so, what seemed like Alex's defection came as a shock.

For nine years, since Annie was two and Alex six, we had lived together as a family. Robb, especially, was distraught. Neither Annie nor I had ever seen him cry before, and recently she told me she can still picture him leaning against our bed in the dark with his head in his hands. She remembers the boat being quiet that day.

The boys

Sailing would be harder for the three of us, especially for Robb, but we knew we'd just have to see how it went. By a strange coincidence, the same week a friend of mine from high school faxed, wondering if we needed crew. His twenty-three-year-old son sought "world adventure." Annie and I would have liked to give him a try, but it was still too early, too painful, for Robb to consider a "replacement," as he put it, for Alex.

⚓

Shortly after I quit work on May 24, Robb hurt his ribs again, maybe cracked one, and developed a severe sore throat. For the next three weeks, we watched a lot of videos as he recuperated, and we continued our provisioning and other preparations to leave. On June 16 we upped anchor for the first time in more than six months, and *Sorcery* headed for the pass with her crew of three.

Instead of sailing straight out into the ocean, we anchored overnight inside the lagoon at Picnic Island. That turned out to be a lucky decision, because we discovered our brand new GPS wasn't working. We'd always relied on SatNav for navigation, but with those particular satellites being phased out, we had to upgrade. Returning to Majuro in the morning, we mailed the defective GPS back to Downwind Marine in San Diego. Generous and trusting cruisers Lisa and Gary on *Almitra* loaned us their spare GPS. The plan was to leave it for them at the marina office in Lautoka, Fiji, where we'd up our repaired one.

FROM WHERE WE SAIL

CENTRAL PACIFIC TO SOUTH PACIFIC

Marshall Islands to Australia
Mid June to Late November 1995

THE first day at sea, a bad gale lasting several hours left us bruised and tired. Several misfortunes arose. We lost overboard the basket with laundry supplies, a water bucket, and the sun shower. The third reefing line got sucked up into the boom, the water temperature gauges stopped working, and the dinghy filled with water.

Kiribati

Tarawa Atoll

Once that storm blew over, fine weather accompanied us the two or three days it took to travel 400 miles to Tarawa, the capital of the island nation of Kiribati (Kir i bahs). Entering the picture-perfect South Pacific lagoon, we couldn't imagine the scene over half a century before, when that peaceful place was the site of one of the most gruesome battles of WWII. Within the span of 76 hours, between November 20 and November 23, 1943, nearly 6,400 Japanese, Koreans (workers, not soldiers), and Americans died, most of them on and around the small islet of Betio where we anchored.

Old photographs show the horror of the beach strewn with bodies. Our friends on Sendaya happened to be there in 1993, on the 50th anniversary of The Battle of Tarawa. They told us about speaking with American veterans who'd come for a reunion. Several vets walked the beach, talking, gesturing, and stopping. One man seemed to be alone, so Ann and Bill joined him, cautiously observing, "You don't seem to know the other men."

"All of my friends were killed," he said.

The Tarawa officials accepted the out-of-date visas we'd gotten in Fiji the year before, and allowed us to stay a few days. Through Annie's knack for finding a girl her age, we met a friendly Australian family. The mother, Kate, drove us around getting charts and other supplies, including replacements for the essentials we'd lost overboard. She organized an enjoyable tea party for me with two of her friends, figuring, rightly, I'd appreciate some "ladies' time" away from the boat. The daughter Michelle invited Annie to spend a night, and then another.

We took the bus to the end of the line, sometimes seeing at the same time the dark blue ocean on one side of the road, the azure lagoon on the other. At a tourist shop we bought big, handmade, traditional wooden fishhooks and short, shark-tooth sabers.

Since no other boats were in the anchorage and the lagoon was huge, we tested one of our spare emergency dye packets. Powder from the little film-canister-sized container formed an orange puddle of maybe 100 yards in diameter. These days I'd think twice about unnecessary pollution. But that was then, and seeing the powder in rescue mode comforted me.

We wanted to see Abemama, a less-visited atoll farther south. Other cruisers had been denied permits to stop there, but our standard M.O. was "No harm in asking." When the official quizzed me repeatedly about why we wanted to go, I fished around for reasons until I happened upon the one that satisfied him: "an educational experience for our daughter."

Abemama Atoll

A long, tiring overnight sail brought us to the atoll and a tiny island village. As we pulled our dinghy ashore, the teacher and all the children from a grade school came running to welcome us. We'd been told by officials in Tarawa not to give the people on Abemama anything, except maybe books, so we gave the teacher our standby, a few *National Geographics*. Later, in the teachers' lounge, we saw stacks of the magazine.

Robb and local children

Along our walk to the ocean side, people invited us up to their platforms to have drinking coconuts. By the time we got back to the lagoon, the tide had gone out, leaving the dinghy stranded. A few yards from the sandy beach, the ground became rocky, so our new 100-pound, 13-foot inflatable with its 100-pound motor had to be lifted and lugged approximately 200 feet to the water. After we'd gotten back on *Sorcery*, a man brought us seven coconuts. We didn't have any other books to give away, so he got a *Geographic* too.

The Calling of the Porpoise

Kiribati and its neighboring island nation of Tuvalu had been British protectorates and then colonies, known as the Gilbert and Ellice Islands respectively, from 1892 until 1976 when they became independent. Before we left Majuro, Susan had sent a book written by a young British colonial administrator, who'd worked and lived in the Gilberts for years in the early 1900s. In *A Pattern of Islands* Arthur Grimble relates his remarkable adventures and includes stories he collected from the previous generation, who could remember "the full glory of the old pagan ways."

Grimble himself witnessed a magical event, The Calling of the Porpoise. His extraordinary, yet credible, account is far too detailed and lengthy to relate, and summarizing doesn't begin to do the story justice, but the essence of the tale is this: The islanders valued human fatness and found Grimble to be "lean and bony like a commoner." A diet of porpoise flesh would cure the condition, and the porpoise could be supplied by a "dreamer" on the Gilbertese atoll of Butaritari.

Unconvinced until the last minute, Grimble marveled as a great herd of "friends from the west," invited by the dreamer, swam slowly right up into the shallow water. The village men waded out, picked up the animals, and carried them ashore. Later in the day the men butchered, salted, and served the porpoises at a feast, though the Englishman couldn't bring himself to eat any. The book as a whole is so plausible that I choose to believe Grimble saw this phenomenon, and also that the magic had an underpinning of science.

Many believed a dreamer still called the porpoises on Butaritari, so one of my few regrets is we didn't try to go and see for ourselves. If we hadn't found anyone who claimed to be a dreamer, I would still have loved to stand on the beach imagining a flotilla of porpoises moving as if in a trance into the lagoon. The reason we didn't go there was simply that I'd thought of the adventure too late. Obtaining a permit at that point would have required returning 400 miles to Tarawa, something even I was unwilling to do.

⚓

With the good weather holding, Robb was eager to press on. The day we left Abemama turned out to be a glorious traveling day, 10 to 15 knots of wind, clear blue sky, headed straight for Funafuti. Susan didn't come up on the radio, but we spoke with *Almitra* and *Panacea*. The winds became lighter, yet we still made progress. One afternoon about half a mile from the boat, a pod of sperm whales put on a spectacular breaching show, leaping clear of the water, then crashing down again.

"Can't we go a little closer to get some photos?" I asked.

"Are you kidding? Apart from the risk of being close to animals of that size, do you see the calf? Do you know how dangerous that could be if we accidentally got between a mother and her baby?"

At about the same time a rainsquall passed over, and we turned our attention to catching fresh water in the scuppers for the water tanks. A bell jingled letting us know we'd caught a fish, a nice skipjack, on the "meat hook" trailing behind the boat. The frequent light winds required us to motor more often than we liked. We only carried 100 gallons of fuel; also, we preferred the peace of sailing to the noise of the engine.

Life was going smoothly. Annie read, listened to tapes, and brought up the idea of her living with another family while we continued cruising. Robb and I humored her by discussing various relatives and friends, but the three of us couldn't come up with anyone suitable, and, much to my relief, the subject drifted away for the time being.

***

On one of the windless days when we were ghosting along at a knot or two under sail, Annie and I decided to take a dip in the two-mile-deep ocean. The idea didn't thrill Robb, but he agreed to be on shark watch.

"What if a gust of wind hits and the boat takes off?" Annie asked.

"I can get back to you," her father assured her.

Sorcery didn't have a swim step, so we attached our boarding ladder to the toe rail on the side of the deck and lowered the solid teak steps over the side. Robb also tied a thick, knotted line to the boat, dropped it next to the ladder, and instructed us to hold onto the rope at all times.

Annie and I eased down the ladder, taking hold of the rope as we slid up to our necks into the soothingly cool, purple-blue ocean. We treaded water and scanned the horizon from the new vantage point. Not more than a minute later, Robb yelled, "Shark!"

"Oh, please," huffed Annie, accustomed to her father's teasing. I already had my hand on the ladder.

"Shark! Two o'clock!" Robb screamed as he pointed in that direction, assuming the bow of the boat to be 12 o'clock.

About 50 yards away, Annie and I could see a fin headed our way, and we both cleared the water in seconds. Once on deck, we all searched for the fin, but saw nothing, not even a ripple. The novelty of being in the ocean with no land in sight enchanted Annie.

"How many people can say they've swum in the middle of the ocean?"

After 15 minutes or so, Robb and I agreed to let her go back in for another few minutes, while I added a second pair of eyes to shark watch. Neither Robb nor I remember it, but Annie swears another fin appeared again in seconds, thus ending the escapade.

⚓

Three days before arriving in Funafuti in Tuvalu, *Sorcery* was running peacefully, if slowly, downwind. That is to say, the wind came from behind, and the sails had been let out perpendicular to the boat. Suddenly the whole boat shook violently, and a thunderous and terrifying crash summoned us up on deck.

The wind had gotten in front of the mainsail causing the boat to accidentally jibe, or change direction. The 22-foot-long aluminum boom with the enormous mainsail had swung rapidly from starboard to port. In the Cheated Death Again column, I added a mental checkmark. One of us would almost certainly have been killed if we'd happened to be in the way of that swinging boom.

Attempting to convince the boat to go faster than three knots, Robb experimented continuously with various combinations of sails and motoring.

"We'll never get there," he moaned.

Revisiting Funafuti ~ a week in July 1995

But arrive we did. I'd been on the last watch of the night, so Robb and Annie let me sleep while they motored into the familiar lagoon. After a cup-of-noodles lunch, and checking in at the port office, Robb and I set off for a cool drink at the Vaiaku Lagi Hotel, while Annie made a beeline for her friends, Alifo and Abner.

That evening we rented the video *Gigi* and bought bread to go with our light supper of pâté, fruit, cheese and wine. The next morning while we were having coffee under the canopy in the cockpit, raindrops treated us to a symphony. First we heard the soothing pitter-patter of zillions of drops of rain in the tall palms in the distance, then the pounding of that watery army as it rushed toward us across the water, and within a minute, the wet crescendo all around us.

That week, Annie, Alifo and Abner were inseparable. When the kids stayed on our boat, they clowned around in the water, played cards and board games, and watched movies. Sometimes we took the three of them to lunch. One day, Annie and Abner paddled up in an outrigger his uncle had made for him. Her bond with the island puppy, though, had not survived the many months of separation. Recently she reminisced. "Buddy had all but forgotten me, and his puppy cuteness had worn away, so my eleven-year-old self didn't put much energy into reestablishing the bond. He was happy and healthy though, so that made me happy."

***

A classmate of Annie's from the year before told her his father went fishing one day and never returned. The family had asked the witch doctor to call the father's ghost and find out what happened. The ghost came and wrote in the sand with a stick, "A big fish hit the boat and the other man drowned." Then the ghost said he was tired and went to sleep. When he woke up he said he'd been eaten by a big fish. At the time, the story made me wish anew we'd gone to Butaritari to look for a dreamer. My fixation on finding a dreamer blocked any presence of mind to search for the witch doctor right there in Funafuti – another missed opportunity I now regret.

In spite of the humid heat, time passed pleasantly, and we accomplished a surprising number of projects: taking slightly outdated and excess medicine to the hospital, calling home, visiting the library and the postage stamp store, provisioning, snorkeling, going out for lunch every day, watching videos every night. Robb had his hands full with servicing and repairing equipment: the tiller pilot, its remote control, the autopilot, and securing the mainsheet turning block which had loosened during that accidental jibe. He put a paddle on the wind vane, which replaced the electric tiller pilot as the interface with the steering wheel.

***

On the day of my birthday and our anniversary, Robb made a sweet card, and we breakfasted on champagne and a cake I'd baked and frosted. I mention the frosting because making it was an anomaly. If anything, I usually created a European-looking, lacey design by sifting powdered sugar over a large paper doily placed lightly on the cake.

That evening we all gussied up for dinner at the hotel. Annie looked lovely and grown up in a white skirt and my black T-shirt with its sparkly New York City skyline. At fifty-three, I was feeling old, overweight by 15 pounds, and frumpy in my full, flowered skirt with an elastic waistband. The hotel staff baked a dear little heart-shaped chocolate cake with white icing and a border of blue flowers. Annie contributed to the day's celebration by sprinkling our bed with paper-heart cutouts.

On our last day there, Tammy, the young lady who sold *laulu* at the kiosk, gave me a shell necklace and earrings. Alifo's family gave Annie a necklace and earrings, a large handmade mat with an intricate design, a necklace for me, and a feather fan for Robb.

⚓

The good sailing weather that had lured us away from Funafuti only lasted a day or two. When the wind died, we ghosted quietly along during the day, then motored noisily at night. The engine overheated when the fan belt broke, but Robb is famous for having a spare for his spares. Later the new belt slipped off – luckily, an easy fix for Robb.

Ninety percent of the time our trusty wind vane steered the boat. So, when the line connecting the wind vane to the steering wheel snapped, it was a big deal. Robb, also known for having backup plans, hooked up the autopilot to steer while he spliced the line together. When we didn't have chores or repairs, we read, and Annie and I dipped once again in the ocean. "Color of water so marvelous!" my journal recorded. "A deep, inky blue – like the ink you buy in jars."

Though Annie was capable of being sassy and rude, mostly she was a big help and added brightness by being eleven and wanting to play. Because she was getting so grown up, any childish behavior, like wanting me to hold her in my lap while I sang "Rock-a-bye Baby," seemed even more precious.

Her father told her nearly every day what a beautiful young lady she was growing into. To hasten that eventuality, she wanted braces for her teeth and to straighten her long, curly hair. She took another little piece of my heart when she talked again about living with another family while we continued cruising.

Revisiting Fiji
Mid July through August 1995

After three slow and quiet days, a strong, rattling wind came up in the middle of the fourth night, requiring all of us up on deck in warm clothes and harnesses until we had set the sails. By morning, within 50 miles of Fiji, the wind was still blowing 20 knots – uncomfortably fast for *Sorcery* to pick her way through the reef that lay scattered between us and the town of Lautoka.

Tiny, uninhabited Navadra Island called to us to stay for the night. We worried a little about being caught before checking into the country. But we needed the rest, and opted to enjoy what might have been pre-jail time by snorkeling, baking cookies, napping, watching *Star Wars*, and getting to bed early. Unfortunately, Robb woke up with a dreadful headache, took antihistamine and aspirin, and went back to sleep. Anxiety always surfaced whenever the captain was out of sorts.

Later in the still blustery morning, we motorsailed, zigzagging through the reefs, into Lautoka. Normally, we would have anchored in the harbor, but the health official wasn't willing to come in a dinghy in such rough weather to inspect our boat. We were obliged to take *Sorcery* into the dock, a nerve wracking maneuver with a 61-foot boat, even when it's calm.

At the marina office we were happy to find our repaired GPS and a new EPIRB, both sent by Downwind Marine. A big box from Susan, plastered with $48 worth of postage, waited for us at the post office. Using the excuse we might be selling the contents, Customs demanded $40 to release the box. In the end we had to pay, but we told each other the videos alone, *Searching for Bobby Fischer* and *Nightshift*, were worth the ransom.

I mailed an authentic sari outfit – including a stick-on red dot for her forehead and pretend gold bangles – to Susan's daughter, Elizabeth, who wore the ensemble on Halloween. Before we knew it, we'd spent over $500 on customs' fees, provisions, eating out, doctors and prescriptions, gifts, boat gear, and having the wind vane welded. Journal report: "Lots of paperwork. Boat a mess."

***

While having dinner at the Lautoka Hotel, we met cruisers Don and Janet Hess. The next day Don invited the three of us on an industrial tour of the town, our only sightseeing that time around in Fiji. He wasn't able to get us into the sugar refinery or the distillery, but Gopal's rambling, outdoor factory of Indian products made up for it. Smoke from wood fires and other exotic scents floated through the air as we wound our way past the endless piles of goods being made and packaged: swarms of noodles cooking in giant woks; stacks of incense sticks being perfumed and dyed blue; heaps of raisins and spices stuffing themselves into tiny packets; yard after yard of fabric dyeing and drying in the sun; clear bottles announcing by color and label the tempting cordials within – green Cardamom, yellow Banana, pink Rose, clear Coconut.

That evening Don and Janet came over for a snack of smoked chicken, salami, cheese, veggies and dip, and to watch our favorite documentary, *Around Cape Horn*. Don and Janet were soon on their way to Majuro, so we arranged with *Almitra* to have Don and Janet take to them the GPS they'd loaned us.

Many a day we participated in the endless rounds of drinks, potlucks, and book and video exchanges with folks we knew on *L'Escargot, Ocean Angel, Kama Lua, Ariadne, Thesis,* and *Jacaranda*. Annie was welcome and often joined those gatherings because unlike a year ago when a tribe of nine or ten little Indians inhabited the harbor, now there were none. But she had made friends with a young woman, Anna, who worked at the marina. Also, three charming young female student doctors from England adopted Annie as a sort of mascot.

***

Eventually, we heard reports of kids on boats in nearby Musket Cove. On the morning we headed over, Annie and I were motoring the easy 20 miles while Robb rested. Feeling quite pleased with ourselves, we beamed when he came up the companionway, facing us in the stern. He turned to look forward and screamed, "Jeez-us! Don't you see the submerged reef? Hard-a-port! Hard-a-port!" He grabbed the wheel and steered until we were well past the danger. Since we'd been moving so slowly, the situation wasn't life threatening, but you never know. To me, there seemed to be no shortage of opportunities to cheat death.

Friends on *Thesis* and *L'Equipe* greeted us at Musket Cove, and we met new people, Trisha and Ed on *Galaxie*, and the Australian boat, *Naiad*, with Sue, Craig and thirteen-year-old Laura. Craig and Robb hit it off and went sailing. Ironically, after my recent fright at the wheel, the men snagged *Naiad* on a reef and radioed me to help by bringing the dinghy. Before I'd fired up the outboard, they'd gotten off by themselves, so I went back to fixing lunch for everyone. After eating, we all decamped to the hut on shore for drinks and showers.

Laura and two other girls, Cassie and Sarah, came back with us and stayed the night. With only minimal warning from me and with Annie's encouragement, one of the girls cut Annie's hair. As I recall her hair was held in a ponytail and the tail cut off. When she reached for her hair in the middle of the night, she panicked, but reminded herself it would grow back. Tough lesson.

Over the next few days, all the girls left Musket Cove, a loss more depressing for Annie than a bad haircut. After a slow motorsail back to Lautoka, the wind whipped up to 20 knots just as we entered the harbor. Robb got the wind generator up and running in time for more wind – not the predicted 50 knots – but enough to allow the generator to earn its keep by charging the batteries. When it was windy we tended to stay on the boat and watch movies. Robb and I liked Ken Burns' *Civil War* series, a subject lost on Annie until years down the road.

Then a happy day. A boat from Tasmania, *Kavenga*, came in with not one but three girls Annie's age. The first night Anna, Claire, and Tani were to stay on our boat, we'd invited the whole family for a 5 o'clock dinner. By 5:30 no one had come, and we couldn't raise them on the radio, so Robb and Annie took off in the dinghy to investigate. An hour later, Robb and Annie seemed to have disappeared. Imagining the worst, I called Port Control, who contacted the police and the hospital.

Tom on *Skywave* finally radioed me to say everyone was at the marina, the girls taking showers, the guys having a beer at Spence's. *Hmm.* I was annoyed, but a glass of wine helped me appreciate the evening when everyone did show up for the meal, which hadn't suffered by being postponed.

A few days later, *Kavenga* had us over for dinner. Afterward, at home, Robb reprimanded Annie about her table manners, then launched into other complaints. He felt Annie and I were against him, and that I, particularly, didn't help enough with the boat. The last was probably true, but I didn't say so. A distance had developed between Robb and me. He noted, quite rightly, we miscommunicated often, and he asked, "Do we ever agree on anything?"

My very thought. Here's an example: He wanted to go to Saweni Bay to save the $2.50 per day marina charge. For me, Saweni would be far too isolating, especially for Annie. In any case, the expense was nominal and included the luxury of taking showers at the marina. For a few days we were all on our best behavior and plowed through lots of chores. In spite of all the boat work, Robb did take some time for himself by going twice on tank dives with a dive boat.

***

Annie developed a bad cold. After several days, though her fever was down, she complained of a pain in her chest when she coughed, a symptom way out of my comfort zone. First response, *Thank heaven we're not at sea.* Second, look up chest pain in *Where There Is No Doctor.* Seemed she could have had a touch of bronchitis, the home treatment for which was rest and treating the cough. Third, plan to take her to a doctor the next day if she was worse or in two days if she didn't improve.

A few days later, her symptoms all but gone, she stayed overnight with the *Kavenga* girls. When the girls and the boys Casey and Brandon from *Skywave* were on our boat, Robb rigged up the spinnaker pole so the kids could swing out and splash down into the water. That activity lasted until something broke on the pole, and Robb had to take lots of time repairing it. The girls spent a night on the wreck Annie had stayed on the year before. The boys participated by terrorizing the girls with firecrackers thrown near the wreck.

Sleepover venue for Annie and friends

About the time all the kids on *Kavenga* and *Skywave* left, Chris and Robin, boys Annie had known from the year before, arrived on *Our Way*. She went to the movies with them and then spent all afternoon on their boat. Annie didn't want us to invite the parents over because she said she thought her dad would be rude to them. That remark led to a serious family conference. Later I learned the parents hadn't been on the boat that afternoon, something against our rules, which may have explained her not wanting us to meet them.

After *Our Way* left Lautoka, Annie asked me some questions about sex. I was pleased she still felt free to come to me and answered as best I could, then ventured nonchalantly, "So, what happened with the boys on the boat?"

"Mom, get a life!" I knew from experience with my own mother that pressing my daughter would not necessarily yield the truth. Whether they'd been messing around or just talking, the innocence that only a short time ago had wanted me to sing "Rock-a-bye Baby," was dissolving before my eyes.

***

Shortly before we left Lautoka, Lisa and Al on *Sannyasi* had faxed from Vanuatu. "We will speed up, slow down, turn around, whatever, so we can see you!" We'd have loved to see them too, but weren't willing to face malaria. "Take quinine!" our friends urged us in a radio call. But we knew the country had other diseases too, like dengue fever, and really big spiders. So, we vowed to meet in Australia where we'd all be spending the hurricane season. Months later, they learned a cruiser they knew died in Vanuatu of encephalitis.

The end of August found us waiting for the weather to calm down and chomping at the bit to leave Fiji. *Kavenga* had returned due to autopilot problems. That gave Annie a little more time with the girls, before returning to the misery of having to leave her friends, again. Letters took weeks, even months to be exchanged. "Imagine cruising if social media had been available," Annie said recently.

Robb became quite ill and started antibiotics for what he knew from experience to be strep throat. I applaud those readers who observe that Robb tended to get sick before a passage. The pressure and stress on him were tremendous. As the day to leave approached, we tried not to cash more money into Fijian dollars than we could spend. The plan backfired a little in that we ended up leaving with virtually no fresh bread, milk, meat, or produce. Oh, well, soon we'd be in a French territory, stuffing ourselves with all manner of fresh food.

New Caledonia ~ September and October 1995

Two 100-mile days and one slower one deposited us after dark at the southeastern pass through the reef surrounding New Caledonia. Rarely did we enter an anchorage, let alone a coral pass, at night. But light from a full moon and the wide entrance, one of the best marked in the world, invited us in.

The wind was occupied elsewhere, so we motorsailed in the quiet moonlight around submerged reefs near the southern tip of the 240-mile long, cigar-shaped island. Then, as if suddenly remembering us, a 25-knot gust rushed in, forcing all hands on deck to lower the main. By the time we arrived at the capital of Noumea, the day had begun.

"That was fun!" I told Robb. We both wondered what happened to the Cheated Death Again woman.

We tied up at the quarantine dock to wait for Customs to clear us, so we could all get off the boat. By late morning, no one had come. Since one person was allowed to leave the ship, I dashed off to the bank for French francs, to the post office, and, as a surprise for my crewmates, to McDonald's. I was ordering in French, or so I thought, until the tall boy in a paper hat behind the register interrupted me. "I speak English."

A hero's welcome greeted me when I showed up at the boat with burgers, shakes, fries, and American catsup. Susan had picked up lots of mail for us at Mail Call, the business in San Diego that served as our address. We dumped the pile of letters from home in the middle of the galley table, and sat around contentedly with food in one hand, and a letter in the other.

"Listen to this!" Every so often one of us blurted out the news: So-and-so has his boat for sale, is engaged, broke his arm, or isn't friends with Walt anymore.

***

A kiosk, part of a farmers' market near the dock, opened before daylight, offering coffee and fresh croissants to the fishermen. We could only manage instant Nescafé on the boat, so Robb and I appreciated a good cup of java. Most places we traveled to didn't know from coffee, but France took possession of New Caledonia in 1853, so the island had ample time to learn.

Annie didn't want to get up that early, so leaving her on the boat the next morning, we left in the dark and by 5 were sitting side by side with locals on stools at the open-air counter. Each of us cradled a warm bowl of café au lait in both hands and inhaled the aroma of croissants heating in the toaster oven. True, you can have a cup of coffee and a croissant in a nice hotel any day of the week, but being at that kiosk before sunup spelled cruising to me. Before we left New Caledonia, we bought four coffee bowls, our only souvenirs.

Noumea was big enough to require a bus ride to get an overview. None of us remembers anything except beach after beach studded with women of all ages, shapes, and sizes wearing only the bottoms to their swimsuits. The women looked at ease, and a few were not above flaunting.

I hadn't gone topless since one afternoon in my twenties with some hippie friends at a river in upstate New York. My journal said I shed my top in Noumea for an hour, but my memory differs. Wearing the last bikini of my life, I lay down on my stomach on a towel in the soft warm sand, unhooked the top, and rolled onto my back.

Annie, clearly abashed, whispered, "Mom!"

"If you're so embarrassed," I said, "sit over there."

But she didn't want to sit next to a topless stranger. Even though I rolled back onto my stomach after just a few minutes, Robb congratulated me on my "daring." My journal elaborated that I was the "oldest, fattest." I knew I exaggerated, yet the facts remained: We were living on pâté, baguettes, cheese, and wine, and had no bathroom scale.

***

September was coming to an end, and Robb wanted to stay longer in New Caledonia. I liked it well enough, but was anxious to get to Bundaberg, on the northeast coast of Australia, in early October to meet up with Lisa and Al. In our next radio call, they told us they weren't able to get a long haul out at Bundaberg, so they were heading farther south to Brisbane. We'd planned on staying in Bundaberg for the hurricane season from the time we met *Spirit of Kalahari* in Fiji. The family lived in Bundy and encouraged us to come, especially because our daughters had become pals. Since the urgency to get to Australia had passed, we agreed to stay in New Caledonia at least until after Annie's twelfth birthday on October 21.

The local youngsters Annie had met spoke only French, but soon a few cruising kids showed up. She and her friend Casey from *Skywave* went horseback riding and swimming in the yacht club pool. Joanna's parents from *Dreamchaser* invited Annie to spend a night with the family at the Meridian Hotel. She hung out with Saul and Dayl from *Rusuri*. The *Zardoz* family, Jacques, Susan and Tamerlan, joined us one evening for fondue. Another day, Susan took Annie and Tamerlan to babysit at the Australian consulate's home, where the girls stayed overnight. Candia and Dave and their small children, Justin and Lana, on *Moonshadow* were there. Single hander Victor from *Windfall* had tea with us, and we met June and Garland on *Swift*.

By the time Annie's birthday rolled around, we knew lots of people, so the day bustled with friends dropping by for tea and cake. She ended up with three cakes and lots of gifts, mostly from us and her grandma. Tamerlan spent the night.

⚓

Robb declared New Caledonia his favorite place so far: the variation in topography from mountains to calm lagoons within an hour's drive; easy cruising; things worked; plenty of shopping; socialized medicine; topless beaches; and we could work there. Above all, they loved Americans. After asking to be sure we were American, proprietors at the market would usually give us little extras, maybe a free bunch of parsley.

Huge black and white blowups of WWII naval operations covered the walls of the office where we rented a car. During the war, New Caledonia had been the second-largest naval base next to San Diego. The owner shared some of his wartime experiences, and shook our hands in gratitude, as if we, personally, had helped in the effort.

In the town square, a 10-foot-high American flag sculpture, recognizing the 50th anniversary of the arrival of Americans in 1942, rippled across the lawn. The year we were there, 1995, a shiny new brass plaque had just been installed in the same park commemorating the 50th anniversary of the end of WWII:

THE PEOPLE OF NEW CALEDONIA
WISH TO THANK THE PEOPLE OF AMERICA
FOR SAVING OUR COUNTRY

We took many a foray out of Noumea to one of the inviting little islands or bays nearby. Each time we anchored, we checked for echovescence, that term we'd coined in Mexico to rate echoes and bioluminescence. During the day we strolled the pristine beaches and hiked green hills on well-maintained trails. High above our heads, an occasional impressive web spanning the 10-foot-wide path suggested the presence of really big spiders. From the tops of the hills, we could see miles and miles out to sea.

In the evenings, with the wind blowing, we were cozy in the boat playing Hearts, and, always, watching something from our movie collection on our beloved 12-inch television.

The Chicken Shit Award

Usually, I let Robb and Annie do almost everything when launching the dinghy. One time I went out of my way to make myself useful, and heard Robb call out, "Mom gets the Chicken Shit Award!" Angry and wounded to the core, I retreated into a silent funk until well into the next day. Finally, I became willing to say what had made me so mad.

"Chicken Shit Award?" Robb hooted. "I said Good Citizenship Award!" Annie backed him up, so I had to let it go.

At Kuendo Bay as we tried to drop a second anchor, a line got cut. Each of us had a part in the mistake. After we anchored, Robb dove for the severed line and retied it. He took the mishap surprisingly well. Earlier he'd chastised me for something I'd done on the boat, but I spoke up, "I know there's more than one way of doing things, even on a boat. If I'd done it the other way, you'd have criticized that."

"You're probably right," he said. "I know that I look at everything you do as wrong because that's the way I was raised."

I counted that as an apology. He told Annie he was sorry for the times he'd been harsh with her and went on to say he was proud of her crewing. Back in Noumea, he bought me flowers.

Medical Emergency

At another little island, we'd been on shore and were wallowing calf-deep in water to launch the dinghy. Suddenly Robb screamed, and began hopping and flailing about in pain. His sandals had thick soles, but something had bit or stung the side of his foot. The wound bled profusely. We helped him into the dinghy, then up onto the boat.

We knew live cone snails inhabited the area because we'd collected a couple of the prized empty shells on the beach. We also knew that their sting was not only intensely painful, but potentially fatal. Heart pounding, I jumped on the radio and put out a call for a doctor. Annie took her dad a pan of water, as hot as he could stand, to immerse his foot. The heat would help relieve the pain and break down the protein of the venom. She gave him acetaminophen with codeine, the strongest painkiller we carried.

Right away a doctor, a fellow cruiser we'd met, responded to my call. She confirmed the situation could be life-threatening, and recommended we order a medical helicopter to evacuate him the 10 miles back to Noumea. She listed the symptoms to watch for: difficulty breathing or speaking, double vision, numbness or tingling of an entire limb, progression of numbness to area around mouth, then to paralysis of the entire body.

"I'm not taking a helicopter," Robb said, "I'm sure it was a stingray."

Honestly, the $10,000 price tag was a drawback, though certainly not if his life were at stake. None of the symptoms had started to appear, so we opted to start motoring and keep a close watch. A helicopter could be requested to pick him up from the boat at any time.

Friends Josie and Stewart on *L'Equipe* had heard our radio call, and let us know they'd have help waiting. During our two-hour trip back, they organized boaters we'd never met, Ron from *Sagittarius* and Tom on *Nerissa,* both of whom had cars. All three men met *Sorcery* and assisted Robb into Ron's dinghy to be rushed to the hospital. Stewart helped secure our anchor, then Tom took Annie and me to shore and drove us in.

The ER doctor cleaned and dressed the wound. This was another country with socialized medicine, so there was no way for us to pay. On the way home Robb said he felt sure something was embedded in his foot. Over the next couple of days, he dug at the site with a knife until eventually he pulled out a piece of what looked to be the tip of a stingray barb.

***

Within the week Robb itched to get out of town again to see a bit more of the country and, I think, to save money. Except for some groceries, and necessities like café au lait and croissants, prices were high. Mostly we only window-shopped, but I did buy Annie a cute little top and for myself a denim dress. My whole wardrobe needed sprucing up. I'd asked lots of pieces to hang on way too long. I loved the way Susan on *Zardoz* dressed, very French, kind of bohemian. Meeting her may have been when I decided I'd like to stay in New Caledonia to learn the language, and have her help me create a French look for myself.

We anchored at Ile Bailly for two nights. Exploring a shallow river on foot, I spied the only bit of trash I ever saw in the country, a champagne label. In a French place, even the litter is classy. The days had become cool and blowy, and we'd transitioned to long pants and socks. Inside projects like varnishing the galley table and engine cover, playing Scrabble, and watching movies became the norm. I studied French and did my exercises. According to my journal, "Being on an endless vacation can at times be a little bit boring."

As if Cruising weren't Primitive Enough

Toward the end of our time in New Caledonia, we rented a car and drove to the mountainous area east of Noumea. The rustic cabin we'd reserved through the forest service was free of charge and about as basic as they come: a bunkbed, a water faucet in the yard, an outdoor toilet, no electricity. A few day-trippers, who'd been in the area when we arrived, disappeared along with their chatter in the late afternoon, leaving only the sound of the gurgling stream next to the cabin.

Being in French country seemed to release us from our collective comfort zone – we all went skinny dipping. Easing into the bathtub-deep stream, Robb yelped, "Ouch! Ouch!" A pesky little inch-long fish was biting his nipple and making us all laugh. The persistent fish and the chilly water soon ended our caper.

By the time we'd built a fire in the pit outside the front door and eaten our dinner, darkness had settled in. Without electricity, we had no option but to climb into bed, Annie on the top bunk and us on the bottom. We all read by flashlight for a while, but didn't want to run down the batteries. Besides, getting into a comfortable reading position proved close to impossible. We spent about 10 hours on the hard, wooden beds with nothing but the clothes we were wearing and our sleeping bags for padding.

A soon as the sun offered enough light, Robb made a fire and boiled water for coffee. I'd remembered to bring instant coffee, but not mugs, so we liberated a small can of peanuts to use as our one cup. We all have good memories of the adventure, a definite change of pace. We felt like pioneers, as if cruising weren't primitive enough. Our home on *Sorcery* was luxurious in comparison.

***

Robb was sold on New Caledonia, at least as far as working through the hurricane season. He's an electrician, and other cruisers assured us his skills were much in demand. If we were there less than the 90 days allowed on our visas, we'd have to work under the table. However, we could apply to work legally by simply extending our visas.

The only school for Annie was taught in French, a prospect our twelve-year-old totally opposed. She lobbied hard to keep moving toward the States. "I want to go to the mall, to a prom, but mostly, to have friends for more than a few days or weeks." Years later, Annie regretted her obstinacy. "I wish you'd insisted I go to school there. I could have learned French! And don't blame me that we didn't stay. If you and Dad had really wanted to, it wouldn't have mattered what I said."

Robb maintains we left because of Annie. Although I adored New Caledonia, I sympathized with my daughter's feelings at the time, and sensed we were coming to the end of the number of years we could claim she'd thank us later for the experience. The issue of not staying, and why, is still a matter of family contention.

With New Caledonia still in sight, a spectacular 5-foot dorado got hooked on the fishing line dragging behind the boat. The electric greens and blues and yellows of the fish mesmerized Annie, and she begged to let it go. Truthfully, it was more fish than we could reasonably eat and keep without a freezer, so Robb agreed. He managed to unhook the mahi-mahi or dolphinfish, as it's also known, by hanging precariously over the back rail, but the fish thrashed, and the hook sank deep into a gill.

Believing the fish wouldn't have a chance, Robb hauled it into the cockpit, where we watched the colors and life fade away. He cut up the fish on deck, packing the meat into plastic containers, which Annie ferried down to me through the hatch over the galley. Discarded fish parts went back into the sea.

After that Annie quit eating fish for a number of years. The fading colors had made her too sad.

FROM WHERE WE SAIL

AUSTRALIA

Third Big Stop
Late November 1995 through August 1996

Bundaberg

L ESS than 1,000 miles from New Caledonia, we reached Queensland on the northeast coast. Our destination, the town of Bundaberg, lay 12 miles up the Burnett River. At the Midtown Marina, we had to tie up fore and aft between two buoys. The marina manager advised us to tie-on headed upstream. Facing downstream seemed safer to Robb, and for half an hour he tried to convince the bucking and pulling *Sorcery* to agree. Ultimately, he turned the boat around and tied on with the bow upstream.

Annie and I got ready for town, but Robb was stalling.

"Robb, come on!"

"I'm not coming."

"What? Why not?"

"I'm too embarrassed because of the problem tying up."

"Nobody cares."

Those fateful words so wounded Robb that our relationship plunged to a new low. We had the good sense to seek counseling, and found a local professional, a wonderful woman, whom we saw every week for months.

"How do you feel about the boat?" Alison had asked me in the beginning.

"I hate the fucking boat. I wish I liked boating and sailing as much as Robb does, but I just don't. I like the places we go, but not getting there."

She said something that set us both on a track to work hard at healing and figuring things out: "You have to want for him what he wants, and want for you what you want."

That first week, some of the boat kids invited Annie to McDonald's and to a movie. The next week she spent a day at school with Dannielle from *Spirit of Kalahari*. That event evolved into enrolling Annie as a ninth grader at Shalom Catholic, a co-ed high school. Technically at seventh grade level, Annie wanted desperately to be in the same class as her friend. The school was okay with that as long as Annie could keep up with the work, which she easily managed. Meanwhile in Chicago, Alex was making the highest test scores in his school.

At Thanksgiving a potluck was held in the park next to the marina. We all chipped in to buy a huge ham, which only *Sorcery*'s big oven could accommodate. The minimalist in me was surprised by the way I fancied up the main dish with a pleasing pattern of pineapple slices, cloves, and maraschino cherries. The worry-wart part of me clutched as the baked, decorated and unwieldy haunch made its way off the boat, into a dinghy, then on to dry land.

We had plenty of mostly traditional food, and several children darted around adding to the family atmosphere. Norm from *Witchcraft* spoke for all of us when he made a speech of gratitude for our blessings, including, in a roundabout way, cheating death.

Robb and I had talked about renting a car and driving to Melbourne on the southeast coast, but considering our ongoing discomfort with each other, he decided he'd rather stay put and paint the inside of the boat. In a generic Christmas letter, I wrote we were planning to put the boat up for sale, in part because of pressure from Annie, who wanted to go home. Then, in a handwritten note to my mom at the bottom, "Don't get too excited about us selling the boat. Annie says doing so would 'kill' her, that she just wants a break."

A change of scene for all of us came in the form of renting a little one bedroom flat with a garage within walking distance of the marina. To paint the inside of the boat, we had to get everything off and have a place to store it. By that time *Sorcery* had moved from the mooring to the dock, making it much easier to take everything, including the toilet, from the inside of the boat to the flat and garage.

The day we moved in, neighbors across the back fence, Alan, Colleen and eleven-year-old Scotty, foretold their never-ending thoughtfulness by lending us something that came in surprisingly handy, a red electric teakettle.

***

Our boat was across the dock from a commercial shrimper. Late one afternoon as they came in, Annie decided to help tie up and shouted for them to throw her a line. The two men on deck smirked and hesitated, doubtful this shrimp of a girl would be much help. They looked up at the captain on the bridge. He grinned and nodded his okay, so one of the crewmen threw her the line.

She caught it, and within a matter of seconds, whipped the line under both horns of the cleat on the dock, crossed the cleat on a diagonal, went under the other horn, and finished with a locking turn. Raising their eyebrows, the men nodded their approval, and no doubt felt a little sheepish about their earlier dismissal of the young sailor. The impressed captain came over with a gift of a bucket full of big Australian tiger prawns. "That's quite a sheila ya got there!"

When I asked Robb now about the incident, he said, "It's one of my very favorite memories of the entire trip. I was so proud."

***

Sannyasi was south of us in Brisbane and Al had flown home to Connecticut to look after their business, a Mexican restaurant. At Christmastime, Lisa bused 232 miles north to spend the holidays with us. Having her around was always a happy occasion. She gave Annie a little stained glass angel. The miniature guardian protected Annie for years, until she sold her first car. Then, in the excitement, she left the angel dangling from the rearview mirror.

The Christmas also stands out in my memory because of the scandalous cookie Dannielle's brother Kevin made. Those two and Scotty came over to make Christmas cookies. I'd prepared a heap of dough, given each elf their share, and let them loose with a rolling pin and cookie cutters.

Annie built a tower of graduating stars and other 3-D constructions, which I was certain wouldn't bake through, but who doesn't like cookie dough? Ten-year-old Kevin created a naked lady, complete with nipples and pubic hair. I always wondered if the cookie went home or if he ate it on the way, but I didn't have the nerve to ask his mom.

The Flood

On January 10 at 2:30 in the morning, Garland from *Swift* woke us up by banging on the front door of our flat.

"The river's flooding! We have to move the boats!"

He was so agitated, and what he said so fantastic, at first we thought he must be drunk. The weather was warm and calm. There hadn't been any rain. But within a minute or two, he'd convinced us about the flood.

"Want a cup of coffee while we get ready?"

"There's no time!" Garland said as he flew off.

Before we reached the roaring, galloping river, floodlights and the din of frenzied shouting told us an emergency was in progress. Boats still tied to buoys were in danger of dragging their heavy moorings and being unable to steer. The marina was preparing to sink the docks, so they wouldn't float up and over the pilings that kept them in place. First, all the boats tied to the docks, including *Sorcery*, had to move or be moved.

Annie was 150 miles south visiting a girl she'd met in New Caledonia, and we'd have to get in touch with her later. I insisted on dashing back the 12 blocks to the flat, making a mental list as I ran: VHF radio, passports, money, food, toilet paper, sleeping bags, a couple of books, anything useful I could grab in a couple of minutes and be able to carry to the boat. Loaded up, I stopped two streets away at Barry and Maureen's house to let them know.

Understandably skeptical, these friends from *Spirit of Kalahari* tried to call the marina, but the line was busy, suggesting something was up.

They offered a ride if I'd wait until they loaded the dinghy onto the top of the car. We hadn't gone a block before one of the lines holding the dinghy untied itself and became entangled in a wheel. I jumped out and schlepped the rest of the way as fast as I could, bags banging against my legs.

As I huffed and puffed down the dock, I could see *Sorcery* being cast off. Robb pointed my way and shouted, "Wait! Please! My wife's coming!"

"You can always get another wife!" a man yelled back, tossing him the dock lines.

Robb hollered for me to go with Garland on *Swift*, which was right beside me and also being cast off that very minute. Garland helped me aboard, and we were on our way. His wife was in the States, so I was able to be helpful, particularly with anchoring.

Swift's windlass, the mechanism for lowering and raising the anchor, was operated manually at the bow. *Sorcery* had an electric windlass with controls at the bow and in the cockpit, which enabled Robb to anchor by himself. Halfway down the river, that feature came in handy when the engine overheated. He anchored at the river's edge and cleared debris from the blocked cooling water intake.

Dodging small trees and other debris, both boats, always in radio contact, motored a few miles to a wide, placid turnout. After anchoring, Robb fetched me, and we turned our attention to contacting Annie, who was due to start home on the bus in 12 hours. We needed to tell her to stay put because buses were being stranded on the flooded roads. Air-Sea Rescue helped us get through on a land line to her and the family she was staying with.

On the second day we spotted a channel marker buoy that had broken loose from its mooring and was bobbing toward *Swift*. Robb and Garland buzzed out in a dinghy. Looking like a toy boat next to the enormous buoy, they nudged it on down the river then notified the Coast Guard. We spent four days sharing the small inlet and potluck meals with two other boats. We managed well, even with a bucket serving as our toilet.

When we finally got the "all clear" to return to Bundaberg, *Swift*'s anchor refused to come up. We dropped the dingy back in the water and

Robb used a chain loop to pull the anchor out from whatever it was caught on. Although Robb protested that we only did what friends do, Garland insisted on buying us dinner. "I'm going to the restaurant at six o'clock and ordering three meals whether you're there or not."

Back at the marina, Robb earned another dinner for diving with zero visibility into the murky water to retrieve *Querida's* anchor. The next day we picked up Annie, smiling as she stepped off the bus at the Greyhound Depot.

Why hadn't there been any warning about the encroaching calamity? A torrential rain had hit many miles upstream. Apparently, the station there had closed at 5 p.m., and the person or persons hadn't realized until hours later that the Burnett would flood downriver. At that point they faxed Midtown Marina, which, of course, was closed as well. Later in the evening someone happened to go to the office, see the fax, and spread the alarm. The flood we experienced rose to 9 feet. In 2013, a flood in Bundaberg peaked at over 27 feet, inundating virtually the entire town, probably including the flat where we had lived.

For many, many weeks, sometimes for as long as 12 hours a day, Robb worked on the boat. When he grew weary of painting, other projects waited for him: cleaning the bottom of the boat; re-splicing the rope-to-wire roller furling line; servicing, with Annie's help, the bearings on *Sorcery's* "coffee grinders," the two big three-speed winches; and replacing the steering cables with my help. He'd decided to replace the cables before heading across the Indian Ocean. In doing so, he discovered the ends of one of the cables was badly frayed and would have been a huge problem if it had come apart underway.

My jobs were to help with the boat work and be a gofer for Robb; bring lunch every day; shop, cook, clean, do laundry, other household chores and boat projects; keep track of Annie as best I could; and entertain my mom during her two-week visit.

Mom, hobbling off the plane on swollen feet, announced this would be her last overseas trip. Then in her mid-seventies, her health was beginning to fail. Throughout her stay she hardly moved out of her motel room on her own, except to have coffee or a bite to eat next door at the Hog's Breath Café. Annie had school and homework, but otherwise spent all of her time with her beloved grandma, even staying overnight a few times.

Bundaberg's downtown, within walking distance of the motel and the marina, had recently been upgraded, thanks to the inspired work of a female town council. The city fathers claimed there was no budget for a renovation, but the women performed the transformation on a shoestring. Many pleasing turn-of-the-century buildings were restored, diaper-changing stations installed in public restrooms, and loads of flowering plants put along the streets.

Mom, Annie and I took short excursions downtown to shop for souvenirs, visit art galleries, and try the local cuisine, like hamburgers with pickled beets. At a tiny zoo we saw a few indigenous birds and animals, and adorable kangaroo joeys peeking out of their mums' pockets.

***

The marina swarmed with boat kids and kids from town. They went to movies, the roller rink, the swimming pool, and hung out on each other's boats. Annie had girlfriends, Dannielle (Danni), Emma, Jessica, Rafi, and Mandy, and some young male friends: Little Nick, Tim, Big Nick, Joe, Aaron, Victor, and Jeremy. One day Joe, Little Nick, another Joe, Aaron and Mandy were on the boat to help dye Annie's hair red. A second piercing had appeared in each of her ears, then a third, for which she was grounded.

A secret admirer left Annie a bouquet of three long-stemmed red roses with baby's breath and a sweet note, "From someone who cares." We worried about what she was doing with the boys, and continued to feed her information on sex, in what we imagined to be a casual, matter-of-fact way. When I overheard Sharon from *White Tunny* tell Annie, "No guy is worth it," I began to understand that twelve was the old fifteen of my youth way back in the '50s.

Annie was reading a trilogy, *The Spy Wore Red*, the true story of an American female spy in Spain in WWII. When Annie told us, again, she was tired of cruising, I asked if she didn't want to see Spain, still a possibility on our route.

"I'm not old like you, Mom. I can see Spain anytime."

The comment was kind of a joke, but once she was really angry and called me a "big, fat slob." A few minutes later she hugged me and apologized, saying I was better than she was because I didn't call her names when I was upset.

⚓

Since Annie was in school and Robb working on the boat, we didn't do much sightseeing. To our great fortune, the largest turtle rookery in the South Pacific was just a few miles from Bundaberg. One evening we took a tour bus to view a hatching of loggerhead babies on Mon Repos Beach. It was dark by the time we arrived, but flashlights weren't allowed because the light would confuse the hatchlings. They needed to be lured by the moon and the natural light at the horizon out into the water. Digging carefully down into the sand where nests of eggs were buried, a ranger gently brought dozens of hatching eggs to the surface.

As soon as the turtles broke free of their shells, the little creatures, smaller than your palm, waddled several yards in a determined, if indirect, route through the sand toward the surf. The advancing and receding 2-inch foamy tide pushed the featherweights back a few times. Eventually, each hatchling figured how to get out into the ocean, where it would swim non-stop for three days to reach the East Australian Current, the turtle superhighway made famous years later in the movie *Finding Nemo*. Only one turtle in a thousand survives to adulthood.

Another excursion was with Colleen, Alan, and Scotty to a distillery right in town. In 1888, a band of local sugar millers turned surplus molasses into fine rum and started a thriving industry. The one thing I remember, from our tour of the Bundaberg Rum Distillery, is clutching the thin rope rail on a high catwalk circling a giant vat, and peering down into a swirling lake of dark, sinister, bubbling molasses. Unlike in the States, no signs advised us not to fall in. We wondered to each other how many people may have slipped, jumped or been pushed to a searing death over the last century.

⚓

"Call my insurance agent!" the skipper of a local boat yelled back over his shoulder after he'd smashed our wind vane as he was leaving the dock. What a disaster. The expensive mechanism did 90 percent of our steering. In the end we "engaged a solicitor" because neither the insurance company nor the owner would pay for a new part. The solicitor eventually got the owner to agree to pay the value of the part prior to damage: several hundred dollars. But the money never came through. He had a year to pay, and knew we wouldn't be allowed to stay in the country that long.

The replacement part we ordered from New Zealand was flown to Brisbane, and then made its way to Bundy on a bus. New Zealand accepted our credit card, but when we needed to order parts from Sydney, right there in Australia, our marina manager had to send the company a check, and we paid him in cash.

***

On the first Sunday in April, a clear, crisp Easter morning, church bells rang out with "Morning Has Broken." The unexpected pleasure of hearing a Cat Stevens' song soothed my soul. At the time, I didn't realize the song is a well-known Christian hymn, so I interpreted the playing of it by a church as being quite cosmopolitan.

***

Just in time for the rainy season and the evening sand flies in mid-April, we undertook the monumental job of moving everything back onto the boat. Barry and Maureen, Alan and Colleen, and a new local friend, Hughie, all had cars and helped us immeasurably. We became more social, having lots of visits, potlucks and book exchanges with our "movers" and with *L'Equipe, Swift, Free Spirit, Bageera, White Tunny, Intercept, Moonshadow*, and I'm sure others. In the evenings, especially when we had company, light from a kerosene lamp and a couple of candles created a cozy atmosphere.

Our Friends, the Pranksters

"You'll never guess what!" Lisa shouted amid excited hugs and hellos as she and Al from *Sannyasi* got out of their rental car. "We stopped at Bustard Bay on the way here, and found a message in a bottle on the beach!"

Al plucked a folded piece of paper from his shirt pocket and handed it to us with a big grin. "Hello!" the note started out. "This bottle was thrown from the sailboat Sorcery between New Caledonia and Australia.

We would love to hear from you! Please write to The Lane Family, #235, 2726 Shelter Island Drive, San Diego, CA, 92106-2731, USA."

But we were way ahead of the pranksters. The letter was obviously a photocopy, and we'd already read in the local newspaper that "Neil Megard had the surprise of his life when he found a bottle containing a message and a tiny American flag pin floating in Bustard Bay." Al and Lisa had found our message tacked on a bulletin board in a bar, and made a copy. Neil never did write to us, but then we received only two other responses from the dozens of bottles with messages we tossed in the ocean over the years.

***

One afternoon, a pleasant and lively Israeli family living in Bundaberg strolled the dock admiring the boats. After chatting for a while, they invited us for Passover, a first for our family. At the dinner, their twenty-one-year-old daughter asked if she could crew with us, and came down to the boat the next day to talk about our mutual expectations.

For her part, Ofri, who had lived for two years on a kibbutz in Israel, was looking for adventure. Since she had no sailing experience, Robb wasn't keen on taking her along. But I envisioned companionship for Annie, as well as help for the passage up and over the top of Australia and then across the Indian Ocean, a total of nearly 8,000 miles. We told Ofri she could join us, at least until we left Australia, to see how things went. If she was still with us, visas weren't needed in South Africa, or anywhere in between. We'd be leaving Bundaberg in mid-May, less than a month away.

***

One afternoon Annie and I became mesmerized by police activity on the dock across from us. We watched as a diver dislodged a man's body which was found clinging to the underside of the dock. His body, stiff with rigor mortis, was still clawing at the air when it was placed on a floating stretcher. No foul play was suspected; the man had simply been drunk, fallen in the water, and was unable to get out. Up until then, Annie had never seen a dead person. Recently she told me it was at once terrifying and fascinating. "We'd been sleeping so close to someone who needed our help, yet we had no idea. That made it sad and scary to me."

***

We started readying the boat for passage: Securing and marking charts; full-on provisioning of food, liquor, prescriptions, vitamins, toiletries, stationery and cleaning supplies, propane and gasoline; vacuum-packing food; and always, stowing. *Sorcery* was loaded to the gunwales for the voyage before our next long stop in South Africa. Robb was still wishing there was another solution besides making this long, challenging trip. We talked about selling the boat when we got there. On my paper calendar, Annie drew a frownie face with huge teardrops on May 10, the last day of school. But she cheered up at the Rollerblading & Pizza Going Away Party we gave for her.

Up and Over the Top ~ May through August 1996

We pulled out of Bundaberg with Ofri on board. Half an hour after we left the dock, the marina radioed saying my mom had had a heart attack and was in intensive care. If this was in a movie, you'd never believe it: We spied some buildings near the shore, anchored, I climbed a hill, and voilà, a phone booth. Using my AT&T calling card, I not only got through to the hospital, but talked to my mom, who was already out of intensive care and on the road to recovery.

Farther on down the river, we anchored near the home of Alison, our counselor and friend. She lived with her husband, Peter, and their sons, Andrew and Dale, in a sunny, sprawling old farmhouse on the outskirts of town, right on the river. High wind warnings out in the ocean kept us there four nights while we visited and took care of last minute details.

Dale, two years younger than Annie, enjoyed showing her the fun things around the property: chasing chickens; swinging on the big truck tire suspended from a tree branch; teasing the harmless but scary looking spider that lived in the outhouse we had to use; setting off fireworks after dark. Each day Alison had us over for coffee and pie or cake.

We worked on the boat, went for walks, played Pictionary and Backgammon, watched movies, fixed fondue, and I called Mom each day from Alison's. Mom was feeble, but stable, and left the hospital before we weighed anchor for the last time. Ofri's parents visited, bringing milk, grapes, chocolate, and an apple tart. Ofri was already proving herself useful. She had ideas for cooking and went ahead and did it. She helped Annie shave her legs and make a friendship bracelet. They took the dinghy to town a time or two.

The last evening Alison invited us all over, and asked me to bring my guitar to join in some after dinner music. I'd hardly picked up the guitar since Mexico and always knew I had more enthusiasm than talent, but I agreed with pleasure. Little did I know they were both semi-professionals, way out of my league. Alison sang haunting renditions of Joan Baez songs to the perfect accompaniment of her husband on his guitar.

By the time it was my turn, I'd had too much wine to realize I should simply have declined to participate. My fingers couldn't negotiate the few chords I knew, and some of the words to the two familiar songs escaped me. Alison and Peter couldn't have been more gracious, but I thoroughly embarrassed myself.

The next morning, we said our final goodbyes and continued down the river. Reporter Sandra Goodwin had been finishing up an article about *Sorcery*, and let the *News-Mail* photographer know when we were motoring out the mouth of the river so he could get an "action" shot. Later our friend Hughie mailed us a copy of the article that was all about the boat and her exciting past as a famous racer. One little paragraph at the end mentioned us and our trip.

Inside the Great Barrier Reef

From Bundaberg we'd be heading north to the tip of Cape York, a total of 1,400 miles inside the Great Barrier Reef, one of the Seven Natural Wonders of the World. The most wonderful parts are underwater. But for us traveling on the surface, we found safe harbor at 15 or so of the 900 tropical islands along the crooked spine of the reef.

***

The minute *Sorcery* nosed out into the open ocean, our new crew member lost her color and felt like throwing up, an unanticipated and unpleasant development for all of us. We insisted Ofri stay on deck, standard procedure for seasickness. That meant we had to climb over and around her in the cockpit as she tried to get comfortable, draping herself in various positions, sometimes lying full length on the cushions.

The wind soon died, requiring us to motor overnight to our first landfall, Hummocky Island. The next day we all took it easy. As I fixed dinner, Ofri became distraught when she saw me pop a slice of raw potato into my mouth.

"Stop! Don't eat that! Raw potatoes are poisonous!"

Though I assured her I'd been eating them for decades and had never once been the least bit sick, she still carried on as if I didn't know what I was talking about.

That evening we joined Australians Frank and Jane from *White Heron* for a restorative gathering around a crackling bonfire on the beach. The following day we sailed to Keppel Island. After suffering from a miserable swell all night in the first anchorage, we moved to nearby Svendsen's Beach for two days. At the resort there, we ran into friends on *White Heron, Kindred Spirit* and *Fair Wind II*. We lunched on a patio where a flock of lorikeets – bright quilts of birds with bold patches of red, blue, green, and yellow – joined us, noisily helping themselves to Robb's French fries.

***

A sloppy, uncomfortable overnight sail to Port Clinton on the mainland again brought seasickness to Ofri, and caused all of us to lose sleep. An accidental jibe swung the heavy boom terrifyingly close to Robb's head. In the morning after anchoring, we sat down to a comfort-food breakfast of Impossible Cheese Pie, something like a quiche.

Chopping up the seas, the wind blew fairly steadily at 20 knots, so we stayed four days at Port Clinton. I watched for saltwater crocodiles while Robb scraped barnacles off the bottom of the boat and the girls scrubbed the waterline. Otherwise, we focused on indoor projects.

Annie and Ofri wanted to make placemat-size courtesy flags for the countries we would visit, so I hauled out the sewing machine and our flag making kit. South Africa and Mauritius had flags with simple geometric patterns, so that's where the girls started, and, as it turned out, ended. They did the laundry. I made yogurt and pancake syrup. As I kneaded bread from a recipe I'd successfully used dozens of times, Ofri opined that I was working the dough far, far too much. "That's not the way they do it on the kibbutz."

Robb had recently painted the entire inside of the boat, but the baseboard area on the walls around the edges of the teak floorboards still needed painting, so we all pitched in. Robb placed a line of blue paint tape to show us where to stop, and warned us not to remove the tape until the paint dried thoroughly. Immediately upon finishing, Ofri pulled the tape off the walls, making a mess of the wet paint.

"Didn't you hear what I said about leaving the tape on?" Robb asked.

"Yes, but I didn't think it would make any difference."

Some aspects of her personality were starting to wear on us. Of course, we enjoyed her peanut butter cookies and the cucumber tzatziki she made from my yogurt. She repaired a rug, re-stitched the Velcro on the back awning, and hemmed some cabin cushions by hand.

After a couple of days on the boat, on a still windy but calmer day, we all piled into the dinghy, and, as we scrambled ashore, an entire army of small, blue-bodied crabs scattered in every direction, leaving the entire beach to us.

⁂

The last day of May we sailed overnight to Thomas Island, then on to the green hills of Nara Inlet at Hook Island. In the early morning we'd set out on foot to see aboriginal cave paintings, but it started to rain so we turned back. We passed a come-hither grassy area next to a pond, and resolved to have a picnic there if and when the sun came out.

For lunch, I attempted to make falafel from a packet of dry ingredients. The balls wouldn't hold together in the hot cooking oil, so I strained the crumbles and spread them on paper towels. The sun appeared, so at the picnic I rolled leftover tortillas into cones, and filled them with the crunchy, spicy falafel along with some yogurt. Everyone loved them, including Ofri, who asked me, "How did you think of this?"

"Oh, I don't know," I said while thinking, *Necessity mothered another invention.*

We hadn't brought swimsuits, but after lunch Ofri stripped down to her panties and tank top, waded into the pond up to her neck, and then, probably thinking nothing of it, dripped back up onto the grass. Being in underwear might not be much different from being in a swimsuit, but somehow revealing her wet underthings in front of Robb was too intimate for me.

Neither Robb nor Annie remembers the incident, so the story probably tells more about me than it does about Ofri. Anyway, back at the boat Robb attended to the ailing bilge pump. In the evening all of us played dominoes, then put a puzzle together.

On the first day of June, a 25-knot wind made a quick trip of our hop to anchor near the town of Airlie Beach on the mainland. For three days we ate out, grocery shopped, filled the water and fuel tanks, and made phone calls. At the Whitsunday Sailing Club we played pool, splurged on ice cream, and had coffee and drinks with friends from *L'Equipe* and other boats.

Ofri met some Israeli girls, one of whom she knew. One day she came back to the boat, announced she had a ticket for the 8:30 evening bus back to Bundaberg, and packed her things.

She didn't explain the decision, nor did we ask, but we weren't surprised. If nothing else, her seasickness concerned us all, and was one of the reasons we hadn't introduced her to being on night watch, a major activity for which Robb and I could have used a third person. After we saw her off on the bus, Annie told us, "I'm glad Ofri left."

When I asked about that recently, Annie said, "You mean that woman who crewed with us? She just wasn't a good fit. I preferred our little family unit."

Recall Scare

In Bundaberg, we'd bought two cases of peanut butter, one crunchy and one smooth, to sustain us on our trip across the Indian Ocean. Halfway up the Great Barrier Reef we heard on the radio that the very brand we'd bought had been recalled due to a salmonella scare. Thankfully, one of our cookbooks stated salmonella bacteria perish when heated to 140 °F for 12 minutes, so baked goods were safe. That was okay, but we always used lots of that mainstay in cold sauces and just plain. Before I figured out we could "cook" the peanut butter in its own jars, without the lids, in a pot of boiling water, we'd had way too many peanut butter candies, cookies, and coffee cakes.

Before reaching the major city of Cairns (Kanz), we stopped at Gray's Beach, and the islands of Upstart, Magnetic, Orpheus, and Mourinyan. Looking back at the charts, it's hard to believe we could find the islands, let alone the anchorages, especially in rain and mist. I remember light rain eating away at one paper chart as I stood in the cockpit trying to figure out where we could land.

But find we did, and along the way caught a Pacific sierra and a 40-inch wahoo, and met up with friends on *Intercept, Kindred Spirit, Fair Wind II,* and *Witchcraft*. After sharing ceviche, made with one of Robb's fish, with *Kindred Spirit* and *Intercept*, I noted in my journal that the evening was fun, and "I'll miss cruising." Shirlee from *Intercept* and I had talked idly about men being from Mars, the frustrations of boat life, and often feeling like incompetent second mates.

Family games, movies, simple meals like potato soup and, once, a chocolate fondue that didn't exactly work, filled those evenings when we weren't underway or with friends. Robb and I had a long, calm talk and were getting along okay. Annie and her dad fought a lot, but overall she was in good spirits. For the most part, she did what we asked without complaint, and seemed to enjoy her math and science homework. Three brutal migraines knocked me down along the 900 miles between Bundaberg and Cairns. Prescription Cafergot pills saved me, and debilitation from the headaches had one good side effect: We always got to stay an extra day wherever we were.

Cairns to Portland Roads

Getting up to a speed of 11 knots at one point, *Sorcery* flew the 60 miles from Mourinyan Island to Cairns. Several of the boats in the anchorage were familiar. Running into people we knew was a decided pleasure of cruising life.

Don and Nancy from *Bag End,* whom we'd met in Mexico, had been there awhile and willingly showed us around. They warned us that Darwin, the last big town before leaving Australia, would be very expensive. So during our three days in Cairns, we shopped a lot, especially for food. Woolworths Supermarket, "Woolies" to the Aussies, who had a nickname for practically everything, delivered our orders to the dinghy. That first night, the *Sorcery* crew dug into a sumptuous, store-bought spread of rotisserie chicken with stuffing, minty tabbouleh, cheese bread, and ice cream.

Nancy steered us to second-hand bookstores and Café Cyclone, a lively coffeehouse. Annie and I shopped for clothes, and always needing to find gifts ahead of time, I bought things for Robb for our July anniversary and for Annie's birthday, still months away. I showed Nancy how to make yogurt, and she and Don joined us late one afternoon for chicken minestrone and garlic bread.

Two of the three nights, Annie stayed with the family from *Siomi*, Alan, Martha, and their two girls Annie's age, Lisa and Amy. After a two-day sleepover, she was too tired to shop, so on our last day in Cairns, Nancy went with Robb and me into town for a few chores, lunch at Café Cyclone, and a final visit to the bookstores.

The morning we left at 4 a.m., my dear husband let me sleep in because I'd had a miserable night with another bad headache. We stayed at the Low Isles for one night, Walker Bay for another. At one point we found ourselves uncomfortably close to shore.

"All hands on deck!" Robb yelled.

Now he says we probably weren't that close, but the potential made our hearts race, and I felt we may have, you know, cheated death. Journal observation: "I need to relieve Robb more so he doesn't get so tired."

At Lizard Island, although the anchorage was fairly calm, the wind was blowing pretty good "outside," 15 to 20 knots with higher gusts. None of us felt well, so we ended up staying five days. Finally, we saw some of what the famous Barrier Reef was all about. We might have missed the experience if Dennis from *Interlude* hadn't pointed out an area right in the anchorage where giant clams could easily be seen by snorkeling.

The clams, measuring 2 to 3 feet across, rest with their openings skyward. From those gaping mouths, protrude thick, wavy velvet lips with intricate patterns in rich dark browns, neon blue-greens, mustardy yellows, and deep purples. Sometimes we could peer down into a siphon as wide as a fist to see a circle of bright-orange clam innards. The snorkeling was the best we'd ever done. The clams alone would have been enough, but hefty crown-of-thorns sea stars, bright-blue sea stars, huge parrot fish, startling lionfish, fantastic coral, and swarms of whimsical tropical fish all shouted, "Look at me! Look at me!" Later we had drinks with Dennis and Doris on *Interlude*, their beautifully kept 74-foot Deerfoot. Of course, they had some crew.

We visited Sue and Jim on *Heart of Gold*, had tea with a British couple, Helen and Neil, on the *Alexandra Louise*, and walked on the beach with folks from *Fair Wind II* and *Kindred Spirit*. Doing schoolwork while we were underway had been difficult, so Annie spent a few days catching up. In the evenings we played Rummy and War, watched both parts of *Fiddler on the Roof*, and for the first time, Annie watched *Red October* with us.

Annie and I hiked to Captain Cook's Look, as the Aussies call the lookout, a four-hour round trip on a steep track leading to the 1,200-foot summit. Captain Cook, the renowned British explorer, navigator, and cartographer had climbed that very peak in 1770. We surveyed the same maze of reefs and islands that confronted Cook as he charted a safe passage out to the Coral Sea. The next day Annie woke up complaining of a sore throat and feeling "icky," but still wanted to go on a hike. Bad blisters repaid her for the effort, so we traded shoes on the way down.

***

Robb needed a haircut. When I cut his hair on the boat, we plugged electric clippers into the generator on deck. But since sweeping up hair on the boat was a pain, our preferred venue was the beach. At Watson's Bay, after giving Robb a scissor haircut on the beach, we all walked a short way up a sandy trail, and washed up at a huge old-fashioned hand pump set in copse of trees.

After Lizard Island we had four "lovely days, lovely sails" in a row. Stopping at Bathurst Bay, Hedge Reef and Night Island, we caught fish for lunch and had soup for dinner. *Alexandra Louise* invited us for drinks made of ginger beer and whiskey. Due to my sore throat and chest cold, we spent two days at Night Island. The first morning I stayed in bed reading *The French Lieutenant's Woman* while Robb made pancakes. The rest of the day we all ate cookies. The next night we set sail again.

Fetching water at Watson's Bay

Robb Gashes his Knee to the Bone

On the morning of June 26, we pulled into Portland Roads, a small outpost of half a dozen houses about 125 miles south of Cape York, the northeastern-most tip of Australia. At mid-afternoon on what was supposed to be a sick day for me, I lay in bed reading. After looking up my chest-cold symptoms in *Where There is No Doctor,* I suspected the cold may have turned the corner into bronchitis. Robb had opened the flush-deck sliding hatch above our bed 5 or 6 inches to let in some light and air.

Suddenly I heard Robb screaming. His bloody leg came down in front of me through the overhead opening. Blood gushed down on me, the book and the bedding. He'd been on deck pushing the suspended dinghy out over the lifelines to launch it, and accidentally stepped through the partially opened hatch. As his bare leg slid through the opening, his right knee caught on the metal latch. I helped get his leg back up through the opening, then ran up on deck.

I like to think I'm good in emergencies, but when I saw the bleeding, messy gash, which looked as if it went clear to the bone, I froze. Robb said, "Get something to elevate my leg, find something for compression, and call Helen."

Annie put a big, soft-rubber boat fender under his knee, while I fetched thick sanitary pads for compression from our first-aid kit. Our friend Helen, on the *Alexandra Louise* anchored right next to us, was a pediatric nurse. She arrived within a minute or two with her medical kit and immediately set to work assessing Robb's condition, giving him a painkiller, then cleaning and dressing the wound.

She dispatched her husband Neil and me to shore to see if we could find a doctor. Annie asked what she could do. Helen, ever the Brit, smiled at her. "Please put the kettle on, dear, and make some tea."

We thanked heaven the accident hadn't happened while we were underway, that a nurse was close at hand, and Geoff, a thinking man's Crocodile Dundee, and his wife lived in the first house we came to. He was the postmaster, the airline agent, and appeared to be the de facto mayor.

Most importantly they had a phone and called the nearest medical facility, the Lockhart River Health Center, a clinic about 25 miles away in an Aboriginal settlement of 600 souls. Later we found out a Royal Flying Doctor had been there at the time we called, but he assumed the nurses could take care of a cut on a knee, and flew off to the next clinic.

***

Annie stayed behind with Helen and Neil while the ruggedly handsome Geoff drove Robb and me to the clinic in his jeep, which had "Taxi Service" neatly stenciled on the side. The 25-mile trip took nearly two hours. As the painkiller began to wear off, each bump in the unpaved, potholed road was agony for Robb. He was in no condition to appreciate the ride through the gorgeous Queensland rainforest. For me the most impressive sights were the reddish-brown, conical termite mounds, some as tall as 12 feet.

Although we arrived just minutes after 5 p.m., the clinic was closed. To open it, Geoff had to round up three people, including the head nurse, who was walking her dog on the beach. After Robb settled into a bed and his laceration examined and dressed, painkillers were administered "with good effect," according to the nurse's notes.

Beatrice, a shy Aboriginal village elder, was sent to make tea for Robb. She asked if I would help, and when we were out of everyone's earshot, she confided, "I've never made tea for a white man before. I don't know what to do."

I assured her the process was exactly the same, and we made the tea together. After almost two hours the head nurse declared the wound too deep for them to close and said Robb would have to be flown to Cairns, 265 miles back the way we'd come.

"I'm not going," said the man who believed he could fix up that sort of wound with duct tape.

"You are," the nurse and I answered in unison.

The clinic arranged for him to fly there the next morning in a puddle jumper from the nearby airport. I tried to pay for everything, but with Australia's socialized medicine even the round-trip plane ticket was considered part of the medical care, and there was no way for them to take our money. As Geoff and I left, Robb was nodding off.

When we got back to Portland Roads about 9 p.m., Helen, Neil and Annie picked me up in a dinghy and had a lasagna dinner waiting. Although they'd planned to leave in the morning, they would stay on another day, just in case. In my absence Annie had scrubbed the deck and washed the towels and bedding, removing all traces of Robb's accident. Her initiative reminded me that since she was eight, I always felt she was someone I'd want to have with me in a covered wagon going West. She and I had some nasty go-arounds, but still ....

***

The next morning, I got on the radio for the Cairns Cruisers Net. "This is Dianne on *Sorcery*. We're up in Portland Roads and Robb's had an accident. He cut his knee very badly and he's flying into Cairns this morning. He's wearing shorts, has no shoes, toothbrush, comb, money, passport or even a book to read. If anyone's still there who knows us, could you please try to find him at the hospital and take him a toothbrush and a book?"

"Hi, this is Yvonne on *Tshinta*. You don't know us, but I'm a nurse and we have a car. I can pick him up from the airport and take him to the hospital." Remembering the generosity of strangers still touches a deep part of me. If her offer weren't enough, someone else came on the line, a friend of ours.

"Hi, this is Stewart on *L'Equipe* and I'll be there too." Stewart was the same man who'd arranged transportation to the hospital in New Caledonia when Robb got stung by the stingray. Later, Robb said he couldn't imagine how he was going to manage when they landed. So, he was never more surprised or relieved than when the door of the plane opened, and Stewart stuck his head in.

"Hi, buddy! Don't worry. Everything's under control."

***

Meanwhile, back in Portland Roads that morning, I heard a knock on the hull and went up on deck to find two uniformed men from the Australian Coast Guard pulled up alongside in their skiff. "We heard what happened to your husband. Anything we can do to help?"

Nothing came to mind, but they offered to extend our cruising permits another month. In a way, them knowing about the accident so quickly was a little creepy. Geoff, I guess.

***

We have all the handwritten notes from the clinic and the Cairns Base Hospital in a brown envelope stamped O.H.M.S., On Her Majesty's Service. The important notes were on page three: "Laceration 26 hrs old. Needs delayed closure on Sunday 30/6/96." Four days away. The delay, standard medical practice, was to assure no infection had set in. Stewart and Josie insisted Robb stay with them. Not only did they have a luxurious boat, Josie was a first class cook. Yvonne, who'd been the head nurse at the biggest teaching hospital in Australia, drove Robb to the hospital each day to have the wound flushed and dressed. On the third day, *L'Equipe* had to leave, so Don and Nancy took Robb to stay with them on *Bag End*.

At one point the doctor brought up the fact Robb was an American, not eligible for free medical care under Australia's socialized medical program. Robb said he wanted to pay. The doctor agreed there was no way for him to do so, but tore up his return plane ticket, thus saving the Australian taxpayers at least the cost of airfare one way. Since Robb and I were in telephone contact, I bought another ticket with a credit card. On the fourth day, the 3-inch L-shaped cut was sutured with two or three dozen stitches inside the cut and on the surface. The doctor wrote that the wound would "require at least 2-3 weeks for it to be satisfactorily healed, if all goes well."

Lots of people, including Jim and Rhea on *Thesis,* the folks on the Tasmanian boat *Kavenga,* and *Insatiable* came up on the radio with advice, offers of help, and well wishes. We heard from our friends Katherine and Rodney on *Orion,* who'd had a horrific trip to Fiji. During a storm a hatch slammed down, cutting of the tips of little Flora's fingers. Norm and Gerri on *Witchcraft* said they would, and did, "put the pedal to the metal" and got to Portland Roads as fast as they could.

For two days before Robb came back, Annie and I shared meals with Norm and Gerri, watched movies on our boat, and visited a sweet local eccentric, Barb Holdsworth, who gave away Heavenly Holy Healing Cloths for free. An explanatory sheet told the history of the cloths, had several reports of miraculous cures, and provided instructions on how to use them for two dozen ailments, ranging from asthma, "Place Healing Cloth on centre of chest for 24 hours," to prostate cancer, "Put cloth into crotch of pants." She gave us a stack of small scraps in various colors and patterns. The next day Annie had a headache "in her eyes." Before remembering the Heavenly Holy Healing Cloths, I gave her an Aleve. Then she lay down so I could place a 1-inch-square of cloth on each closed eye. We laughed ourselves silly, and her headache went away.

Barb also gave us a packet of Barrier Reef Star Sand with its unbelievably teensy, plump, star-shaped skeletons hidden among grains of sand. Her collection of plaster casts of footprints from "animals unknown to science" was thought-provoking, but we didn't find time to go with her to see any of the actual footprints in the dirt.

***

The afternoon Robb was to return, Norm and I had dinghied to shore to wait for him. We watched anxiously as the tide receded farther and farther every minute, leaving ever more coral between us and the water. By the time Robb arrived, the water was 70 feet or so away from the dinghy, the sun had gone down, and no one else was around.

At the right moment, a fisherman appeared. He and Norm lifted the dinghy with the heavy outboard motor out to the water, while I helped Robb hobble over the coral and into the dinghy. Robb needed to rest for a few days, so having Norm around was terrific. He entertained Robb for hours on end with tales of his adventures as a Vietnam-era fighter pilot.

One of the best accounts was the one about flying a Wild Weasel aircraft. In brief, the task of a Wild Weasel was to bait enemy anti-aircraft defenses into targeting it with their radars, whereupon the radar waves were traced back to their source, allowing the Weasels to precisely target it for destruction.

When Jack Donovan, a former B-52 electronic warfare officer first heard about the mission, he said, "You want me to fly in the back of a little tiny fighter aircraft with a crazy fighter pilot who thinks he's invincible, home in on a SAM site in North Vietnam, and shoot it before it shoots me? You gotta be shittin' me!" The acronym YGBSM became part of the Wild Weasel patch.

Moving On

Robb loved the stories, but after four days he was anxious to move on. Hurricane season was coming, and we had to get across the Indian Ocean. On July 4, we left Portland Roads. Robb was able to steer the boat and manage the anchor from the cockpit, but Annie and I dealt with the sails for the next 145 miles as we day-sailed up and around the northeastern tip of the continent. Robb often had to tell us what to do, starting with the 15 or so steps required to take a reef in the main, but we did quite well.

On the second day we approached the Escape River to anchor for the night. The pass was deep enough, but we'd have to be careful because of the uneven, hard rock bottom. As we eased through the pass I spotted giant termite mounds silhouetted on the top of a ridge, and I sat in front of the depth meter "for just a second" to take a photo. It was probably less than a minute, but long enough for the depth to go from 30 feet to eight and for *Sorcery* to slam to a hideous, noisy, jarring halt.

Dianne and a termite mound

Still confined to the cockpit, Robb yelled to Annie to unfurl the headsail and sheet in the main to make the boat heel over. She Who Panics in a Crisis ran below to call for help on the radio, but wasn't able to raise anyone. I thought if we gave our coordinates, maybe someone could tell us the direction to head for deeper water. I also hoped anyone already anchored there would offer to do something if they could, but the anchorage was around the corner and no one responded. The shaking and noise inside the boat was terrifying.

Robb used the engine and the rudder to get the boat rocking back and forth. After several agonizing minutes, he was able to get us free.

He told Annie he was proud of her for jumping into action, which, of course, made her feel good. We motored to a safe spot, stayed the night, watched an episode of *Star Wars*, and then took off at first light. Annie remembers this:

> Later, the other people in the anchorage told us they heard us, but didn't come because they were afraid of crocodiles. I didn't blame them. With *Sorcery's* starboard rail underwater, a croc could easily have walked right up on deck. Dad said that was ridiculous. I still felt sad no one tried to help. I thought about the time in the hurricane in Mexico when a man called for a ride to his moored boat, but we didn't answer because we knew it wasn't safe to dinghy to get him, and we didn't want to tell him no.

After negotiating a rain squall through the nerve racking, half- mile-wide pass at the tip of Cape York, we reached the calm anchorage at Possession Island. Ten days had passed since the black plastic outside sutures had gone in, and it was time for them to come out. The inside stitches would dissolve. Annie stood by as I ordered: "Cotton! Alcohol! Stitch cutter! Scissors! Tweezers! More cotton with alcohol!" I felt a little as if I'd missed my calling.

That afternoon Robb wanted to try taking a walk, his first in 10 days. On the beach, as we passed a swampy creek, we joked it looked like a crocodile should live there. Then, realizing being chased by a croc would be no laughing matter, we headed back to the boat. We'd heard a healthy human can outrun a croc, but Robb could hardly walk, let alone run.

We told the story to our Australian neighbors, Lee and Val, retired prawn fishermen who lived at Possession on their boat *Jessica*. We'd seen them walking the beach with their pet duck waddling along behind. When we asked if crocs were around, they answered with two questions: "Did you ever notice that log near the beach in the morning? Did you notice it's not there in the afternoon?"

Annie made cards for our ninth anniversary and my fifty-fourth birthday. We spent the day relaxing and listening to Pink Floyd's *The Wall*, the CD I'd gotten for Robb in Cairns. As we were savoring a bottle of champagne, Camembert, pâté and soda crackers, Val showed up with a whole armload of pink wild orchids. In the evening we watched *Hook*. Robb apologized, "I thought we'd already be in Darwin by this date and celebrate there." I assured him I couldn't have imagined a better way to have honored the day.

Two days later, as we headed out, we spoke with *Sannyasi* – headed to Indonesia; *Witchcraft* – reporting light winds; and Rod from *Lady Ruth* – relaying the happy news that lots of mail awaited us in Darwin.

Darwin

Thank heaven we'd gotten a head start on meals with the food we'd prepared while still at anchor: a loaf of English muffin bread, a big pan of scalloped potatoes, curried beef, a dozen pickled eggs, a three-bean salad, and jello. Four rough overnights, through the washing machine of the Arafura Sea, brought us halfway across the top of Australia to Darwin, just after dark on the fifth night.

We headed straight to the Darwin Sailing Club to get our mail, a bonanza of two boxes full of goodies from Susan, a dozen letters, and a nice note from Dennis on *Interlude*. He included tickets for free beers at the Dinah Yacht Club. That first night we dug into crocodile burgers, and piled our plates high from the $4.50 fresh salad and hot vegetable bar, the first of numerous meals from the pub-style offerings on the Darwin Club's outdoor patio.

Most evenings we arrived early enough to marvel at the magnificent, red-orange sunsets that colored the entire sky. The city must have been close to the edge of the earth, for every setting sun was enormous. Southern Hemisphere, mid-winter weather, refreshingly cool nights, perfect.

***

The layover at Darwin was a big deal. Although we'd be stopping at a reef and four islands before reaching South Africa, we had to prepare for a voyage of more than 6,000 miles that would take us three months. The first task was to find a yard to haul out for routine maintenance and needed repairs.

"Looks like a giant croc chewed on that keel!" the owner of Spot On Marine observed as a Travelift hoisted a dripping *Sorcery* free of the water. The chomping had taken place during our brief but close encounter with rocks in the Escape River.

Since we lived on the boat, the biggest downside of hauling out was not being able to use running water, including the toilet. Anyone not willing to opt for the bucket had to go down the ladder and walk over to the office restroom, something we didn't do after dark. In a different bucket, dirty dishes got lowered over the side to the ground where a hose supplied the water. But the upsides were terrific. We had shore power, didn't have to use the dinghy to get to and from land, took proper showers at the club, and the boat was stable and quiet.

We often ate out, but also cooked on the little propane barbeque perched over the stern railing. In the packaged meat section at the grocery store, marinated kangaroo steaks nestled matter-of-factly between cuts of beef and chicken parts. My family was always up for experimenting, so I bought a package of that local fare – kangaroos were raised for food – and cooked the meat on the "barbie." At dinner I didn't say anything, but watched Robb and Annie as we ate. Initially they rated the meat as "nice." Then silence. Another bite. Another chew.

"What is this?"

"Kangaroo steak."

"Oh! Interesting."

Ever so carefully we each finished our steak. Actually, we liked it well enough to try again, but kangaroo didn't make a third round. The taste, color, and texture proved a bit too gamey, dark, and unusual.

Gordon, Kym, Veronica, and Deeanne in the yard office helped with every question and problem we brought to them, and even gave us car rides into town. I'd hoped Veronica would drive us, as she once hinted, to the Aboriginal village where her mother lived. When her mother was five years old, she'd been taken away from her family and never saw them again. From the early 1900s until about 1972, thousands of aboriginal children were removed by government policy to live in institutions, a sad chapter in the country's history.

Remembering Sweetheart

Kym, the office manager, told us about a crocodile trap placed by the city not far from the yard. Based on his belief that having a look would be safe, every day or two Annie and I took the dinghy up the estuary to check on the 12-foot-long wire cage, half submerged in the water. The job of a dead chicken, suspended inside at the far end, was to lure the reptile past the raised gate at the entrance. A simple mechanism would drop the gate behind the croc as the chicken met its second fate.

We never saw a croc, trapped or otherwise. Those forays came before we learned about Sweetheart the Crocodile. In the 1970s the 17-foot reptile had become notorious for a series of attacks on fishing boats, outboard motors, and dinghies. The animal was caught alive, but drowned while being transported when it became entangled with a log. At a museum in town we paid our respects to the stuffed Sweetheart.

***

The yard made a few small repairs, but Robb did the bulk of the work, not only restoring the lead keel, but the massive undertaking of cleaning and painting the boat bottom and topsides. I focused on household chores, shopping, and paperwork. I made a canvas cover for the dinghy fuel tank and worked on a new wind scoop until the sewing machine quit. It took a couple of hours, but Robb brought the machine back to life.

To get to town we hitched rides, borrowed a car, took a bus, or as a last resort, called a taxi. For being so far-flung in the world, the town struck us as lively and colorful. One day we happened upon clowns on stilts, part of some of the best street theater I ever remember seeing.

We shopped, dealt with the bank, picked up photos and new film. After dropping off the printer for repair, we lunched on fish and chips with vinegar, made phone calls, and sent and received faxes. Annie, who'd became a die-hard Michael Jackson fan in Bundaberg when she read about him in a tabloid left in the laundry room, bought one of his CDs. I found another one to secretly save for her birthday. A phone call with Alex revealed he'd made Honor Roll again and had a job for the summer at West Marine in San Diego. We were so proud of him.

***

As much work as we had, we found time to socialize with friends: *Witchcraft*, *Alexandra Louise*, *White Tunny* and Rod from *Lady Ruth*, whom we hadn't seen since New Zealand. Frances had flown home from there and Rod had gotten crew. People on two other boats in the yard, *Bufran II* and *Cheshire Cat*, sometimes joined our activities, gave us rides, and loaned us their cars.

We met the New Zealand family on *Windora*, also headed for South Africa. Dennis gave us two tickets for the Darwin to Ambon Race Dinner at the Dinah Yacht Club. My notes claim Robb and I looked good, me in my purple pants outfit and Robb in his new Bundaberg shirt. We sat with Rod, who would be in the race to Indonesia.

Annie's new acquaintances, fifteen-year-old Marika from *Bufran II*, Kym's two daughters, his niece, and Angie, Rod's former crew, entertained her with invitations to a carnival, a sleepover, movies and shopping. At home in the evenings she started watching with us a few of our tapes in the *Civil War* series. The films piqued her interest, but sometimes she just couldn't sit through the desperately sad scenes.

After we'd knocked off a few projects and made headway on others, we felt we could take a day off. Driving a rental car to Litchfield National Park, a peaceful getaway in the rainforest, we swam in water-filled rock holes, fed pretty birds, and stopped at a pub for cold drinks and a few games of pool.

At the small Territorial Wildlife Park, trainers gave talks within a few feet of us with their birds, snakes, and a kangaroo joey being fed from a baby bottle. For the Bat Chat a ranger had chunks of fruit in a cup attached to her belt, and a black bat hanging upside down from her arm. Throughout the talk, the bat dug into the cup, tossing out bits of fruit right and left in search of his favorite, the grapes. A small restaurant served us lunch on a table under a sprawling banyan tree.

***

Back at work, we took the heavy, folded mainsail in for re-stitching, but the sewing man had called in sick, so the sail didn't get fixed until Cocos Keeling Island. Robb repaired a hole in the dinghy, covered the raft with two coats of high visibility lime-green paint, and stenciled "T/T SORCERY" (Tender to Sorcery) in 2-inch black letters on both sides. Annie and I received lessons from the salesman on how to use our new dinghy outboard, a 15hp Evinrude. Robb claims the invaluable instruction ended my war with the outboard, while I insisted having a new outboard was also a factor. *Kindred Spirit* sold us some spare Benmar autopilot parts from their old autopilot.

The Tooth

At Crocodylus Park, we gasped as giant lizards leapt clear of the water to get food. On her outstretched arms Annie held a limp, yard-long juvenile, its jaws taped shut. In one room, flaps covering full-color photos warned of the gruesomeness about to be revealed. A tooth in a crocodile skeleton looked identical to a 2-inch fang Annie had found on a beach in Mexico. We brought the tooth in to the museum where an alarmed researcher grilled us.

"Where exactly did you say you found this? Mexico? Are you sure? This tooth is from a Crocodylus porosus, an endangered species."

A world map showed the range of those crocodiles included Baja and Mexico's west coast, an unsettling fact we hadn't known all those years we traveled in Mexican waters.

"You can tell the tooth was not long out of the croc's jaw by the brown traces of gum tissue you see here," he said, pointing to the gum line.

The chance of an Australian Customs agent discovering the apparent contraband was unlikely. But to be on the safe side, the researcher, believing our story, prepared an export permit from the Convention on International Trade in Endangered Species. The tooth and permit are among our most treasured souvenirs.

Our visas were about to expire, and the "bridging visas" the yard manager had tried to arrange didn't come through. Rationalizing that we were spending loads of money in the country, we momentarily considered skipping out. In the end we fell back on our "clean wake" policy. I took a bus to Immigration to pay a total of $435 for three visa extensions for two more weeks.

Sorcery splashed the week before we left. We checked out, fueled up, and filled the water tanks. Annie'd been fighting a high fever and other strep throat symptoms, so we started her on a round of antibiotics. During the two extra days we stayed until she was clearly on the mend, we made our final trip to town for money and provisions, had showers and a meal at the club. Always finding one more thing at the last minute, Robb discovered the compass light, which hadn't been used since the night we arrived, wasn't working, and fixed it. About noon, on Tuesday, August 27, we pulled away from Australia and headed west.

THE INDIAN OCEAN

Australia to South Africa
September through November, 1996

THE journey of 6,000 miles across the Indian Ocean began with a 520-mile hop from Darwin to Ashmore Reef on the western edge of the Timor Sea. The trip took five days, half that time motorsailing over the hot, nearly windless, featureless water. Two incidents broke the monotony. First, on a moonless night we passed a gigantic offshore oil rig looking fierce with its forest of long legs and intense multi-colored lights.

Here's what Annie remembers of the other happening:

My watches usually started at 4 a.m., when it was still dark. To pass the time, I'd listen to my Walkman down below, and then, as usual, check the horizon every 10 minutes. At last check, there'd been nothing.

But the next time, I saw flames, or lava, or something, a mile or two straight ahead. My mind thought volcano because the shape was triangular, and the light appeared to pour down in a fluid, constant motion. But it couldn't be a volcano - no ash, no smell of smoke, no noise. Yet the light behaved as only fire could. For a moment I felt crazy.

Volcano or not, what if there was an uncharted land mass, and we ran aground? I stood still, quietly panicking, while my mind raced to understand what I was seeing. I didn't scream, because I wanted to have some facts before sounding the alarm. Not more than 20 seconds passed, but I couldn't make any sense of it. I thought I'd better get Dad, and quickly.

I ran below. Dad was sleeping on the cushions in the galley so he'd be close to the cockpit if I needed him.

"Dad!" I shook him awake. "There's a volcano ahead!" For a second I could see the look in his eyes that said, "This better be serious. For real? You're going with 'volcano'?" Who could blame him? I was nervous because what if this was something really simple? What if nothing was there when we got up on deck? How would I explain that to an exhausted dad? What if I couldn't be trusted with watches anymore? But I knew I'd done everything right. I understood and believed the importance of scanning carefully and slowly every 10 minutes. So when we were all up on deck, I was relieved the "volcano" was still there, and that Dad was having trouble figuring it out too.

Using binoculars, as we got closer we could make out a stationary, traditional Indonesian fishing boat with a big fire in a brazier on deck. Without electricity for running lights or a radio, the men had lit a fire when they saw us headed their way. That's why I hadn't seen anything on my last look around. The flickering light from the caldron of flames had lit up the tall, quivering sail, expanding the appearance of the fire to many times its actual size.

When we passed the boat, we were close enough to see a man at the bow protecting the miniscule flame of a Bic lighter. We glimpsed the shadowy faces of men standing on deck watching us, and sensed their fear. Can you imagine being in a small old wooden boat, and having a huge vessel barreling down on you in the middle of the night? We passed them quietly. No one waved or smiled. I expect they were simply thankful we hadn't hit them, because we hadn't changed course all that much.

Altering our heading would have cost time, so we never wanted to deviate any more than necessary for safety. With the autopilot off, Robb, an excellent helmsman, was at the wheel.

Ashmore Reef

Using handwritten instructions we'd gotten from another cruiser, we made our way to the anchorage through an unmarked channel, a maze of barely submerged coral heads. Unlike other reefs we'd been to, hardly more than great circles of rocks, Ashmore Reef was a small, low lying, uninhabited tropical island. An expanse of white sand, ending in a thin fringe of green vegetation at the horizon, welcomed us. We'd barely dropped anchor before we took off for the beach. Fluffy white clouds with flat, dark bottoms hovered low over the island and were reflected in immense puddles of water.

Beachcombing was amazing because when the tide went out, the beach surfaced fast, stranding oversized and unusual sea life. Annie picked up a chocolate chip sea star that extended way past her open hand. In rows atop each of the five orange arms, dark brown horns looked very much like the creature's namesake. And unlike the dinky little helmet shells in our collection, we came upon proper head-sized helmet shells. Four-foot-long snakes found themselves stranded on the beach, and from the boat we watched as other snakes swam through the water. Ashmore was famous for its sea snakes. Most of the 14 species there were poisonous, but because they had tiny little mouths and weren't aggressive, the likelihood of being bitten was minimal.

The stranding that concerned us was a 200-pound Loggerhead turtle, leaving a tank-like track as she panted and puffed her way to the water. We assumed "she" because the reptile was covered with sand, as if she'd been busy digging a hole, laying her eggs and hadn't realized the tide was going out and it was time to leave. The sun beat down, and the turtle had at least a quarter mile to go. In the end, our belief in letting nature take its course overcame our strong urge to lift and carry her to the cool water.

Timor Fishermen

Though commercial fishing was illegal in this Australian territory, fishermen from Timor were allowed to use their traditional nets and wooden boats as they had done at least since the 1700s. The men came in to Ashmore Reef to rest and get water from an artesian well. Handmade and weathered single sails were blue and white stripe, green and white stripe, or blue–on-blue check. One boat sported a festive patchwork of all three colors and patterns in its sail. The sides of the wooden hulls, rising only 2 feet above the water, were painted in decorative combinations of greens, yellows, blues, reds, and whites.

Without engines, the colorful 35-foot boats had to anchor under sail, which made for remarkable shows. Unable to go straight into the wind to drop anchor, the boats tacked toward the desired spot. Once the anchor dropped, the wind pushed the boat back to tug and secure the anchor. We were on deck watching such a maneuver when the anchoring boat came so close we grabbed our boat hook, ready to fend off. At the last second, the oncoming boat whipped around and tacked the other direction.

Steve, an Australian researcher and the reef's caretaker who lived on a research boat and checked us in, told us the Indonesian boats sail from Timor in 24 hours by using only the stars, the moon, and the green glow on the horizon. The six men on each boat were away from home two to three weeks, from time to time a couple of months, and sometimes forever. On a flat sandy spot under one of Ashmore's two palm trees, piles of white coral rocks defined a modest fishermen's graveyard with two carved and painted waist-high wooden pillars. A scattering of packets of tobacco, cigarette papers, matches, individual clove cigarettes, and empty miniature glass bottles – the size found in hotel-room fridges – completed the memorial.

When two fishermen rowed over in their small boat with a nautilus shell to trade, we invited the men aboard. Steve, who happened to be visiting us, spoke their language.

"They can't use money, but they'd like some milk."

"Okay, but we only have powdered milk."

When he relayed the information, their faces broke into smiles as they handed us an 8-inch Tiger Nautilus, with its rusty-tan, wavy stripes. We also gave them batteries for their flashlight, but it still didn't work.

One man spoke a few words of English, and wrote down their names, Yahya Bulan and Iban (Ibrahim) Loko, in a little book we kept of boat names and people we met.

***

Of the handful of boats in the anchorage, we knew two, *Witchcraft* and *White Tunny*. We beachcombed, snorkeled and had potlucks with our friends. One evening we watched Kurt Russell in the comedy *Captain Ron*, a must-see for couples cruising with children. Gerri and Norm brought over a scrumptious carrot cake and ground beef from their freezer for a spaghetti potluck dinner. We were glad to know someone with a freezer, and ice, when Annie burned her foot stepping on the recently-used barbeque while hoisting the American flag. We'd learned long ago to only fly flags at anchor because they quickly shredded if flown underway.

Annie did schoolwork, baked brownies, and spent time with the two youngsters, Yotam and Maya, from *White Tunny*. One morning while Annie, Sharon and the kids went to shore for a swim and to explore, I made Irish Soda Bread muffins and Greek Egg Lemon soup, a snack for when everyone came back. Before *White Tunny* left, heading through the Red Sea to their home in Israel, we had a going-away potluck. In honor of the sea snakes, I fashioned dough for Italian bread sticks into sea snake shapes: long and thin with the tip of the tail pinched to perpendicular. As luck would have it, we had black sesame seeds which made dandy snake eyes.

Shortly before we left, Steve let us send a fax home from the boat on which he lived, making it the most unique place, the boat and the remote reef, from which we'd sent a fax. We topped up our tanks with water from the well.

***

When we left, we followed a different maze out of the anchorage with Annie at the bow watching for coral heads, me at the wheel, and Robb up in the spreaders, again reading aloud from handwritten notes.

"Three coral heads to the right. Five to the left. Wait! Wait! Do you think that one there on the left just breaking the surface counts as number four?"

At least once, we came to a dead-end and had to circle back, but finally we were free and clear and underway.

Two weeks later, the next journal entry appeared: "First 1,000 miles were great."

Cocos Keeling Island

The distance from Ashmore Reef to Cocos Keeling is 1,772 miles, give or take. One day we covered 210 miles, but much of the time the wind wasn't strong enough to heel the boat, an aggravation for Robb, but fine with me. My journal doesn't have much to say about the passage, and we remember the time as being when we indulged in our exciting new discovery, books on tape. Other cruisers had given us a few tapes, and we'd bought more in Cairns, but the passage to Cocos was the first one suitable for the activity.

On slow, quiet sailing afternoons I'd bake a batch of cookies. The scent wafting throughout the cabin would lure Robb and Annie to the galley. We'd sit around the glossy, varnished table set with cookies piled high on our sunflower plate, an exception to the no-glass rule. One of us would push the play button on the black tape recorder, while someone else set the white plastic darkroom timer for 10 minutes. We'd settle back into the cushions to listen to something like Pat Conroy's *Beach Music,* Paul Theroux's *Milroy the Magician,* or John Grisham's *The Chamber.*

Every 10 minutes when the timer rang, we'd pause the recorder, and take turns dashing up on deck to check around. Except for the soft lapping of the boat moving through the water, all was quiet, and as far as the eye could see in any direction, nothing but blue water, blue sky, perhaps a few distant white clouds. *Sorcery* was a tiny dot, snug in the center of the universe. Annie, who remembers the cookies, but not the books, adds this, "The ancient Chinese philosopher Lao Tzu once said, 'A good traveler has no fixed plans, and is not intent on arriving.'" I'd say on those afternoons we were pretty good travelers.

Some days, when there was no wind at all, the boat rocked lazily from side to side, fittings and lines clanging against the mast. A couple of weeks out, Robb became concerned about something we'd never worried about before: the possibility of running out of fuel before we reached our destination.

I suggested we take a piece of paper, sit in the cockpit, and work out a plan. We had roughly 700 miles to go, and about 90 gallons of diesel left. Each gallon would take us maybe six miles. Six miles times 90 gallons equaled only 540 miles, 160 miles short of our destination. Robb suggested we run the engine, which heated up the cabin, two hours each night when the weather was coolest to charge the batteries and make some headway. The rest of the time we'd simply wait for the wind to come. We had plenty of food and water.

No sooner had we committed plan to paper than the wind picked up to about 20 knots, creating big, rolling swells. Someone had to be on deck at all times, sails needed changing as the wind shifted around, and the motion of the boat took its toll, so the last several hundred miles exhausted us. We arrived with fuel to spare, but no energy. I slept 11 hours the first night and 10 the next.

***

Cocos Keeling, another Australian Territory, is made up of three postcard-perfect islands, Home, West, and Direction. They are set in a loop of reefs and smaller islets around a lagoon with a deep, wide entrance.

Yachties were allowed to anchor only at uninhabited, palm-covered Direction Island. We took full advantage of all the amenities for travelers: a toilet, two tanks of non-potable rainwater, a hammock, a clothesline. A barbeque grill stood on the beach near two picnic tables under an open shelter festooned with curious flotsam. There was a telephone booth. We needed to call our bank because we'd received a message over the single-sideband radio that our credit card had been cancelled due to suspected fraud. I dialed the string of numbers on our International Calling Card, and presto, the familiar singsong: "This is AT&T. How may I help you?"

"I just have to tell you where I'm calling from. This is a solar-powered phone on a deserted island in middle of the Indian Ocean!"

No doubt she'd received calls from places far more exotic, and in any case, was in no mood to chitchat. "How may I help you?"

In the balmy weather we washed our hair and clothes at the beach, then rinsed everything with fresh water under the tap at a tank. By the time we'd hung the last bit of laundry on the lines strung between three palms, the first item had dried. Robb cracked open coconuts for us to drink and speared fish for dinner. Both the laptop computer and the printer decided to quit working. Robb revived the computer, but we were without a printer until South Africa.

⚓

We'd first met Lee and Beth from a different *Windfall* in Bundaberg, but barely knew them when Lee came rowing over on the second day. He found Robb sitting cross-legged on deck with a leather "palm" protecting his left hand and a sailmaker's needle with special Dacron thread in his right. He was reinforcing by hand the mainsail seams that had not gotten done by machine in Darwin.

"I can help you with that." Lee nodded toward the sail, an untidy heap of over 700 square feet of heavy canvas piled on deck.

"No thanks, that's okay."

Lee rowed back to his boat. Minutes later he reappeared with his canvas ditty bag, the sailor's toolbox, and climbed on board. Sitting cross-legged near Robb, he pulled from the bag his own leather palm, needle and thread and commenced to stitch. After that, we spent many an hour with Lee, a warm and witty legal-aid attorney with a high tolerance for lawyer jokes, and his lovely wife Beth, an artist and midwife.

The first time Beth and Lee came over for tea, Annie baked some excellent bread. Later, Beth passed on to Annie, who was approximately the same size, some clothes that Annie loved. We gave Lee and Beth "lots of stuff," though I'm hard pressed to remember what that was. They reciprocated with two huge bottles of rum.

Beth taught us Dictionary, a simple and hilarious game. One person looked up an unusual but real word none of us knew. Each player wrote out a definition, then everyone tried to guess which was the real meaning. There was a system for scoring, but we were always too busy laughing, especially at Lee's priceless definitions, to bother keeping track.

Pictionary, another favored game, was always girls against boys. In our most memorable game, the final card was an All Play. Lee and Annie each looked at the same card and started sketching. Lee drew a door on the left, an eyeball on the right, a dashed line going from the eye through the door. Annie drew a stick figure of a torso with an outline of a shirt and boobs where they should be.

"See through!" Beth and I screamed. The girls almost always won.

Lee and Beth

Beth, who'd been a vegetarian for years, found out she was pregnant and suddenly couldn't get enough animal protein.

"Are you going to finish that?" Beth eyed her husband's steak just as we sat down to dinner. She had a dream of hanging whole cooked chickens on the clothesline, and licking the grease as it dripped down her arms.

Because Cocos had no hospital, local women weren't allowed to give birth on the islands. For the happy event the government flew women to Perth on the west coast of Australia. When the local authorities heard Beth and Lee planned to have their baby aboard *Windfall*, they insisted the couple sign a waiver stating if anything went wrong, the Australian government would not be asked to fly them out.

Beth did have at least one fear. As a petite woman, she worried the baby's head might be big, too big to easily exit her body. An Australian nurse, the wife of a local doctor, promised to help, although doing so was forbidden. And Beth's mother would come. We were apprehensive for our friends, though we knew them to be intrepid. They'd chosen to sail around the world without any electronic navigation, using instead a sextant to determine their bearings from the sun and the stars.

***

We all dinghied to Home Island, a Muslim-Malaysian community of about 400 people. The little settlement included a museum, a few shops, and a mosque. Women wore head coverings and long, colorful dresses in gypsy-like layers. An old fellow in a black hat taught us a few words of Malay, and steered us to his brother, who made and sold tortoiseshell jewelry. I knew about the ban on trade in these shells. But rationalizing that the brother was an individual, the tortoise already killed and eaten, the price right, and the likelihood of getting caught minimal, I bought two delicious translucent rings for Annie and myself. I wouldn't do that now. Not that I'm necessarily more law abiding, but these days I have a stronger empathy for animals that are simply minding their own business.

Another day we all visited West Island by leaving our dinghy at Home Island, then taking the free ferry across the lagoon. From the ferry landing a bus, also free, took us into town, home to more than 140

Australian government families. West was the commercial center: police and customs, a post office, an airport, a dive shop, propane, gas, diesel, provisions, and other facilities. Starting with lunch at a nice little restaurant, we spent a leisurely, if tiring, afternoon in the heat taking care of some business, shopping, and wandering around. The most notable sight was a stunning 50-foot-tall Mongoose Fan Palm. The tree was two dimensional – a giant, opened, Chinese folding fan.

⚓

We got to know other lively and appealing people too, Mike and Jane on *Aqua Symphony*, Phil, Lynda, and their young boys Cliff and Luke on *Windora*, and the French family, Nicole, Christian and thirteen-year-old Adrien on *Adélaïde*. With a dozen cruising boats in the lagoon, the barbeque potlucks on the beach, book exchanges, and snorkeling at The Rip, the pass leading into the lagoon, never stopped. After one such snorkel, *Windfall* and *Aqua Symphony* came over to our boat for hot buttered rums and to watch *Searching for Bobby Fisher*.

Toward the end of our two weeks in Cocos, we had a big beach potluck with boats including, to quote from my journal, "an old (in their 70s) couple, *Windfall, Music, Angelos,* and a Norwegian hippie boat with three guys and one gal, all of whom went topless on their boat." Going on the premise, I suppose, that it never hurts to ask, the Norwegians invited Annie, all of twelve years old, to spend the night on the beach with them. She didn't.

***

The day we intended to leave, the winds were very light, and Robb woke up with a raging headache, so I called Customs to re-check us out. The following day didn't bring any more wind and none was predicted, but Robb felt better, the fuel tank was full, and we had to get moving. Nearly 2,000 miles separated us from our next stop.

The first few days the winds remained light, yet we never resorted to motoring. *Sorcery* was a good light-air boat when she had even a little something to work with. Then, during the last half of the trip, *Sorcery* made her best time ever, 217 miles in one day. Rough seas seemed to make Robb a little seasick. That new development concerned me, not only because I hated to see him feel bad, but so much depended on him. I often referred to my husband as a single hander.

Each day we talked on a radio net with boats ahead of and behind us: *Aqua Symphony, Gwenaskel, Music, Interlude,* and the German boats *Stromer* and *Fradilira.* We listened to more books on tape and had loads of new reading from the book exchanges on Cocos. Annie, the snippy preteen, was sometimes the little girl making silly faces. Overall in good spirits, she became cuddly, even took naps with me.

One night, Annie happened to wake up to find her dad had fallen asleep while on watch. She simply took over and let him sleep. On that particularly long passage, we'd hoped to be able to cut down to looking around only every 15 minutes at night. But surprised by the number of huge merchant vessels we saw or heard on the radio in that vast expanse of water, we decided against it.

Once I called to a big ship visible in the distance. After several minutes, a man speaking minimal English responded, then a long silence. Finally, another fellow came on speaking more English and eager to talk. They were from Sri Lanka.

"Can you see us?" I asked, giving our position.

"No."

"Do you keep a visual lookout for small ships?"

"No, we don't."

"Do you have radar?"

"Yes!"

"Are you using it?"

"No."

Later we learned from a Merchant Marine friend of ours that although big ships are required by law to have radar, often, as a money-saving measure, they didn't use it. The Sri Lankan man asked about our boat and crew, then expressed alarm that a boat our size was in the Indian Ocean.

"It's dangerous out here! It can get very rough!"

"I know, but here we are."

"You've been lucky. Why don't you go more south?"

Rodrigues

With 11 days and 2,000 miles behind us, we eased through the surrounding reef of Rodrigues (Rod reegs). Anchoring in the quiet harbor would have been fine, but we got lucky and docked at the wharf, hooked up to shore power, and side-tied to *Stromer* the entire nine days we were there.

A couple of afternoons the lady on the boat invited Annie and me over for *mate*. Yerba Mate, a traditional tea in some countries in South America and the Middle East, is usually shared with friends. One sips the tea from a beautiful, small, round bowl through a special metallic drinking straw with a flattened strainer at the end.

***

The people of Rodrigues were an exotic mélange of Indians, Chinese, Blacks, and Indonesians. In the busy little town right at the harbor, some of the buildings made of corrugated tin dressed themselves up with bold 3-foot-wide stripes, sometimes at a diagonal, of vivid orange and blue, or blue and white.

Along the unpaved streets, bicycles leaned against the buildings. Small, non-threatening dogs slept and strolled at will. Live chickens for sale were stuffed under large, overturned open-weave baskets, a gunny sack thrown across the top for shade. From fancy wrought-iron balconies, strings of fresh sausages stretched horizontally in the dusty air to dry. Green plastic ties pulled the sausages up at intervals in uneven loops, bringing to mind Arabic calligraphy. Round, rectangular, and square Coca-Cola, Fanta and Sprite signs in primary colors dotted the outside and inside walls of businesses.

Provisions could be delivered to the boat and were cheap: Bread 10¢, eggs 12¢, sugar 25¢ a kilo. But the best deal came frozen from India: tender filet mignons in the shape of small baseball bats for $1.85 a pound. We yachties took turns in the morning making the two-minute bread run, delivering warm baguettes from the bakery up the street to our friends lounging in their cockpits with mugs of coffee.

Since restaurant meals cost only three to five dollars, including a drink, we ate out nearly every day at El Capitaine, El Paille en Queque, or Le Gourmet. Octopus, the island specialty, came in a variety of ways:

with spicy tomato sauce, in a stew with garlic and mystery ingredients, or plain grilled, to name a few. We tried them all, and settled on curried as the best.

Which Way is Mecca?

One morning while I shopped at Mahmood's, the blue- and white-striped grocery store on the corner, Omar, the manager, came up to me.

"Do you have a compass on your boat?"

"Yes, of course."

"Could you please bring it to me?"

"Bring it to you?"

"Yes, we need to check the magnetic variation at Rodrigues to orient the new mosque we're building."

After explaining the compass was built into the boat, I invited him to come by and we'd figure out the variation. We agreed on noon. At 12, a young man appeared with a handwritten message on the store's letterhead. Omar asked if he could come at 5 instead, and to "Please answer to the bearer of this note."

At 5 on the dot, Omar, his wife, son, and father arrived at the boat. To thank Robb for calculating, with the help of the GPS, the correct direction to Mecca, they invited us to their home the following day. Sitting around their parlor, we drank tea and listened to Omar talk about religion. He was a born-again Muslim, she a Christian. The spiritual orientation of the silent children and the two or three other adults wasn't discussed, but the whole family dressed in long tunics and loose trousers, headscarves for the females. Stacks of spicy falafel and samosas were passed around, and a packet of them presented as a gift to take home.

***

For $3 per person, 10 of us yachties took an all-day private bus tour, much of it along the breathtaking 23-mile perimeter of the island. From the vantage point of a couple of hundred feet, the ocean appeared black-blue in the distance. A wide band of thick white froth broke on the surrounding reef protecting the shallow aqua water closer in.

On a rise against the backdrop of the ocean, drying octopuses, 5 or 6 feet in length, hung from a line, their heads stretched flat with sticks, their long arms swaying in the breeze. We hiked into the mouth of a cathedral-like cave, continued on toward the light, then out into forest of palms. The driver stopped at a kiosk where we bought soft drinks to wash down the lunches we'd brought with us.

A little rain now and then cooled the otherwise warm, sunny days. The usual visits, potlucks, and chores kept us busy. *Windora* was there. Adrien on *Adélaïde* and Annie became good pals. We'd hoped to do our laundry on the big supply ship, but that didn't work out. We gave clothing to a church, and I helped people make yogurt. On Saturday we shopped at the farmers market. Sore throats sprang up in the cruising community. Jane on *Aqua Symphony* got it first and became the sickest. Robb got a bit of a scratchy throat, but Annie and I escaped.

Antoinette Decides for Us

Although we had no way to earn money, no school for Annie, or any place to buy supplies to work on the boat, we'd thought we could happily have stayed in Rodrigues for many weeks. However, on October 17 at 1 in the afternoon, just a little over a week after we arrived, the decision to move on was made for us.

Claus on *Stromer* spread the word that Tropical Cyclone Antoinette, 1,000 miles to the northeast, was moving toward Rodrigues at 15 knots. The local weather people warned us storms on that track usually hit Rodrigues and, at the current speed, that would be in two and a half days. With unknowns and variables, such as the possibility Antoinette could pick up speed, we decided to head to our next destination, the island of Mauritius.

The sudden need to leave stressed Robb, but we had a routine for getting ready, and in three hours we were on our way out the pass with *Stromer, Solfrana*, and *Adélaïde*. *Windora* stayed until morning to get further reports. The only thing we hadn't been able to do was top up our water tanks because two dead cows had been found in the reservoir. However, the generous locals allowed each boat a few jugs of precious trapped rainwater. In any case, *Sorcery*'s water tanks weren't low, we might be able to capture rain water underway, and our next stop was a mere 360 miles – three or four days – to the west.

Mauritius

Arriving too late in the day to be allowed into the harbor at Port Louis, we anchored out in calm water. Early the next morning, we entered the animated panorama of a big commercial harbor, painted in shades of gray by a heavy mist. Ships of all sizes sat in place or moved about the harbor – serenely if a big vessel or noisily if a smaller one. As the morning haze lifted, the majestic craggy mountains in the background revealed themselves to be green.

We spotted a place to dock behind *Interlude*, but as we approached, our forward gear, which had been acting up since Darwin, went out again. Noticing our predicament, a Coast Guard dinghy eased us into place. Later, *Adélaïde* side-tied to us, then *Windora* onto them, and *Solfrana* on the outside. Our four-boat raft-up lasted until the two outer boats found places of their own. *Aqua Symphony* docked right around the corner.

The following morning, Annie woke up on her thirteenth birthday to a pyramid of white eggless cupcakes lit up like a Christmas tree with colored candles, including at least one that re-lit. A little glass bear she'd admired in Cairns sat on the top. We gave her two Michael Jackson CDs, a wallet with a five-dollar bill, a pair of yin-yang stud earrings, a fake nose ring, the game Cluedo, a whoopee cushion, and bunches of batteries and rolls of film.

Her pal Adrien got the day off from schoolwork in honor of her birthday. Two of the many balloons they blew up found their way under the shirt and onto the chest of that quiet and droll French boy who behaved nonchalantly as if nothing unusual was going on. The two kids entertained us the rest of the day with the whoopee cushion and other antics. For a late afternoon birthday potluck with our friends from five or six boats, I baked lasagna and a chocolate cake. Others brought salads, garlic bread, homemade candies, real French crepes, and cards and little gifts for the new teenager.

Mauritius got mixed reviews. Starting at the bottom, the water in Port Lewis was absolutely filthy. All the yachts had a miserable time getting the oil sludge off their hulls. We understood we were in a commercial port, but we felt cruisers were made to feel unwelcome. Although *Sorcery* wasn't asked to move, other boats were, and sometimes more than once. One rainy night a boat came in and side-tied to *Adélaïde*. Officials came by shouting, "You must leave! It's forbidden to come in at night! It's too dangerous!"

"But we're already here! Going back out would be dangerous!"

The argument, however rational, fell on deaf ears. The new boat left, in the dark and the rain, to anchor outside the harbor.

At Immigration, our spear gun had to be relinquished until we left the country. Rodrigues had required the same thing, but retrieval was easy because the island was small. Mauritius was a different story. And for the first time in our travels, cruising yachts had to pay a port fee based on their tonnage. That was one of the few occasions we wished we had a smaller boat.

As we stepped off the water taxi that had taken us to shore, the driver warned us the city was dangerous.

"Thieves handcuff people! Then rob them!"

"We'll be careful," we promised as we walked away, asking over our shoulders for the directions to the post office.

The city was excitingly foreign. On their heads, young men carried huge baskets overflowing with what must have been 100 pounds of produce destined for the extensive Old Market near the port.

We followed the crowd and earthy smells into the dark, cavernous building complex. Endless rows of tables held stacks of artfully arranged, fabulous looking, high-priced fruits, vegetables, meats, and fresh and dried fish. Gigantic squash were seeded, halved and displayed with their orangey-yellow flesh sunny-side up. Other items for sale covered the walls and hung from the ceiling: Indian saris, western clothing, flip-flops, baskets, shopping bags, towels, toys, shoes, kitchen equipment, a tricycle, who knows what all. Only sarongs were cheap.

⚓

After a couple of days, we cruisers moved 10 miles up the coast to calmer and cleaner Grand Baie. Robb had fixed the transmission, but *Windora* and *Adélaïde* followed us just in case. We made it into the bay before the gears went out again. Luckily, we were able to drop the hook near the yacht club. Robb found the heat exchanger had corroded through, possibly due to the warmer water, allowing saltwater into the gear box. At Grand Baie, he installed blades that gave us only forward, which took us all the way to South Africa.

The small town of Grand Baie was a pleasant and restful stop. Jane and Mike from *Aqua Symphony* came over for coffee and almond cake. At the yacht club we gathered for drinks in the evenings, and held a book exchange one afternoon. We got water there, though not much, because of a water shortage on the island. It took Robb, Annie and Adrien the better part of a day to clean the sludge from *Sorcery*'s hull – and that was only around the waterline. We took the laundry out to be done, a rare and welcome reprieve.

When we were in Rodrigues, Annie had met Virginia, a seventeen-year-old girl who lived in Mauritius. With their tan skin and long, dark, curly hair, the two could have been sisters. She'd given Annie her phone number and invited her to visit. Virginia and her urbane parents came the same day we called and drove Annie and me to their gorgeous home right on the shore. After serving coffee and cake on their patio, the parents drove me back to town. The next afternoon, they returned Annie and stayed for drinks and hors d'oeuvres.

***

The best of Mauritius was an all-day tour in a minibus with *Aqua Symphony, Music,* and *Adélaïde*. A 300-year-old botanical garden, billed as one of the most beautiful tropical gardens in the world, was not overrated. The picture that sticks in my mind is pond after pond covered with Amazonian water lilies. The perfectly flat, round pads were a yard across with raised edges like giant green tart pans. Just off the pathways, monkeys sat peeling and eating little bananas.

On another part of the island, high on a breezy hill overlooking unspoiled valleys and mountains, we visited one of the many Hindu temples, this one white with gold domes. On an outside terrace, we bought snacks: samosas, falafel, and deep-fried breaded chilies. A shy man in western clothes was selling five cowry shells, each the size of a fist. Two women with red dots on their foreheads and wrapped in bright saris, one of pink and one of red and gold, carried offerings on small brass trays.

Dressed all in white – long, loose pants, a tunic, and a scarf – a young man dozed in a chair, his head drooping forward, fingers interlaced, bare feet propped on a rail, a book open on his lap. Puffy white clouds floated behind him in a blue, blue sky. That day we understood a little of what we'd read on the label of a wine bottle, "Mauritius was made first, and then heaven, and heaven was copied after Mauritius. Mark Twain."

***

One day, Lynda from *Windora* and I tended dinghies while Jane, Robb, Phil, Mike, and two other men drift dived. *Interlude* invited us to lunch with their crew at the Grand Baie Yacht Club. Another day we took steaks to a barbeque on *Interlude*. On a shopping trip with Jane and Nicole, I bought Annie two cute T-shirts and some leggings for myself in a nice shop. We all had lunch at an inexpensive, open-air Chinese restaurant on the main street, and then bought sarongs from a hawker on the beach.

⚓

Things between Robb and I had dipped to another low. He thought, and I half-heartedly agreed, we should separate in South Africa. He'd stay to work, fix the boat, and get crew. I'd fly back to the States with Annie. At his suggestion, we told Annie what we were discussing. She cried, said she'd rather have her dad than friends. Later on she asked who she and I would stay with until things got sorted out, how the money would be divided, if her dad and I still "do it," and wished she had someone like her friend Lisa in Darwin to talk to.

I felt numb. Still hoping we could find a way back, I apologized again for the mooring episode when we'd arrived in Bundaberg, which is where I felt the relationship had frayed to the breaking point. He said for him it was before that, in New Caledonia when I'd challenged him on his dealings with Annie. Going back even further, Robb said he felt I always sided with Annie. Talking diffused the tension for the time being. Once again, we swept the unresolved issues under the rug.

***

After a jam-packed week, Jane, Mike, Annie and I took a bus, a two-hour round trip, to the Immigration Office in Port Louis to check out. No one was in the office, so after waiting an hour, we went to lunch at a nice looking Chinese place with not-so-good food. We stopped to watch dozens of huge tunas being loaded onto a truck, their frozen bodies white with frost. Immigration gave us a three-hour runaround. They didn't want us to leave from Grand Baie, though they'd allowed *Music* do so. In the end they gave both *Sorcery* and *Aqua Symphony* clearance to leave from there, but said I'd have to come back to Port Louis on our last day to collect the spear gun. I kept talking until they finally agreed to let me take it with me.

As we motored out of Grand Baie on the day we left, the Coast Guard pulled alongside to inform us Immigration had changed their mind: They insisted we leave from Port Lewis after all. "Are you on your way to Port Louis?"

"Yes," we lied. Apart from the time-consuming and unnecessary trip back, we didn't want to subject our boat to the oil sludge again.

Apparently believing us, they sped off in another direction. Even though we had proper exit papers, we felt a little like criminals sneaking away.

Réunion

A single overnight passage from Mauritius delivered us to the town of Le Port, on the northwest side of the island of Réunion. Even without reverse, anchoring went smoothly. As soon as the hook took hold, Robb launched the dinghy and found a place for *Sorcery* to side-tie next to *Gwenaskel.*

After all the official hassle about leaving Mauritius, Immigration at Réunion didn't even ask for our exit papers. Bernard and Beatrice, the French and Brazilian couple on *Gwenaskel,* brought over a baguette and introduced us to the Brazilian national drink, *Caipirinha,* made with rum, lime juice, sugar, and – always a real treat for us – ice. That evening Annie and I played Pester, a silly card game.

At 6 the next morning *Adélaïde* and *Windora* pulled in. *Windora* side-tied to us, and seven people – three of them young boys – piled onto *Sorcery* for a couple of hours. My gregarious husband invited them all to come back later in the morning, then *Windora* again in the evening, for a total of about five hours of visitors that day. Although I was tired, I hadn't begged off because I liked the people, and Robb particularly enjoyed the company of the two men, Phil and Christian, both intelligent, funny, easygoing fellows.

***

When we made the long, hot walks into town, locals sometimes offered us rides. We thanked them with cigarettes and little American flag pins. To get our two propane tanks filled, we had to go to a big industrial complex, which sold propane by the tanker load. They gave us free refills, apparently because our 20-pound tanks weren't worth charging for. Sometimes such projects took up most of the day. By the time we figured out where we needed to go, how to get there, actually found the place, arrived during business hours, talked to the right person, and gotten the deed done, the morning or afternoon had often slipped away.

In the evenings we watched movies, a few from *Adélaïde's* collection, and twice we showed *Around Cape Horn* to people from other boats. Adrien, endearing himself to Annie, translated a Michael Jackson article in a French magazine, and then the two of them watched *The Addams Family.*

***

A big run-around to several agents ultimately resulted in us renting a car for two days to go sightseeing. Just outside of town we encountered our first point of interest: a billboard touting a certain brand of mattress featured a supine, 24-foot-tall woman covered with nothing but a hand towel across her groin.

"We're not in Kansas anymore," Robb observed. We believed the fact that the island is a department of France explained the spicy advertising.

Réunion is one of the planet's hot spots, and seeing a volcano or two was a must. We were on our way south along the coast to visit *Aqua Symphony* at a marina in Saint Pierre. Mike and Jane had invited us to stay overnight so we could drive at first light to a nearby volcano. Usually at mid-morning heavy fog moved in at the higher elevations, obscuring the scenery and making driving hazardous.

When we arrived at the marina in the afternoon, our friends took us to a market selling produce and handmade products from Madagascar. We'd heard drumming was all the rage with teenagers in the States, so Annie picked out a drum. Although I'm not religious, some rough, unpainted wooden figures for a simple manger scene spoke strongly to me, echoes from my childhood. I didn't get the figures, but have since regretted it. I did buy a small dish of dark wood carved to look like a coiled snake as well as several whole vanilla bean pods, a few for ourselves and a few for friends, to stick into containers of sugar to add a delicious scent.

After we'd stopped for drinks at a waterfront bar, back on *Aqua Symphony* Jane prepared a satisfying spaghetti dinner using plenty of garlic, and served with red wine. She laid out colorful ski sweaters, scarves, hats, and gloves for us to borrow for the early morning cold, which would be in the 40s.

At 4 a.m. the next day, we headed to Piton de la Fournaise, the peak of the furnace. At the time I didn't know that particular volcano was considered one of the most active in the world. In those days a great deal of our information came by word of mouth. We were horrified, for instance, to hear that cruisers, some of whom we knew, purposely walked right up to a hot caldera in Vanuatu, then grabbed their children and raced downhill as the volcano spewed out rocks, some the size of baseballs. Every year the volcano managed to kill several tourists in just that way.

The volcano we came to see had a habit of being active virtually every year since 1900. But in 1996, when we were there, it hadn't blown in four years. A lifeless environment stretched in all directions. We hadn't heard about or seen any sign of an eruption, so we crossed the desolate gray sand plain near the top of Fournaise. Rocks the size of volleyballs were painted white and stationed every 15 feet along each side of the road to help people find the way back if they got fogged in.

Hiking up and looking down into the four-mile-wide caldera, we saw a gigantic, smooth operculum of igneous rock formed when the last lava flow sealed the opening. Witnessing an eruption would have been sensational. Yet we found our adventure, as it was, vastly pleasing and dramatic enough. The fog started to roll in.

On the way down the wiggly road, we saw many gingerbread cottages, and a few dog houses, with white wooden "lace" hanging from the eves. At a rustic chalet we stopped for a *petit déjeuner* – a carafe of coffee on a table with a flowered tablecloth, bowls for drinking the coffee and hot chocolate, warm croissants wrapped in cloth in a basket, butter that appeared fresh-churned, pots of jam.

After returning the clothes to Mike and Jane, we hugged our last goodbyes and promised to keep in touch. They'd be going north through the Suez Canal to the Mediterranean, while we were headed south around the Cape of Good Hope at the tip of Africa.

Continuing on our drive around the perimeter of Réunion, we ran into a traffic jam the last few miles before home base. Deciding our time would be better spent stopping at another waterfront bar with a view of the ocean, Robb and I each ordered a *pastis*, an anise-flavored French *apéritif* and played pinball with Annie.

We slept in our own beds until 4 the next morning, and then drove to an older, no longer active, yet spectacular volcano, Piton Maido, its steep mountains blanketed with green. From a walkway on the side of a mountain, something could be seen 3,000 feet below in the bottom of the valley.

"What are those white specks?" I asked the young Frenchman leaning next to us on the railing.

"Oh, those are houses," he explained, clearly prepared for the question. "After the slaves were freed in 1848, white people who couldn't abide Blacks being equal moved there. The only way out is by walking, donkey, or helicopter, so most of those people have never seen the ocean."

"Wow. What about inbreeding?"

"It's a terrible problem that's led to severe mental and physical disorders." He was knowledgeable, and we were full of questions, but the fog started coming in, so we excused ourselves and moved on.

After hiking back to the car, we drove to a hotel where we treated ourselves to an elaborate breakfast, followed by a few friendly games of pool. In town we changed more money into French francs, an hour's project, got groceries, and returned the car.

***

On Thursday, November 14, after a busy two-week "rest," we started the 1,600-mile trip to South Africa. As we motored out, Adrien, shrinking ever smaller, waved madly from the top of one of the huge concrete blocks that formed the breakwater. The picture of that dear boy tugged at my heart. In life, whether on land or sea, you can't be certain you'll ever see anyone again. But when cruising, all of us were on the move, so the chance of not seeing someone ever again was very real.

The *Adélaïde* family stayed in Réunion for several months. As a computer programmer, Christian had helped develop some of the first voice-recognition software for the French government, and he found work in Réunion. As it happened, we did see them again on our last stop before we left South Africa.

⚓

The passage started off easily enough, the winds light and the air hot. Mostly we read, and Annie did schoolwork. The computer had stopped working again. Robb colored my hair. Each day we checked in on a radio net with other boats underway, *Windora*, *Gwenaskel*, and Peter on *Friendly Rival*.

Ten days later, a cold front came through bringing miserable seas. But in less than 24 hours we lost the wind again, and hoped we'd make it to South Africa before another cold front caught up with us.

On Annie's watch the mainsail chafed through where the reef point is attached to the boom. The clew, a big ring sewn into the sail, had pulled out previously and been repaired, but had come out again. With no way to make the repair underway, we had to take a double reef, leaving less sail area when we needed it for the light winds. As upsetting as that was for Robb, he recovered quickly, and tackled the next problem: an oil leak at the mast where the vang, a moveable, multipurpose arm, supported the boom.

As we neared the South African coast, we began getting intermittent weather reports from Alister's net out of South Africa, 14316 and then 7045 LSB at 11:30 Zulu time, and joined a daily roll call with him. We seemed to get the most wind of the entire Indian Ocean passage just as were making for the entrance to Richards Bay. It was already dark, and we were flying along at 11 knots. With the boat running parallel to the coast and dodging massive vessels as we crossed the shipping lane, I shouted to Robb,

"Isn't this where we're supposed to go in?"

"Yes!" he yelled back. "We will if I can slow this boat down enough to make the turn!"

The calm waters of the continental shelf helped *Sorcery* reduce speed. At 3:30 a.m., 11 days after leaving Réunion, we entered the well-lit commercial port, and anchored for the night just outside Tuzi Gazi Marina in Richards Bay, our home for the coming year.

FROM WHERE WE SAIL

SOUTH AFRICA

Last Big Stop
Late November 1996 to March 1998

THREE days before Thanksgiving we arrived in Richards Bay in KwaZulu-Natal Province. The town of 40,000 is 90 miles north of Durban on the east coast of South Africa. The following day we got a ride to a huge supermarket in a mall, 10 minutes away through the green countryside. Balancing washtub-sized bundles on their heads and adorable, pudgy babies on their backs, a few traditionally-dressed Black women mingled with the crowd at the mall.

The supermarket, though very Western, gave a few clues we were somewhere else. Loaves of bread came unsliced. A slicer stood by in case you wanted to do it yourself, but no sign warned you the management wasn't responsible if you cut off your own fingers. Elated to find frozen turkeys from Canada, we bought a 25 pounder in anticipation of a potluck on our boat. When we got in line, cart filled to the brim, our bounty became an embarrassment. Many people, who looked as if they couldn't afford to buy much at one time, held what they were buying in their hands. Shoppers ahead of us gave a few small South African rand coins to the Black man bagging groceries, so we did the same.

Twenty or so people showed up for our Thanksgiving feast, some of whom had never experienced the American holiday. Nevertheless, they fearlessly prepared dishes like pumpkin pie and green-bean casserole, without knowing exactly how they were supposed to taste. Didn't matter. Everything was delicious.

At the supermarket, we'd picked up the Credence Clearwater Revival album *Platinum*, and we played it at nearly full blast for after-dinner dancing on the boat. If we'd held a contest, the trophy would have gone to the self-described "wild woman" Sheila and her partner LeCain from *Perelandra*. They danced their hearts out. Among others joining us were the German couple from *Fallado*, the Austrian couple from *Tamara*, *Gwenaskel's* French and Brazilian couple, the *Windora* family from New Zealand, and *Aqua Symphony*. We were happy to see Mike and Jane again before they headed to the Med.

After Thanksgiving, the turkeys, already cheap, went on sale. They kept going down in price, and we bought one probably once a week. In those days, I made soup and stock from the carcasses. As we began to get turkeyed out, we started sharing the ones we bought with *Windora*. We all gave out before the birds did, but it was a good run. We had especially appreciated a whole real turkey after having been in the Marshall Islands, where the closest thing we could find to a gobbler was a five-pound bag of turkey tails. In other countries we always made an effort to sample the local fare. But seeking out a recipe for tails-of-fowl never crossed my mind.

⚓

Officially, the first month at the wharf was free, but we were never approached for payment. Apparently, some people were charged, others not. Meanwhile, daily life became easier with hookups for water and electricity, and a handy little mall at the end of the dock where we could buy a few groceries, fresh fish, make calls, and send faxes. We left our dirty clothes at the laundromat with Zandilie, an amiable young Zulu woman who washed, dried, and folded our clothes for about a dollar a load. The Australian couple who owned Quay Walk Travel let us use their address to receive mail.

No one would accuse the city of Richards Bay of having charm, but it proved to be a wonderful place for us to rest and get things done. As things settled down, Robb and I realized separation wasn't the solution for us. By December our days had already taken on a back-to-real-life aspect: endless appointments with doctors, dentists, optometrists and hair salons, enrolling Annie in school, ordering transmission replacement parts from Germany, and sending our mainsail and jib off for repair to Doyle Sailmakers in Durban. Kentucky Fried Chicken had never been on our radar, but food options were limited. We became a little bit hooked; the chicken tasted so good and reminded us of home.

Overall, South Africa was inexpensive, the cheapest of our big stops, and some things cost even less than in California. Ten dollars, for instance, covered a visit to an excellent dentist or doctor. One item, though, did give us sticker shock: $3,700 for a new laptop computer and printer.

We turned to Susan in San Diego to try to find a power board for our ailing Toshiba. "If it's more than about $50, our second choice is a used laptop for around $500. If we have to bite the bullet and get a new one, please send it marked 'Yacht in Transit - Warranty Repair.'" We assumed the duty on a new one would be astronomical.

⚓

South Africa has 11 official languages. In KwaZulu-Natal the Blacks often spoke three: Zulu, English and Afrikaans. Afrikaners, the white descendants of Dutch settlers spoke Afrikaans, a Dutch dialect, and English, but rarely any Zulu.

The Zulu language, although difficult, can be enchanting. The one word for hello, good morning, good afternoon and good evening is *sawubona*, literally meaning "I see you." The response is *yayboo*, "Yes." When we used the plural *sanibonani* to greet a group of Zulus, the people grinned and giggled, we thought with surprise and pleasure that we knew the plural or for that matter, any Zulu at all. Or maybe our pronunciation simply tickled them. We didn't learn many words, but we got a lot of mileage out of the ones we knew.

Year-End Holidays

Christmas in the Southern Hemisphere is hot, sometimes beastly so. On Christmas Eve eight of us went caroling in summer clothes to the boats at the marina and shops that were open, then gathered on *Sorcery* for rum punch and plates of food brought by our neighbors. I'd done lots of baking, so when anyone stopped by we had special holiday treats.

Since there were a few children, including Phil's two boys, he gamely put on a bulky Santa suit, complete with hat and beard. Despite sweating profusely, he was a trouper and even let the adults, who may have had a little mulled wine, take turns sitting on his lap for a photo. In the heat, our typical Christmas dinner did seem heavy and out of place, but we all appreciated the semblance of a holiday at home. Later, a South African acquaintance told me that on Christmas the locals sit by the pool with a cool drink and eat fruit salad.

***

On New Year's Eve, we were already asleep when the sound of explosions pulled us into full alert mode. Being in South Africa, even in those relatively calm Nelson Mandela days, we were alarmed and raced up on deck in our pajamas. Lo and behold, the marina was the epicenter of fireworks for the town. Roaming the docks, hundreds of people oohed and aahed as each burst of color lit up the sky.

To add to the festivity, all the pilot and tugboats tooted their humongous horns and shined every last light. That was the first year the government had allowed the Zulu population to set off fireworks, and they indulged with considerable pent-up energy. When sparks started landing on our canvas awning, we knew we had to stay up on deck, bring out our emergency champagne, and enjoy the evening, an effortless and memorable New Year's Eve.

In early January, we received a letter from Beth and Lee letting us know all was well, the baby expected at the end of February.

Robb Gets Work

Prior to leaving San Diego, Robb had worked for 25 years in all phases of electrical construction as a union journeyman wireman, foreman, and as a troubleshooter. The week after Christmas he started working for Psitron Electric as a supervisor at an aluminum smelter plant, and later on at a new automated bulk-unloading system for ships at the port.

The majority of the men in his charge were Zulus. Peter, the Rhodesian owner of Psitron, told Robb, "Don't expect too much from the Blacks," and added, in so many words, that they were sullen and unmotivated. Robb had the opposite experience. They worked well for him, a fact he attributed to treating them as equals.

Working at the smelter plant was mostly a hot, dirty business. He had two pairs of coveralls, one to wash and one to wear. Each day after he came home, you'd see me down on my hands and knees on the dock with a scrub brush and soap, scouring the greasy soot out of the pair he'd worn that day. After they'd been hosed down and wrung out, they were hung on the lifelines to dry.

Wheels

In the new year, Peter sold us his wife's old Ford Escort for $4,000, and said they'd buy it back for the same amount when we left. The car was a blessing, though it required a new battery on day one, and I had to relearn using a stick shift. Since I drove Robb to work each day, he gave me free driving instruction – tough on both of us. Thankfully, Jane on *Aqua Symphony* took over. A patient teacher, she helped me overcome some bad stick-shift habits. After several sessions with her, people riding with me would say,

"Gee, your car seems to be running a lot better!"

The car suffered a few traumas. Once when three ample ladies were with me, I drove over a fair-sized rock in the middle of a dirt road in town. The extra weight in the car caused the undercarriage to get stuck on the rock, damaging the gear box in such a way the car lost reverse. As the women disembarked, the car, heaving a sigh of relief, lifted, and I drove straight to a mechanic.

One day I found a place among all the cars parked helter-skelter in a dirt lot at a mall. As I backed up a little, the right rear wheel dropped into a big hole. Two Black fellows ambled over to offer help. They simply picked up the back of the car and set it on solid ground. I tipped them each 10 rand, about two US dollars, half a day's pay, not much to me, but hopefully a lot to them. Most of the businesses had Not Hiring signs posted in their windows.

Another day, as I drove along a road on the edge of town, the exhaust pipe fell off. No sooner had I pulled over than an older Black gentleman driving a Port Authority car stopped and helped me. I pulled out my wallet.

"Here, let me give you something for your time."

"No, no, that's okay. But would you please write a note to my supervisor telling him what I did?"

By May the car needed almost constant repair, but it soldiered on until we left at the end of the year. Peter and his wife were as good as their word and gave us $4,000.

Annie's Life in Richards Bay

On January 21, Annie entered 10th grade at the only school in town that taught in English, John Ross College, a private, co-ed, quasi-religious institution. The thirteen-year-old wore a proper uniform: white shirt with an emblem, gray skirt, clunky black shoes, and a maroon blazer. On certain, much-anticipated days, students were allowed to wear "civies" if they donated two rand, about 50 cents, to a charity. Her classes were Afrikaans, Business Economics, English, Math, Physical Science, and Technical Drawing. Although Afrikaans was required, she was exempt from being tested and used that class time as study hall.

Black students were in the same classrooms, but there was virtually no social intermingling. Nearly everyone shunned Annie's friend Lee-Ann, who was dating a Black boy. Before getting to South Africa we wondered if our daughter, Egyptian by birth, might experience racial prejudice.

Annie only reported a couple of incidents. One girl told her flat out, "I can't be your friend since you're not white." A boy asked, "Are you Black? It doesn't matter, I just need to know."

"I'm Egyptian," she answered. "You decide."

Recently she told me, "I didn't want to be his friend if the only reason he would talk to me was because he thought I was white enough. He was really obsessed about it, and just wanted me to give him the okay. At the time, it really showed me racism is taught, not born."

Annie didn't like being late or missing a day, and rarely did either. One day in March, at a stoplight on the way to school, the Escort quit running. A police car happened by and the patrolman, probably thinking I'd want him to call a tow truck or at least a mechanic, asked if he could help.

"Yes, please! Can you take my daughter to school?"

Annie claims to have been mortified by being dropped off by a police car. Robb and I had gotten our first-ever cell phones, so I managed to get rescued.

***

Our student had always done well in school. Therefore, when the first grades came out her father and I were startled to see that her highest grade was a 72 percent in math. When I met with her teachers, I learned 40 percent constituted a passing grade, and that 80 percent was the equivalent of an A. The generous scale was used nationwide to bring the educationally challenged into the mainstream. Class grades for the subjects she took averaged 50 percent. Nevertheless, we insisted on two hours of study each day during spring break to bring up her grades.

Annie's Technical Drawing teacher told me the class had no textbook, and most of the students had already taken at least a year of the subject. Not one book on the discipline existed in the school library, the public library, or either of the two bookstores in town. She was determined to take the class because she wanted to learn how to design a house. Although she failed the class, the teacher gave her an A for effort, and offered to tutor her. Once a week Annie went in for an hour after school.

Pleased overall with Annie's work, the English teacher wanted to enter a subtly anti-apartheid poem of hers in the annual Alan Paton Award for Non-fiction. Our daughter, the budding poet, didn't want her work submitted without a copyright. Even though the teacher provided information on how to apply for one, Annie never followed through, and I grew tired of nagging. She didn't enter the poem, and now doesn't remember anything about it.

Alan Paton, I found out later, was a lifelong anti-apartheid activist, a poet, and the author of a favorite book of mine, *Cry the Beloved Country*. If I'd known how prestigious even entering the competition was, I'd have encouraged and helped my daughter, who had other things on her young mind.

Second-term grades showed improvement in three classes, down in one, and failure again in Technical Drawing. She said she'd fallen off on tutoring, but planned to renew her efforts. She asked me to buy study guides for Business Economics and Physical Science. The English teacher rated Annie "the most improved pupil in the class, in attitude, application, participation, and grades." She said Annie had even brought a couple of other students up with her.

For Business Economics, students had to start a business. Knowing how to macramé friendship bracelets, Annie decided to make and sell them for her project. A kindly woman in Dorothy & Fay's, a little shop near us, didn't charge her any commission for leaving a display board of bracelets there. The enterprise could have been a way to make some spending money; a bracelet sold for about $1.50. But each one took two hours to make, and, as friendship bracelets weren't known in Richards Bay, they didn't sell well.

Mid-November brought finals and the end of the school year. A note from the school stated the pupils did not have to attend school for two weeks on the days they didn't write examinations. The note went on to say the concessions were made to enable the students to study and not to "galavant" in town or on the beach. The third and final term she did extremely well, improving in everything, and not only passed, but received a B in Technical Drawing. Thus, she completed her first full year of school since the second grade.

***

Activities for young people in Richards Bay were scarce. After-school programs consisted mainly of sports. Annie tried a little basketball, but didn't want to do anything athletic, not even swimming, though she was an excellent swimmer. There was no one to rollerblade with.

She joined choir, and from the choir teacher took piano lessons at school, where she was allowed to practice as well. Once a week she had a one-hour computer class with Future Kids, a business that taught word-processing, databases, graphics, CompuServe, and the Internet. Annie and a friend went once to volunteer at the SPCA, but she didn't want to go back.

She had lots of overnights, movies, and other activities with several girls from school: Goretti, Mandy, Joannie, Jodie, Lee-Ann, and Lucinda. Except for Goretti and Mandy, they didn't really click. Annie's best friend, the delightful fourteen-year-old Afrikaner Vivienne, lived on a boat at the marina with her conservative family. They homeschooled their children and had them work full-time at their two businesses, a shooting range and a Chinese take-out restaurant. In spite of those constraints, the girls managed to spend quite a bit of time with each other.

Annie's social life revolved around the Game Center at the marina. When the bowling alley's automatic pin re-setting machine jammed, she and her friends set up the pins as people were playing. The kids didn't get paid, but they got a kick out of doing something out of the ordinary. She occasionally deigned to play a game of pool, ten pins, or laser tag; however, the main purpose was to meet and hang out with other kids.

***

Many of our visits to the dentist involved having a retainer made, and routinely repaired, for Annie's teeth. One day, forgetting she'd put the appliance in her lap, she stepped out of the car and the retainer fell into a dry, litter-filled storm gutter at a shopping center. I asked for help at a nearby government office. Within minutes, a Black fellow showed up with a crowbar, pried up the heavy metal grate, then walked away.

The gutter was too deep for me to reach the retainer. As I was about to get down into the hole, a dignified young Zulu man stepped out of the crowd, and said, "I will get it for you."

He did, and I thanked him with a ten-rand note. When we arrived at Annie's computer class and told Mr. Carraso what had just happened, he took the device to be sterilized at the hospital where his wife worked.

The racial prejudice Annie witnessed outraged and saddened her. One evening she'd been invited to have dinner with a friend's family. After the long meal, a man complained he still had to drive his worker home. People laughed as they realized the Black man, not being allowed in the cab of the pickup, had been left for two or three hours on the hard flatbed with nothing to eat after an entire day's labor.

Another time she and I were in line behind a Zulu man buying lunch, only a few things, but too much to easily carry, and he asked for a paper sack. "No. You don't need one," snapped the clerk as she turned to help us. We too had only a few things, but she automatically handed a bag to each of us. We had to continually remind ourselves we didn't have to look too far back into our own country's history to find similar behavior.

How I Got the Mother of the Year Award

When we were in Australia, Annie had heard Michael Jackson was going to perform in South Africa during the time we planned to be there. She begged to go see him. At the time, the event was a long way off, and we'd be on the east coast of a really big country, but I said I'd take her if we possibly could.

As it happened, Jackson was to appear down the coast in Durban the week before Annie's fourteenth birthday. Many Afrikaners, including Viv's family, wouldn't go to Durban, even in the daytime, because they considered the big city too dangerous.

Robb had no interest in going, but our young friends, Jim and Shannon on *Reefer,* were taking their boat there anyway, and were keen to see the concert. Since the show would last until 10:30 p.m., they invited Annie and me to stay the night. Even though the event was midweek and Annie hated missing school, she was more than willing to make a two-day exception for her heartthrob.

The entire way to Durban we drove on the left side of the highway, through heavy rain, with windshield wipers that helped only halfheartedly when they worked at all.

"We literally couldn't see forward for periods of time," Annie remembers, "but Mom was a badass and didn't even hesitate."

The road signs didn't always match up with the map and written directions we had, but luck and a few educated guesses delivered us straight to the marina. That evening Jim and Shannon took Annie and drove our car to the concert, while I stayed with their two toddlers, Savana and Marina. The entertainer lived up to all expectations. The next day Annie and I took care of some business in Durban then drove in sunshine all the way home.

***

For Annie's birthday the following week, I cut out a photo of Michael standing with outspread arms and made a miniature "Happy Birthday, Annie!" banner to go between his hands. The construction was held up by two bamboo skewers; one end of each skewer was taped to a hand, and the other end stuck into a cake. We had a few small, wrapped gifts for her. But the big gift had been attending her first ever concert and the experience of a lifetime: seeing Michael Jackson in person.

Mildred

On weekday mornings, after dropping Robb off at work, a yachtie neighbor at her job, and Annie at school, I gave rides to Zulu women walking along the road. A few were on their way to a job. But the majority, young and old alike, asked as soon as the car door closed, "Do you have any work?" I didn't, but they were always grateful for the ride, and many bestowed a "God bless you" as they got out.

Mildred, my dear Zulu friend

That's how I became special friends with Mildred, a Zulu woman in her fifties. Like most Richards Bay Black ladies in her age group, she was sturdily built, wore ankle-length flowery housedresses, and tied a turban around her head. Every day of the year she got up at 4 in the morning to go to work. After I'd learned about her religious side, I asked if she went to church on Sunday. "Oh, I almost never get to go."

Mildred's feet hurt her a lot, and of course it was no wonder, she walked for miles in worn-out flats. Sometimes she caught a bus part way, but it didn't always come. And when the fare went up by five cents, she stopped riding altogether. She felt she couldn't afford it on the $120 a month, about $4 a day, she earned cleaning offices and restrooms at the mall near our marina.

Whenever I mentioned her pitiful salary to an Afrikaner, they'd pause, then confirm that was about right. Once I drove her to her home in a little settlement way out of town. She didn't invite me in, but showed me where she cooked the meals outside, and told how going out in the dark frightened her because a leopard prowled the neighborhood. Considering the shabby homes they stepped out of, the cleanliness and good grooming of the Zulu people was impressive.

Even on the weekends I picked up Mildred if I saw her. Knowing what time she usually started walking the two miles from the main road to the harbor, I sometimes pulled over on the grass near the top of the road until she came. One day while waiting, I'd already picked up a friend of hers, a large Black policeman in his uniform with a badge. Unless Mildred had pre-approved him, I never gave a ride to a man.

Peter, who'd sold us the car, was driving by and pulled over to check on me. Putting his hands on the driver's side window sill, he leaned down, and eyeing my passenger in the back seat, asked me, "Are you okay?"

"Oh, yes. This man is a friend of my friend, Mildred. We're waiting for her so I can give her a ride to the marina. She works there."

Satisfied enough I wasn't being held hostage, he drove off. The next time Peter saw me though, he gave me an earful on the dangers of giving rides to Blacks. The advice was not without foundation. On the other hand, our own experience told us the majority of the traditionally-Christian Afrikaners were blatantly prejudiced. Mildred said they had no heart. "Are you a Christian?" she asked me one day.

"Oh, not exactly," I hedged, little expecting the grand compliment that followed.

"You're nicer than most Christians I know."

Nelson Mandela

In 1994, two years before we arrived, Mandela had been inaugurated as president. Sadly, most Black people I spoke with thought Mandela was a good man, but that he wasn't doing enough, and was, in fact, responsible for the rising crime rate. For one thing, he had failed to solve South Africa's land ownership inequality as promised, and many Blacks were angry.

We thought the unrest might get worse before it got better. At the time though, the country seemed stable, and we didn't feel threatened. In any case, traveling by boat, we always knew we could leave a place fairly easily, unlike people wanting or needing to escape by plane, vehicle, or their own two feet.

At the library a poster advised how and where to apply if you had committed or been the victim of a political crime – including rape, torture or murder – during the previous violent and repressive white rule. The Truth and Reconciliation Commission had the power to offer amnesty and reparations to qualifying individuals.

In addition to posters around town, announcements about the Commission came over the radio. I heard a broadcast of a white policeman who'd murdered Blacks in a township a few years before. He'd gone back to speak to the families, to ask their forgiveness. Hearing him talk and the people's responses reduced me to tears. He sounded sincere, but who knows? Some individuals, saying they had to move on with their lives, forgave him. Others declared they could never forgive, what he had done was too horrible.

Two similar, but unrelated incidents were our biggest scares. The first occurred one night after we were asleep. The sound of floorboards creaking in the main cabin, a matter of steps away from our bed, woke me up. Annie was staying overnight with a friend, so I was pretty sure it wasn't her. The steps got closer. Peering into the darkness, I saw what looked like the shape of a person right next to our bed.

Alarmed, but still hoping it was my imagination, I touched Robb enough to wake him, and told him in a calm, low voice that someone might be in the boat. Springing out of bed, he nearly bumped into a dark-skinned Indian man who just stood there.

"What the hell are you doing here?" Robb shouted.

"Jus' havin' a look."

"Get the hell off our boat!!!" Robb stepped toward the man, forcing him to back up.

"I'm jus' havin' a look."

"Get! Out! Now!" Robb screamed in his face.

"Could'ja please show me how to get outta here?"

Robb said he almost laughed, but the adrenaline was still pumping, and he kept marching the fellow off the boat.

A few months later, Robb and I were reading in bed with the hatch above slid wide to the warm, starry night. Suddenly the faces of two white men appeared in the opening. They stared with curiosity, as if we were animals in a zoo. Yelling obscenities and imperatives, with me right behind him, Robb charged up on deck like a raging bull. He rushed at the men as if to push them into the water. They stepped back, but held their ground with the now-familiar defense, "We're just havin' a look."

It was clear they were drunk like the previous intruder and, like him, didn't have a clue why we were so angry.

"This! Is! Our! Home!" Robb screamed.

"What if we came up to your house and looked in the window?" I demanded.

The exchange continued, us shouting, them explaining, until one man, the argument having sobered him a little, asked, "Is there anything we can do to make this right? We have a plane and could fly you to our property up north ...."

Well, that might be interesting, went through my mind. But Robb overrode my thoughts. "Just. Get off. This boat."

⚓

Transmission parts Robb had ordered from Germany arrived with a shop manual written in, of all things, German. Kicki, a Scandinavian gal on *Wanderer III*, side-tied to us, helped Robb and Phil by using what German she knew to provide literal translations of the words. Sometimes the men had to translate the translation. For example, "forehead of the shaft" puzzled her, but Phil understood the phrase to mean the front of the shaft.

Phil had projects on his own boat, but when he started working on *Sorcery*, he dropped everything else and finished in a couple of days. The transmission worked flawlessly. Since he wouldn't accept any money, we took the family out to dinner. We always gave them rides, and even loaned them the car.

***

By the time our new computer and printer arrived in February, my life felt too full to consider writing free-lance articles for the local newspaper. Of course, that was the same month we also became the proud owners of a new video cassette player and television. We didn't get TV reception, but used the TV and VCR to watch legions of movies. My mom sent episodes of *M.A.S.H.*, which she knew we loved, and other shows, particularly for Annie.

A local store offered an irresistible rental deal of four videos per week for 24 rand, about $5. The public library also had excellent tapes, but they could only be checked out for two days at a time. We particularly appreciated the many fiction and non-fiction films about South Africa's history and politics, including the exciting 1964 classic *Zulu* with Michael Caine. We watched an abundance of films depicting anti-apartheid themes and lives of activists. The availability of such films surprised and pleased us.

The Animals

Many fascinating animal shows were filmed in nearby Kruger National Park. People warned us Kruger was overcrowded with tourists and suggested we visit smaller game reserves, of which there were literally dozens in KwaZulu-Natal alone. Once we settled in, whenever work and school permitted, we headed to a game park. Often Annie's friend, Viv, came along – fun for all of us.

In town, just off the main road, the Croc Rock Café connected to a sanctuary. An elevated walkway meandered through a natural swamp loaded with crocs. Outside of town, we routinely visited Richards Bay Game Reserve. We did see a few animals there, but mostly we looked forward to a pleasant walk while hearing and seeing evidence of wildlife. A splash in the river meant a croc had slithered in. A wide circle of flattened-out tall grass showed the recent resting place of a hippo.

We visited the small, family-owned Return the Cheetahs to the Wild Project, only a day trip away. Rarely seen in the wild, three of the world's fastest land animals, 0-60 mph in four seconds, came right up to the fence. A tame zebra moseyed around, allowing us to pet him. Especially up close, the African animals were so far outside of our usual frame of reference, they hardly seemed real. They were too big, too colorful, their shapes too unlikely.

Speaking of zebras, Quay Walk Travel had a magnificent zebra rug for sale. The agency owner assured me the skin was from an old stallion that had died of natural causes on the farm of a family she knew. Assuming that to be true, the logic of not wasting the skin seemed obvious, and to my husband's and daughter's horror, I wanted to buy it. In the end, I didn't think I could carry off explaining a zebra skin rug to my liberal friends, or probably even rationalize it to myself once we left Africa.

Lasik Surgery

Cruisers were getting Lasik eye surgery in South Africa because the cost was close to half of the going price in the States. In spite of the reports of successful operations, Robb expressed concern. But I trusted the doctors, using the flimsy reasoning that if a South African surgeon had performed the first heart transplant in the world, how bad could the medical system be?

An ophthalmologist in Richards Bay determined me to be a good candidate. He could do the measurements and "mapping" in town, but for the procedure, I'd have to meet him in Durban at a hospital where the Lasik machine was. When the time came, March 15, we asked Viv to come along. She wanted to, but her parents wouldn't allow her to go into such dangerous, crime-ridden territory, even though we'd be there in the daytime, and swore she'd never be out of Robb's sight.

After my surgery, with a little metallic sieve taped over each eye, we proceeded to a nice restaurant for lunch. A couple of days later, when the protectors came off, my legally-blind-in-California eyes had perfect distance vision. The joy of being able to see unaided after all those decades, and the convenience of not having to deal with contacts and glasses can only be fully appreciated by those who've had the experience. Robb momentarily considered the procedure, but I think even the bargain total price of $2,000 for both eyes, not to mention the words "eye surgery," put him off.

Dung Beetles have the Right of Way

An hour and a half drive out of Richards Bay brought us to a medium-sized game park and a bonanza of wildlife. We sighted nine different animals, including rhinos with babies, warthogs with babies, baboon families, herds of Cape buffalo, zebra, impala, and, my personal favorites, two comical dung beetles rolling a 4-inch ball of elephant poop across the road. I got down on my elbows and knees in the dirt to try to take the perfect photograph of the fast-moving couple.

"Dianne! Get back in this car before a lion gets you!" Robb demanded more than once.

Ultimately, I gave up, but I do have a fine photo from a magazine. Besides helping to keep roads clear and depriving flies and parasites of a place to lay eggs, we learned these beetles play a remarkable role in agriculture. By consuming and burying manure, they aerate the soil and recycle nutrients. Road signs tell you, "Dung beetles have right of way. Please do not drive over dung beetles or elephant dung."

Overnight in a Tree House

In early April, Quay Walk Travel booked us for our first overnight, and an A-No.1 adventure: a stay in a treehouse at Bonamanzi, a small, private game park. Viv's parents had agreed to let her go; then two hours before time to leave, they told us she couldn't go after all because they found out she'd been smoking and was grounded for the weekend.

Our negotiating skills kicked into high gear. "We understand. We don't smoke. We don't allow our daughter to smoke. But we've already paid for the night at the treehouse. We'll keep a close eye on Viv and make sure she doesn't smoke during the trip." And finally, "Annie will be heartbroken if Viv can't go." They caved.

Arriving at noon, we checked in at the park office before driving the short way to our tree. This was not a resort. We brought all our own food. No other people, or even other tree houses, were in evidence. Honoring our commitment to not let Viv out of our sight didn't work out. To the girls' delight, our accommodations for the night were two humble cabins, one story up a steep flight of stairs in a gigantic tree. Robb used a length of line to tie onto our bags to haul them up over a balcony.

After a quick bite to eat we set off on foot to explore. In the bigger game parks people weren't usually allowed to walk around unless they'd hired an armed guide. But this was not an enclosed park, where there would likely be a greater concentration of animals. Bonamanzi had recently removed its northern fence in the hope of attracting elephants. Strolling through the still air, inhaling the bouquet of warm scents from the grasses and earth, we saw in the distance, like a painting, a few impala, wildebeests, and ostrich.

Back at the cabins, I prepared an early dinner in the tiny semi-enclosed kitchen at the base of the tree. A small patio with a table and four chairs connected the two cabins. As we lost the light, we switched on the bare lightbulb dangling over the table and played cards and Parcheesi in the quiet balmy evening.

"You know what would be great?" Annie asked after a while. "Hot chocolate!"

The three of them looked at me.

"Okay, okay, I'll go," I said, pushing my chair back. As I started down the stairs with my flashlight, loud rustling told us fair-sized animals were scattering back into the trees.

If the girls smoked, they didn't burn the cabin down. On our morning walk we found fresh leopard prints on the dirt trail. Farther on, we came upon the bloody carcass of what was left of a small antelope. Reporting the carnage when we checked out, we were told a big cat had probably made the kill in the night, had his or her fill, and gone off to sleep. The hyenas had not yet moved in to finish off the remains.

"What's the purpose of the leaf rake propped against our tree?" I asked.

"Oh, if you rake all the sand under the tree at the end of the day, in the morning you can see by the prints which animals came by."

You couldn't have told us that yesterday? If it hadn't been for school and work the next day, I'd have lobbied to stay another night, just so we could rake. As we drove out of the park, I reached into a backpack and out hopped one of the little miniature frogs that had kept me company in the kitchen. We left her by the side of the road and hoped she could find her way back.

⚓

This, from a letter home, tells where our heads were at the end of April:

Our plan is still to stay until early December when school's out, spend Christmas in Cape Town, then head for the Caribbean, and home. It will have been six years since we left. Hopefully, we'll like the East Coast, and Annie can finish high school there. If not, we go to the yet-unformed Plan B. One idea would be to sell the boat, buy a camper, and drive across the country. Another plan would be to sail through the Panama Canal to San Diego. Meanwhile, I'm making all those hot buttered rums and mulled wines we didn't have when we were sweltering last Christmas.

Before getting to South Africa, I had no idea how much we'd love the animals. Once there, we could hardly get enough of seeing them in the wild, even if the wild was actually a really, really big enclosure.

A Forest of Gray Wrinkled Knees

"Where can we find the elephants?" we asked at the guard station as we pulled into Hluhluwe (Shloo <u>shloo</u> ee) Umfolozi Game Reserve, the oldest proclaimed natural reserve in Africa. "Up there!" The cheerful Black ranger pointed to the top of a ridge, where a line of elephants stood outlined against the sky.

As Robb inched the Escort along, I gave a running report, "They're coming down the hill ... Can't see them ... They're coming up toward the road!" We'd already stopped before the herd came into view.

"They're crossing the road!" I couldn't help stating the obvious as they began to lumber to the other side of the dirt road not more than 100 feet in front of us.

The girls squealed as maybe 20 females and youngsters of various ages, followed by the colossal adult male, stopped walking and turned their attention to us. Two females pawed tentatively at the dirt with their great round feet. A baby mimicked their movements, and a juvenile male took it upon himself to frighten us by trumpeting and flapping his big ears. The herd began easing toward us. We teared backing up, because we thought the maneuver might cause them to give chase.

"Don't anybody move," Robb said. "No photos. No talking." And after one last breath of his own, "No breathing."

The horde sauntered our way until a solid forest of gray wrinkled knees surrounded the car. We'd heard of terrifying elephant-car encounters: an elephant crushing the hood of a car with a powerful foot, a six-ton beast sitting on the hood of a car, or lying on top of it. I thought about how we would have failed our young charges who, even though teenagers, still trusted us to protect them.

Annie remembers one elephant, most likely the oldest female, inspecting us closely. As the matriarch, she decided we weren't a threat, and gave the troop the okay to move on. Annie gained an immediate and lasting respect for these intelligent, benevolent beasts. Two little ones, trailing behind and still curious, took a few steps our way, but were reined in by the trunk of one of the females standing rear guard. Within seconds, the entire procession dissolved into the thick foliage at the side of the road.

Driving to a lodge a little farther along, we rushed in to have a cool drink and congratulate ourselves on being alive. A man and woman came in and sat next to us. "We were in the car behind you and filmed the whole thing." They offered to mail a copy to our address in San Diego, but if they sent one, it never arrived. Anyway, the great and useful film would have been from inside our car. From the moment the elephants started toward us, I'd felt numbed by the horrific possibilities and wasn't truly present.

***

Poaching is an ongoing problem. The demand for animal parts remains high and the South African people poor. Two months before we were at Hluhluwe, a rhino had been killed near Mambeni Gate, the very entrance we had passed through. According to the newspaper, three teachers, a policeman, and a student prison warden were arrested for trying to sell the rhino's horn to undercover policemen.

Wild Animal Auction and More Game Parks

Known for its tiny eyes and poor sight, the rhinoceros lifted its massive head. We could see the nostrils quivering as the beast picked up our scent. In the blink of an eye, the animal charged, ramming its 20-inch horn through the space between two thick wooden bars of his cage, about 10 feet from where we stood. If we'd had the nerve, we could have stepped up and touched the deadly instrument. But witnessing the wild animal smelling us had been scary enough. All that angry weight barreling toward us at close range left us a little shaken and wary of getting any closer.

It was June, and we were back at Hluhluwe Game Reserve, this time to see the 2,000 animals on view prior to their auction in the nearby town of Mtubatuba (Muh tuba tuba). Robb hadn't been able to go, so Annie and I rode the 50 miles with Australians Rob and Robbie from *Bardoo*.

The black rhino that charged us was in a huge and sturdy wooden crate painted a blueish green, a stencil of a rhino on the side, bars on one end. Presumably, the other five black rhinos and 44 white rhinos to be auctioned were each in separate crates, but we didn't see them. The zebras, ostriches, giraffes, warthogs, various antelopes, and three types of wildebeests were each in game pens with their own kind. The terrified giraffes thundered together non-stop from one end of their enclosure to the other, while the other animals appeared to be more resigned.

We had to sign in to walk around and look at the caged creatures. And only licensed and authorized people, organizations, or countries were allowed to even apply, let alone bid in the auction. At that time South Africa wouldn't let Australia buy rhinos to start a park, but did sell them hundreds of thousands of dung beetles. Twenty years later, in 2016, South Africa agreed to sell 80 rhinos to Australia to help save the animals from poaching and the threat of extinction, possibly within the next 10 years. Seeing the auction would have been fascinating, but for some reason we couldn't manage to get to Mtubatuba that day.

On the way home, we stopped at a display of handmade items for sale under the trees by the side of the road. Sparkling in the light, dozens and dozens of long, beaded necklaces dangled from lines strung between branches. Scores of masks, bowls, small tables, drums, and figurines, mostly of animals, were spread out or stacked on mats.

The most striking baskets were woven from brightly-colored, copper-core telephone wire stolen from telephone lines. Not wanting to support actions undermining the country's infrastructure, we didn't buy any of those baskets. The telephone wire beauties have become quite famous, and expensive. Websites claim that stolen wire is a thing of the past, and an annealed steel-core wire that "looks just like telephone wire" is now manufactured specifically for basket making. Baskets made for an organization may use purchased components, but I suspect wire for baskets made and sold by individuals in far-flung villages is still of the "recycled" kind.

⚓

The following month, Viv came with us for several days to stay in two different reserves. The first, Ithala Game Park, 160 miles northwest of Richards Bay, claimed to have four of the Big Five: the African elephant, Cape buffalo, African leopard, and white and black rhinoceros. Incidentally, the term Big Five refers to the degree of danger involved in hunting the animals, not their size. Because Ithala lacked African lions, the fifth of the Big Five, all the animals at the park, including humans, felt safer.

On our hikes we took in gorgeous panoramic views from high ridges over deep valleys, but saw no animals other than silly-looking warthogs. I don't remember being disappointed in not seeing more animals. Just being in those settings was intoxicating, and for two nights we stayed in comfortable cottages with bathtubs and fireplaces. Annie and Viv had their own cottage, included in the price of ours.

***

Leaving Ithala, we zigzagged 150 miles north to the Kingdom of Swaziland, a tiny independent country within South Africa. From time to time, a family compound – made up of a four or five round huts and square sheds, a corral, a handful of goats, and a tree or two – appeared in the middle of nowhere. By the side of the road a woman offered a few souvenirs for sale. I bought a handsome straw tote bag that's held up beautifully over the years.

***

In Swaziland, we stayed three nights at the Mlilwane Wildlife Sanctuary in a private lodge. I say lodge because lots of wood and stone figured in the inside and outside construction, and, at least by boat standards, all the rooms were huge. Antlers held up the ends of the curtain rods. A picture window in the master bedroom overlooked a valley.

In the morning, two ostriches came to peer at Annie and Viv through the screen on the porch where they slept. Besides those big birds, a tall heron, a dozen warthogs, and several small antelope had the run of the camp. A gigantic pile of fluffy feathers turned out to be a male ostrich sitting close to, but not on, four enormous eggs. Apparently, the female took over at night.

From horseback we saw great herds of zebra and wildebeest. An open Land Rover took us to the top of a mountain at sunset. Every night a central campfire provided a meeting place for guests, who sat around the fire on a ring of logs. On two evenings, locals in traditional Swazi costumes danced and chanted by firelight.

Warthogs nuzzled in the dirt as close to the fire and the people as they could without being swatted away. If you let them get too close, the friendly, shaggy things would drool on your clothing. In the morning, as

I walked by the still-warm remains of the fire, there sat a warthog on his rump, incredulously, upright on a log, just as he'd seen people do.

At the camp restaurant, the adults' favorite dishes were wildebeest sausage seasoned with clove, warthog chops just to say we did, and *phuto*, a stiff corn meal mush we ate with our fingers. French fries and a little salad satisfied the girls. The restaurant overlooked a hippo pool, where huge, smooth gray boulders around the edge became hippos sleeping in the sun. At 3 every afternoon, about 20 feet from where we watched from behind a low retaining wall, a man with a bucket of grain lured a shiny, wet hippopotamus the size of a Volkswagen Beetle out of the water. Fearless chickens and a couple of warthogs stole as much grain as they could, flapping and scampering just out of the way as the enormous hippo jaws snapped at them.

Warthog looking for a snack

So busy at Mlilwane that we never drove anywhere, we decided to stay another night. Our little lodge was already booked, but they found room for us in traditional, domed beehive huts. From the outside, the straw huts appeared authentic and sparse. Stooping practically in half to enter the low front door, we found the inside to be clean, modern as any motel room, and cozy with plump feather pillows and comforters. Again, the girls had their own hut. Staying off the boat was always a treat, and the uniqueness of our vacation dwellings enthralled us.

Annie and Viv at the short entrance to their hut.

The fearsome visage for sale in the gift shop looked to me like something you'd see in a museum. Crudely carved from dark wood, the mask, twice the length of a human face, sported a scraggly beard of coconut fibers and two human-looking, but oversized, real teeth, perhaps from a donkey. Later in the day, actually my birthday, Robb surprised me with the mask.

Annie bought me a tiger eye necklace I'd admired, and Viv gave me a handy set of coasters with pictures of elephants. For myself I bought a witch doctor's fortune-telling kit, real bones and stones, with instructions. The girls, eager to learn about their future love lives, let me practice on them. Back in Richards Bay, Robb took the mask to a dealer who told him she was certain the item was authentic, not made for tourists. The one thing I regret not buying was a knife with a warthog tusk handle. At the time, $50 seemed way too expensive. Now I'd have to pay around $300 to get one on the Internet.

Under the Knife

After our vacation, I made an appointment with a doctor to renew my prescription for hormone replacement therapy (HRT). An ultrasound, routine there for HRT, revealed a 2½-inch mass on my left ovary. Although possibly only fluid buildup, the doctor recommended the node be removed. Everything about the doctor and the clinic seemed just like home, so I had no qualms about going along with his recommendation.

Under general anesthetic, he performed laparoscopy. Two small incisions in my abdomen left the entire area black, blue, and exquisitely tender. After a night in the hospital, I spent a few days at home on the main salon cushions because climbing up onto our bed was too painful. Robb tied a rope from the salon's overhead handhold so I could pull myself up. After several days the pain went away, and after a few weeks, the bruising.

Some people have questioned my foolhardiness for doing that in South Africa. But recently, a friend told me when she'd traveled and worked in Kenya and other African countries in the '80s and '90s, she was always warned to never go to a local hospital, but to get to South Africa if she possibly could.

Here Come the Elephants! Here Come the Elephants!

Even without Vivienne, our next excursion, four days at Hlane (Huh lah nee) Royal National Park in Swaziland, was almost too much fun.

At the first camp, Ndlovu (N'dloh voo), two female ostriches, as tall as we were, welcomed us as we got out of the car. Then, with an air of familiarity, one sashayed directly toward me.

Dianne? Is that really you? I can't believe my eyes!

When her avian lips came to within a foot of my mouth, I shouted, *sotto voce*, at Robb, "Take the picture! Take the picture!"

She had long, long eyelashes, and huge, dark eyes. At 2 inches in diameter, ostrich orbs are the largest of any land animal. Later I learned the curious birds sometimes like to have a close up look at things. Not knowing at the time it was a routine inspection, I was a little nervous that her intention was to peck at me, but I didn't want to move until the close encounter was recorded.

***

Our little lodge was within a 100 yards of a watering hole where we'd be able to observe blue herons, rhinos, giraffes, antelopes, and elephants as they came to drink. Shortly after we arrived, a mama rhino and her baby grazed just a stone's throw from us. Only two skimpy strands of barbed wire separated us from the rhinos, or any other critters that might wander by.

At dusk, we'd just about given up on seeing the animals at the watering hole, when I spied a small herd of pachyderms emerge from the bush and plod to the water's edge. Sounding every bit the circus barker, I announced, "Here come the elephants! Here come the elephants!"

All the other animals came too, but the elephants, being so big and active – wading, splashing, drinking – dominated the show. We'd never witnessed anything quite like it. Such scenes added to my shrinking sympathy for zoos. I'd always appreciated being able to see wild animals up close, but had given no real thought to the animals' loss of freedom.

As the evening settled in, we lit lanterns and candles for light because the cabin had no electricity. That single lack allowed us to feel like we were roughing it in a bush camp.

***

Early the next morning we hired a guide, and he joined us in our car on the Big Cat Tour. He didn't carry a gun like I'd hoped, but of course we were in the car virtually the entire time. No sooner had we driven through locked gates than we saw the king of beasts and his big family lounging in tall grass not 30 feet from the road.

"You don't want to do that," the guide advised Robb, who'd started rolling down the window to take a photo. "See that juvenile creeping up on us?" The young stalker continued to prowl after the car each time we moved a bit forward.

Barely recovered from that thrill, we came upon more big cats: three cheetahs, about 50 feet off the road, eating away at a large antelope they'd just killed. By walking up to within a few feet of them, the guide demonstrated that feeding cheetahs had no interest in humans. He said it was okay for Robb to get out on the opposite side of the car to take a quick photo. We'd have missed seeing the third type of big cat, two magnificent resting leopards, if our escort hadn't pointed them out.

After two nights at the rustic camp, we stayed two more at Bhubesi, the modern one with electricity. On the map, the distance between the two camps was less than nine miles. However, the drive took over an hour because the roads were poor, and we stopped to watch two boldly marked, hinge-back tortoises lollygagging across the road.

Cheetahs with antelope dinner

Bhubesi camp consisted of three cabins, each the size of a small house, all overlooking the river, and all locked. Annie was feeling poorly, so I left her and Robb with the luggage and headed back to the office. By the time I got there, they'd figured out we needed a key and had sent someone to let us in.

In a letter home I explained that by going outside the park, I'd found a shorter way back. These days I can't imagine doing that. If anything had gone wrong – a locked gate, getting lost, running into an animal, a flat tire – I'd have had no way to contact anyone. And if it had grown late, Robb did not even have a phone to tell people to look for me along the path we'd come. Anyway, the Sea Goddess seemed to watch over me even on land. That night Annie had a fever, but no other symptoms. After a 12-hour sleep, the fever vanished. She said she felt fine, and was ready for the next adventure.

***

We drove to Mkhaya Game Reserve south of Hlane for an all-day tour in an open Land Rover. They claimed to get you closer to the animals than anywhere else. It must have been true because we came within a few yards of elephants, rhinos, and giraffes. As two bull elephants sparred with entangled tusks and trunks a mere 50 feet in front of us, one of them backed up against a small tree and snapped it like a twig. The guide walked us to within 15 feet of a rhino mother and her calf enjoying a mud puddle.

Close enough!

From the vehicle we saw plenty of hippos and a few lethal-looking Cape buffalo. Elegant little impalas, a type of antelope that grows only about 3 feet high, watched us as we drove by. From time to time, a small herd of them sped along, leaping as high as 10 feet and as far as 30, racing to or from something only they knew about. Giraffes, taller by far than any we'd ever seen in a zoo, ambled along, munching on leaves high up in the trees.

***

Lunch that day was an outdoor braai of wildebeest sausage, warthog chops, heaps of fresh salads, bread hot out of the oven, and fruit salad with cream. "Braai" literally means "barbecue" in Afrikaans, and in South African culture it's more than just a cooking style, it's about the coming together of the community.

The next morning, before heading home, we went on the Big Cat Tour again, seeing a large pride of lions: a male with his harem and a profusion of offspring. At lunchtime we stopped at a Portuguese restaurant which served the best food Robb and I'd had since arriving in Africa: a seafood curry and baked fish in mushroom sauce. Annie was happy with a burger and fries.

Nothing like a mud bath with your baby

My Afrikaner Friend

In addition to Mildred, I had one other local friend, Lorraine, an Afrikaner. We met through an ad I'd put in the *Zululand Observer* asking anyone interested in an overeaters support group to call me on my pay-as-you-go cell phone. Even though I've never weighed more than 20 pounds more than I do now, I'd fretted about my weight since college.

Before we left San Diego, I'd gone to a few Overeaters Anonymous (OA) Twelve Step meetings and felt right at home. Lorraine had never heard of the Twelve Step program, and I didn't know much about it myself, but she grasped the concept immediately. That very day we were on the road to establishing weekly OA meetings that ran from mid-July to mid-December. She recruited a number of women who eagerly joined the group.

An International OA Conference was coming to Johannesburg in October. Lorraine and I both wanted to go, though she was quite anxious as she'd never been out of Richards Bay. But we could stay with her daughter and son-in-law in Jo'burg, and that added a measure of comfort and safety for us both. During the course of our 300-mile bus ride, she told me, matter-of-factly, that until Mandela had taken over, and Black sitcoms started appearing on TV, "I didn't know they could love each other the way we do."

Knots of families, couples, and swarms of nicely dressed individuals milled around the cavernous, clean and modern bus station. Reflecting the makeup of the country, the overwhelmingly majority, easily 90 percent was Black. Visibly nervous until her daughter's husband came, Lorraine said she'd been afraid with all the Black people there. On the drive to the house we talked about safety in the city.

"Nothing to worry about," the son-in-law said, patting the glove box, "I've got a gun right here."

Lorraine's daughter, a small gracious woman in beige satin lounging pajamas, welcomed us with a glass of wine, delicious warm soup, and a loaf of fresh bread. As we settled in for the night, she told us not to walk past a certain line in the house because an alarm would summon the police.

At the packed, virtually all white OA conference, which lasted most of the day, an American woman currently living in Zimbabwe was the inspired speaker. Lorraine and I stayed another night at her daughter's before taking the bus home from our thoroughly satisfying weekend.

In December, before we left Richards Bay, the OA group had a going away tea for me at Lorraine's home. I was a little apprehensive that the South African part of the women would kick in and we'd have all kinds of cakes and goodies. But, no, we had hot or iced tea and cold, perfectly ripe sliced fruit served in china dishes. The beautifully set table held vases of flowers from the garden. The women gave me a lidded box covered with sunflower wrapping paper. The Love Box, as they called it, was packed with thoughtful things to help me on the voyage home: inspirational booklets and tapes, bookmarks, sweet-smelling soaps, a white washcloth tied with a pretty ribbon, and envelopes with cards from each woman with notes telling how much the program meant to them, and thanking me for bringing it to them.

Two Thanksgivings

On Thanksgiving, *Sorcery* marked her one year of being in South Africa by hosting a potluck with Kandis, Michael, and their two teenaged sons from *Potlatch*, a Swiss man, a French family, an American man, and an Afrikaner, Dr. Kruger, our local family doctor. Although we didn't socialize with him, the doctor was a friendly fellow and offered the use of his family's country house for a holiday. I'd love to have gone, but Robb was uncomfortable staying in anyone's home, especially if we barely knew the person.

As always, we had much to be grateful for: health, family and friends, perceived political and financial security, the opportunity for our six-year adventure. Then another blessing. Back in April we'd received a letter from Beth letting us know all was well. Daughter Daiva had arrived aboard *Windfall* on March 2. On Thanksgiving Day we heard on the radio that the family had stopped in Madagascar and would be in Richard's Bay in two days. When they came, we were so delighted to see our friends and meet their adorable eight-month-old baby, we arranged another Thanksgiving. Our two families prepared a turkey dinner with all the festive trimmings and racked up another holiday for the books.

⚓

December brought the rainy season, with some precipitation nearly every day. I have no idea why, but one dark evening I found myself driving alone during a heavy downpour. The landscape of Richards Bay featured great open spaces interspersed with industrial, commercial, or residential development.

At an isolated bus stop with no light and no shelter, a small huddle of Zulus, a man, a woman, and a young girl, all drenched and miserable looking, appeared in the headlights. I simply couldn't leave them there, and the one time I gave a ride to a man without Mildred's approval turned out okay. I lived to tell the story, and the people were so very grateful.

On a sunny day in the middle of December we enjoyed one last excursion to a local game park. Otherwise we busied ourselves preparing and provisioning for the 1,000 miles to Cape Town at the tip of South Africa, and after that, the 6,000 miles to the States. Unsure how convenient provisioning in Cape Town would be, we took advantage of having a car and bought several months' worth of non-perishables.

The grocery store at the marina started carrying Old El Paso Mexican food products, perfect for cruising: soft flour tortillas, taco shells, seasonings, sauces, canned green chilies, packets of rice and bean mix, refried beans. Excited to have Mexican food, I prepared chilaquiles for breakfast, and a few days later, a Mexican dinner for Peter and his wife, Judy. They'd had us over for a veritable feast: hors d'oeuvres, a huge pork loin, roast potatoes, four or five fresh salads and cooked vegetables, and a dessert of fruit salad with cream.

During that evening at Peter and Judy's, I could hardly take my eyes away from her diamond solitaire drop earrings. Of course, South Africa is known for its diamonds. *What an incredible souvenir that would be! Who knows? Maybe they're less expensive if you buy them here.*

My husband picked up my hint and surprised me at Christmas with the most lovely stud earrings, five emeralds with diamonds.

"Oh, they're fancy-schmancy!" Robb remembers me saying. "I just wanted fancy." He encouraged me to exchange them, but the Indian store where he'd bought them didn't carry just plain fancy.

***

Beth and Lee's daughter didn't appreciate Christmas per se, but we loved having Daiva around. She smiled, waved her chubby little arms at all the activity, squealed and produced other sounds of approval. Tearing the wrapping paper from her gifts, she revealed her inner kitten by having more interest in the crinkly paper than the gifts. Since we'd be back in the States by the next Christmas, I bequeathed to Mildred the fake tree that had served us so well the previous six years.

The last weekend before we left, Goretti and Mandy invited Annie for a going-away extravaganza featuring a slumber party, a movie, lunch at a restaurant, and a big Michael Jackson scrapbook they'd lovingly assembled.

Robb, of course, had his hands full readying the boat after its year-long respite. Many months before he'd sent the tiller pilot and remote control to Navico in the States for repair. When the units came back in early December, he had to fax Navico:

The remote control is worse than when we sent it. We are
returning it to you. Please repair and hold it until we notify you
of a location to which to send it. We must get underway. As
we have already invested nearly $400 in freight, the least you
can do is repair and return it to us free of additional charges.
This has put us at some hardship at sailing down the infamous
African East Coast.

Apparently, the fax hit a sympathetic ear, because in the nick of
time we received what looked to be a brand new remote.

From the sail locker Robb hauled the voluminous mainsail through
the hatch and then fit the heavy canvas onto the boom and mast. The
main had been sent for repair to Doyle Sails in Durban a year earlier,
shortly after we'd arrived. They'd returned it in the spring, but after
checking it, Robb discovered they'd neglected to stitch down the biggest
patch, and the sail had to be sent back. A couple of months later we
received the repaired-again main, but the sail's troubled story had not
yet ended.

On New Year's Eve, almost ready to depart, we moved the boat to
another location at the wharf to make our exit easier. Beth and Lee
planned to leave at the same time, so *Windfall* side-tied to us, and we all
stayed up until midnight watching the fireworks.

Three days later, when Robb started the engine and *Sorcery* finally
headed out to sea, Annie sobbed uncontrollably. She wrote to her
grandma, "Richards Bay was the hardest parting I've ever had to deal
with, especially with Vivienne. But there is a happy side to the situation
– I'm going home – going to see you."

I wept for gentle Mildred, of whom I'd become so fond. Thinking
about her hard life pained me, and I didn't want to leave her behind. In
a storeroom at the marina, we sat close together on a wooden bench to
say goodbye. I gave her $100. Her English didn't go much beyond
everyday conversation, but I did catch that someday we would meet "in
the wind."

Down the South African Coast
January to Mid March 1998

The South African east coast, also known as the Wild Coast, is as dangerous and tricky as its nickname implies. The strong south-flowing Agulhas current heads straight into sudden, frequent and strong storm fronts coming up from the Antarctic, thus creating huge, boat-shattering waves. In a museum, a map of South Africa indicated the places where every ship was known to have been lost for the last 100 years. The coastline was solid with black dots.

The trick for negotiating the trip safely was to head out on the tail end of a low, and hope to get to one of the few acceptable roadsteads before the next storm hit. In the 1,000-mile stretch between Richards Bay and Cape Town at the Cape of Good Hope, originally the Cape of Storms, only four, maybe five, towns offered safe harbor.

Captain Robb decided to avoid all that by tacking way out past the current, then tacking back in near Cape Town. However, on the first afternoon underway, he felt seasick. The tacking maneuver would have added many, many miles to the already lengthy passage, and he said he simply couldn't do a long non-stop trip. We chose not to go into the first port, Durban, because of recent crime reports at the marina. Instead, we made for East London, 335 miles away. We'd be hopping down the coast with all the other cruisers, and getting to see more of the country. Not a bad option for me.

Our passage took about a month, but only a week of that produced smooth-enough seas for sailing. The rest of the time *Sorcery* holed up in four different anchorages, and waited for the wind to slow down and come from the right direction. A dozen other cruising boats were doing the same thing. Besides having Daiva to fuss over, Annie got to go boogie boarding, hang out, and watch videos with four or five kids her own age from other boats.

While *Sorcery* was making her way down the South African coast, Alex was crewing on a yacht delivery that took 41 days from San Diego, through the Panama Canal, to Grenada in the Caribbean.

East London

Once inside the harbor, we tied onto a mammoth tire, 8 feet in diameter, hanging from the concrete wharf. *Windfall* side-tied to us. To reach the landing, our then-agile selves climbed up and over the tire. In the evenings, the yachtie crowd usually gathered for a potluck on the wharf. Once someone organized a chili cook-off, a fun and welcome change of fare.

The town offered a few things to do. In the natural history gallery of the museum, the preserved original coelacanth, a prehistoric fish that lived in the Indian Ocean for 400 million years, fascinated me. Years ago I'd seen one at the Scripps Aquarium in San Diego, but here was the body of the first living one ever found. Until that specimen got hooked on a fisherman's line right there in the East London harbor in 1938, the scientific community had thought the fish to be extinct. The museum also displayed an extended family of mannequins elaborately dressed in traditional African clothing, most of it covered with beautiful beadwork. A small zoo allowed us to hold baby animals.

Early on the morning we left East London, a row of eight or nine Black men sat near the boats with their legs dangling over the edge of the wharf.

"Do you have any food?" a man asked.

The amount of bread and cheese we gave them was so inadequate, yet they smiled and thanked us. Even then a part of me knew we'd almost certainly be able to get more bread and cheese at the next stop, but my cruiser's hoarding instinct had kicked in. Now I regret not being more generous.

The Mainsail Gives Up the Ghost

We'd been over a week at East London, and were finally able to head out to Port Elizabeth, 150 miles farther south. On a beautiful day, we left in a loose pack of boats engaging in a friendly race. Suddenly, *Sorcery's* 15-year-old, much-repaired mainsail started coming apart with a loud and alarming *pop-pop-popping* of the stitching at one of the upper seams. In a matter of seconds, the sail, held only by the part still attached along the boom, blew out and tumbled overboard. Without the sail to catch the wind, the boat slowed. Robb yelled, "Dianne! Take the wheel!"

He and Annie rushed to the starboard rail and started hauling the already-heavy material, now holding the additional weight of water, up over the lifelines onto the deck. A shark followed about 10 feet away, hoping for something of interest to eat in all the commotion. Once they'd secured the shredded sail to the deck, Robb hoisted a storm sail to take us the rest of the way. As if to soothe us, a whale the length of the boat surfaced close to us four times.

Port Elizabeth

Robb asked around at the yacht club and made phone calls to find the best place to have a new sail made in Cape Town. Even though we were nearing the end of our trip, and the cost estimate for a new sail was $3,380, the man entrusted with our lives wouldn't even consider going 6,000 miles without the essential mainsail.

He faxed our friend Sam Minervini, who looked after our financial affairs in San Diego. Our usual withdrawal amounted to only $200 cash every couple of weeks, and Sam would need to help us deal with the Bank of America when the suspiciously big charge from South Africa came through on our Visa.

The social highlight in Port Elizabeth was a Sports Afternoon organized by one of the yachts. All of us – from *Alegria, Chenoah, Comme un Cheval Fou, Flambouyant, Moony, Naomi, Odyssey, Potlach, Refrega, Schakles, Susan Bright, Tinker,* and *Windfall* – laughed ourselves silly engaging in a number of contests on the lawn of the yacht club.

Robb played the Farmer and I the Wheelbarrow in a race we lost the moment we started. Robb's job was easy, but my arms collapsed the second he pushed my legs forward. After that I focused on Guess the Number of Jelly Beans in the Jar, a contest I almost won, by the way. Robb also competed in Golf Putting, and coached, to everyone's amusement, the lovely Brazilian lady from *Refrega* on the proper way to hold a golf club.

A Three-legged Race, Hat Tossing, Egg Throwing & Catching, and Pin the Flipper on Something entertained us for hours. Even if there had been other contestants, Daiva would still have easily won the Beautiful Baby contest. Annie helped set up and run the games, but wouldn't participate until the whole crowd shouted for her to join in. All the hilarity and engaging in a completely different activity proved therapeutic for the fleet.

This town's museum complex featured a snake house, underwater marine viewing, a dolphin/seal show, and a regular museum, which held a surprising number of interesting historical items, including another wonderful costume exhibit with more African beading.

Addo Elephant Park

The best part of that stop, though, had to be our drive through Addo Elephant Park in a rental car with Beth, Lee and Daiva. At one point we drove over one of South Africa's famous tire-puncturing 6-inch thorns, and had to stop while the guys changed to the spare tire.

For a while we grumbled because we didn't see any elephants. But after one peeked over the top of some tall pink flowering shrubs, we began to see them everywhere. With a long lens, Annie photographed wrinkly pachyderm parts: a tail with stiff black hairs from which bracelets are made, a head shot, a mouth munching a leafy twig. Scores of the wonderful animals milled around a waterhole: bulls, juveniles, tiny babies, and affectionate females standing close, sometimes with their trunks intertwined or the ear of one lopping over the head of the other. Taking less than a minute out of their busy day, bull elephants mounted cows from behind and both lovers moved around a bit, until he succeeded or gave up – hard to tell which.

Like most parks, Addo had blinds: sheds with horizontal slits in the walls to view animals up close without being seen. We came to a substantial blind surrounded by a stockade and overlooking a watering hole. To gain entrance, we had to climb up a stile over the 20-foot-high fence. Inside the shed, benches on three sides allowed viewing through the slits while seated. No other tourists were there.

Since no animals were in sight, I rushed back to the car for the binoculars we'd forgotten. On my return, stopping at the top of the stile, I marveled at the forest, stretching to the horizon like a dark green sea. My eyes caught a movement, a lone elephant, looking massive even at that distance, lumbering along a barely visible trail toward the water hole. By the time I'd scrambled down the stile into the blind, he was already there, maybe 30 feet away, having the time of his life in the muddy puddle.

Toward the end of January, we left Port Elizabeth for Plettenburg Bay. The good weather held, so we anchored there for only one night before continuing another 100 miles to pretty little Mossel Bay.

Annie and a 70-pound lion cub

Mossel Bay

Except for small, white, two-story Mossel Bay Yacht Club, no development marred the natural shoreline. We settled ourselves among the several yachts bobbing in the harbor.

After resting up a day or two, we went exploring. Not far away, we visited some caves. At a small zoo we played with a very young cheetah the size of an enormous house cat, and we learned it was the last weekend the public would be allowed to hold the three-month-old lion cubs. Juggling 70 pounds of soft wiggles was a challenge. Annie and I each held a cub, but could barely hold on long enough to have a picture taken – a dangerous undertaking, since they were, after all, wild animals. However, we did hold them during the hottest part of the day, when they were laziest.

The Ostrich Farm

I'd written to my mom. "Hopefully, we can go on a tour of an ostrich farm tomorrow, but if the weather is good, we'll have to leave." Luckily the winds weren't right, and a bunch of us took off to see the ostriches. Robb didn't go, but Annie and I got to feed them corn kernels and ride them around a corral. We tucked our knees under their big, fluffy wings and held the reins tightly as the frantic animals surged and bucked around the enclosure. Later I read how extremely hard carrying a rider is on the ostrich's thin, delicate ankles, and wished we hadn't done it.

The farm was beautifully green and open. Simple wire fences separated the birds by age. Several tall, peaked shelters provided shade for a dozen or more eggs nestled in the sand. The need for the peak became obvious when a male, with his great long neck wandered in to inspect the eggs, turn them a little, and then settle down over the nest. The guide encouraged us to stand on one of the enormous eggs. At 6 inches high, 5 inches wide, and with a shell 1/10 of an inch thick, each was sturdy enough for an adult's weight. For lunch we sat at tables under a tree, and dined on tasty ostrich burgers. At the gift shop I bought, for the cost of two dozen chicken eggs, one fresh ostrich egg, which in fact equaled 24 chicken eggs.

Back on the boat I got on the radio and invited everyone in the anchorage to a yachtie potluck breakfast the following morning. *Sorcery* would supply the egg. Trevor Lotter, the yacht club manager, let us use the kitchen and dining area with a long table where we could set out the buffet. The next morning, nearly the same assembly of cruising folk as for the Sports Afternoon – *Adélaïde, Chenoah, Flambouyant, Moony, Naomi, Potlach, Refrega, Saoirse, Storm Along, Susan Bright,* and *Windfall* – turned up with sausages, ham and bacon, pitchers of orange juice, thermoses of coffee, tea, and milk, butter, jams, and homemade breads.

When I pulled out a small hammer to break the egg, Trevor stopped me. "Don't you want to save the shell?"

"Sure!"

"Okay, wait a minute." He ran off, returning with a ¼-inch drill and, with Lee holding the egg in place, bored a hole in the top.

"You want scrambled, right?" Trevor started shaking the egg over an electric skillet, already sizzling with butter.

We all declared the egg tasted, as did the burgers the day before, like chicken. Everyone signed their names and boat name on the shell with a black magic marker. Trevor added his name and the date, Jan 30, 1998.

Drilling our breakfast egg

Simon's Town – Last Stop in South Africa

A brutal combination of wind on the nose and choppy seas convinced us to pull into False Bay on the east side of the Cape of Good Hope. Simon's Town, quiet and picturesque with a scattering of white New Orleans-style wrought iron balconies, stretched itself out along the shore. The False Bay Yacht Club welcomed cruisers, offering handy access to phone and fax, food and drink, fuel and water. *Windfall* came in too, and we all stayed two and a half weeks while North Sails, a big international sailmaker, constructed, in record time, a new custom mainsail for *Sorcery*.

The day we arrived, a man from North Sails, with whom we'd been in contact, came to take measurements and get a deposit for the work. We located a dentist to make a new retainer to replace Annie's broken one. With other people working on those two projects, we turned our attention to preparing for a long passage and to exploring.

Climbing Table Mountain in Cape Town was *de rigueur*. With that in mind we rented a car with Lee and Beth, packed a lunch, and drove to the beginning of the path. The two men charged ahead, leaving Beth, Annie, and me juggling the baby and a backpack of paraphernalia. The sun was hot and the trail steep and rocky from the git-go. We'd barely started when Beth, who carried her daughter everywhere, asked Annie if she'd take the chubby cherub. But my daughter couldn't tote the nearly one-year-old more than a little way. Beth and I opted to ride the aerial cable car to the mountain top, while Annie dashed off catching up with her dad and Lee.

Sitting in the shade at the first cable car landing, Beth got into a conversation with an Indian couple who admired the baby. The fact we were traveling on boats enthralled them. Handing Beth a card, the man told her to get in touch when the boat was up for sale. Shortly after *Windfall* landed in Florida to await the birth of their second child, they contacted that man. And – this never happens – he bought the boat.

***

Our best view of Table Mountain emerged from the windows of the train we took into Cape Town. Against the backdrop of a bright blue sky, green hills footed the high rocky plateau with its iconic white-cloud tablecloth swaying and drifting down the slopes. We'd gone to see how the new sail was coming along and were told it would be delivered on Friday, February 13.

With its crowds and tall buildings, Cape Town appeared to me much like other big cities, except for wide, tree-lined sidewalks with endless rows of mats displaying a vast kaleidoscope of souvenirs. I regret not visiting the former prison on Robben Island where Nelson Mandela spent 17 years. Had I been the Mandela fan I am now, I'd have made every effort, spared no expense to make the pilgrimage, a mere seven miles from Cape Town by ferry.

At the Cape of Good Hope Nature Reserve, Robb and Lee darted away like mountain goats over the rocks to stand where the land met the open ocean at the southern tip of the African continent. We four females stayed behind because of the daunting terrain and the icy, unrelenting wind. When we grew bored of hanging out in the shelter of the comparatively warm gift shop, we retired to the car. A resident troop of baboons, the size of pre-teen humans, entertained us by cavorting all over the parking lot. They munched on found food, groomed each other and themselves, inspected their own private parts, and copulated on top of the cars.

One sunny and blessedly warm day we took a 15-minute bus ride to Boulders Beach, home to a sizable colony of African penguins. Without an iceberg in sight, the knee-high birds have adapted to a warmer climate and waddle happily in the white sand. Another day we drove around visiting friends on boats in other marinas, all the while congratulating ourselves on being in what we thought was prettier and nicer False Bay.

⚓

Simon's Town will always be remembered as where we acquired a "mailbox in the sky." A young American single hander brought up the subject of communication while cruising. With a note of alarm he asked, "You don't use email?"

"No, we don't know how."

Whisking us off to a funky Internet Café, he helped us set up with Hotmail our first ever email address. For the next few months, until we reached North Carolina, the email address was ours to have but not to use, because we only managed to get Internet access once. Besides, we didn't know anyone's email address, or if they even had one.

***

At the Simon's Town Museum we learned about the devastating effect of the Apartheid government's Group Areas Act of 1968, only 30 years before. Under that Act more than 7,000 of the town's "people of colour" were forcibly removed from their homes. Many of those people, including Muslims, had deeds to their property from the time of British rule, but nevertheless were relocated to other parts of the Cape Peninsula and beyond. Families were literally split as some were removed and others were able to stay in town – all based on their skin color. We, a family of mixed skin colors, thought with horror what something like that happening to us would have been like.

As if sailing and maintaining a boat weren't enough of a workout, Lee kept up strength training whenever they made landfall. At Cocos Keeling, he'd fashioned equipment from materials at hand. Some kind of rod or a sturdy stick with rocks, or maybe coconuts, tied on the ends, for example, became a weight bar. In Simon's Town he and Annie discovered the Moss Muscle Gym, and after one of their workouts posed for a photo showing off their sweaty and bulging biceps.

Lee and Beth intentionally sailed around the world without a GPS, relying on dead reckoning and celestial navigation. During our last weeks in South Africa, Robb asked for Lee's help in refreshing his celestial navigation skills, and Lee spent many an hour with him reviewing the nitty-gritty. A copy of Lee's recent email to me with his informative and entertaining description of the process is attached in the Appendix. Here's one quote:

> And with the boat pitching, rolling, and yawing, it
> happens frequently that just as your star – or your backup star
> – comes out from behind a cloud and you have just barely
> enough horizon left, and you find the star in the scope of
> your sextant, the star suddenly disappears behind one of your
> sails. I believe this is the origin of swearing.

In a letter to my mom I wrote, "We've had fun in South Africa, but are eager to get going. Next stop: St. Helena's Island where Napoleon was exiled the last time!" My policy was always to be upbeat with Mom, but I remember actually feeling like that. Quite a different tune from the one years earlier, when I never wanted to leave no matter where we were and dreaded the next passage.

The day we were preparing to leave, the man from North Sails showed up. The huge balance charged on our Visa wouldn't go through. With a few phone calls and faxes to the States and our friend Sam's help, the problem got resolved. Our good fortune never failed to amaze us. What if Sam had been out fishing? The bank refused to acknowledge our legitimacy? What if the old sail had given up the ghost, not within reach of a big city, but thousands of miles from anyplace where the work could be done? Little did we know, trouble still lay ahead for us and the ill-fated mainsail.

On February 21, with the winds right and the new main unfurled, we headed west around the cape. An overcast sky completely obscured Table Mountain, but that breathtaking full-color view from the train still lingered in our memories.

THE SOUTH ATLANTIC

South Africa to the States
March to June 1998

THE South Atlantic lived up to its reputation for predictable and consistent southeast winds. For sailors, that translated happily to very few sail changes. We did do some wing-on-wing, but basically, two tacks, one starboard and one port, took us nearly 2,000 miles from Cape Town to St. Helena in 12 days.

As soon as we'd gotten underway, Robb, eager to test his dusted off celestial navigation skills, covered the readout on our GPS with a flap of paper. He took a sight with the sextant, calculated our position using the Sight Reduction Tables and an Almanac, then studied our faces as Annie and I peeked under the flap. A time or two in the beginning our worried eyes grew big as we looked from the readout to Robb. But his calculations were actually excellent, certainly close enough to have gotten us to the island. Having a reliable method to determine our position should the electronics fail reassured us.

Missing the tiny 47-square-mile St. Helena Island, one of the most isolated inhabited places in the world, nearly 1,000 miles from anywhere, would be a minor disaster. On that point, Lee wrote:

> We only ever missed one landfall – Niuataptopu in Tonga – because we had three days of solid overcast, and when we

got a sight finally, realized we had sailed past the island and had to beat back for a day to get there.

After we met up with Beth and Lee at St. Helena, I asked Beth how Lee was when approaching a landfall, especially one as tricky as this. "He's a nervous wreck," she said. Years later, Lee responded:

> I'm not proud of the fact that I was occasionally anxious about making landfall. But I liked using the sextant, not just for celestial navigation, but for measuring distance off. We watched the birds which fly out from land in the morning, and back to land in the evening, to fine tune our course to an unseen island. I got to know some of the brighter stars fairly well, and I am glad for that.
>
> If the most important thing is being safe, you definitely need a GPS, or two or three or four. But we ended up feeling that having this kind of relationship of dependence on the stars, sun, birds, was a higher value than the benefits we would get from having a relationship with a GPS device. I wouldn't recommend it for everybody else, but it worked for us.

Though staying alive was our family's higher value, we greatly admired our friends. St. Helena's was the last time we would see them for many years. They tried land living, had two more children. Then, after visiting us in San Diego one Thanksgiving, they bought another boat and sailed to Saipan in the Western Pacific, where they still live and work.

St Helena Island ~ a Week in Early March

To get onto the land at St. Helena from the rough open bight where we anchored, we always used the water taxi. It picked us up and maneuvered through sloppy seas to within 2 or 3 feet of the stone wharf. Grabbing one of the knotted ropes dangling from an overhead bar, we swung from the taxi onto a stone ledge, wet and slippery with algae.

From there we walked into Jamestown, a settlement of about 4,000 spilling down through a narrow valley. The only access to the island was by sea, and the supply ship that delivered goods every three months had been delayed. We tourists were asked not to buy butter and other staples running short for the Saints, as they call themselves.

Ten of us, including Kathleen and Brian on *Renaissance* and the Swedish family on *La Pinta*, piled into a 1929 Chevy touring convertible with a green patina and four rows of seats. A day's tour of the wildly beautiful volcanic and tropical island took us past dense green valleys; lingering mists silhouetted the closer trees. At the first stop, we met the island's most famous resident, 166-year-old Jonathan, a 2-foot-high giant tortoise. He'd been brought from the Seychelles in 1882, when he was already 50 years old. Still alive and well in March 2016, at 184 he reigns as the oldest known living land animal on the planet.

Jonathan and Annie

At the next stop we learned that in 1815, the British exiled Napoleon to this inescapable island. We wandered through Longwood House, the charming property where he'd lived. Especially interesting to me were the canopied field-bed where he slept and the pool table where rumor has it his autopsy was performed. Annie recalls, "It must have been a pleasant exile." The site he'd chosen for his burial, a lush green glade where he often walked, is marked by a wide slab of concrete enclosed by a classic, black wrought-iron fence. In 1840 the body was moved to Paris to be enshrined in monumental and ornate *Les Invalides*. Having seen both burial places, I can say the former is far and away finer.

On the road again, a light rain shower started. I asked the driver, "So, do you ever put up the top when it rains?"

"Naw," he said over his shoulder, "not usually." Then, as if he'd turned a dial on the dashboard, the drizzle slowed to a halt.

Near the end of the tour, from the old fort high on top of a hill, we looked down on the toy town, the anchorage with its miniature boats, and the island's greatest physical challenge, 699 stone steps dropping steeply to the town. In 1829, the Saint Helena Railway Company built a cableway to lift supplies from the port up to Ladder Hill Fort. The cable cars also carried large quantities of manure, which accumulated in stables, streets, and stockyards, out of Jamestown to be used by inland farmers.

In 1871, the cableway was rebuilt as a long, steep staircase. Robb and I climbed up and down the 11-inch-high by 11-inch-deep steps once. Annie and other younger ones made the trek a few times. These days the stairs are lit at night, and every year timed runs are held with people coming from all over the world to try to break the record of 5 minutes, 16.78 seconds.

Most other days we walked around town, ate a few meals out, and did what provisioning we could. To remember the island, I bought a little white bookmark from a woman who made them by tatting, a delicate form of crochet. The marker keeps my place in a book of inspirational thoughts I read from nearly every day.

***

After only a week, the time came to leave. On March 12, we'd upped anchor and had just hoisted the mainsail when, with a terrible whipping movement and violent tearing sound, the canvas of the new sail ripped clear along the hem at the foot. We dropped the sail and re-anchored. Immobilized with disbelief and despondent beyond words, Robb sat below decks with his head in his hands. Knowing he needed time alone, Annie and I called the water taxi, grabbed a hand-held radio, and went into town to wait in a little restaurant where fellow yachties hung out.

Robb discovered he hadn't properly secured the shackle near the clew at the back of the sail before we left South Africa. During the ensuing 2,000 miles, the shackle had worked loose, eventually allowing the force of the wind to tear the sail away from the hem attached to the boom at several places. After he'd duct-taped the edge of the torn sail to prevent further fraying, and jury-rigged the canvas to the boom, we got underway.

During the night the repair started to come undone. Unaccustomed to working with a loose-footed sail, Robb contacted someone on the radio who recommended the sail not be held too firmly in place, but be allowed a certain amount of play. With that adjustment, the sail carried us all the way to North Carolina.

Perhaps to cheer Robb after the sail disaster, dozens of tuna gathered around and underneath the boat as we pulled away from St. Helena. Only once before during our entire trip had we seen such a large school of tuna. We found the abundant sea life recounted by cruisers in past decades to be a phenomenon of times gone by. Robb threw out a trolling line and in less than a minute a nice-sized fish, thinking he'd found something to eat, unwittingly became our dinner.

Fernando de Noronha, Brazil
A Week at the End of March 1998

Two of Annie's notes in our logbook reflect the essence of this passage: "comfortable and fast," and "The clouds are amazingly beautiful with the moon." A sample from my more prosaic notes: "If motion uncomfortable, or speed > 9.5k for ½ hr, or if <7.5, wake R."

That type of detailed directive from the captain came about after to an incident early in our sailing days on *Sorcery*. The boat had been zipping along under sail on my night watch when Robb woke up.

"What's going on?" He'd screamed, looking at the speedometer, "We're doing 15 knots!"

"I know, isn't that great?"

"No! You'll tear up the gear!"

"What? I thought the boat was designed to go fast?"

"It is." Robb's voice carried exasperation. "But we have to make it last for at least 40,000 miles. We've got to slow this boat down."

⚓

Ten days' sailing took us 1,700 miles to the easternmost point of the South American continent. In 2001 UNESCO designated Fernando de Noronha, a spectacular archipelago of 21 rugged emerald islands and islets, as a World Heritage Site.

Ordinarily we'd have tried to make a trip to the mainland. However, Noronha lies 220 miles offshore of Brazil. Going in would require more traveling, and we didn't have that much time. We needed to be in North Carolina by June, before hurricane season. Besides, we didn't need a visa to stay on the islands. We'd heard the process of getting one was expensive, in part because of bribery, or *mordida*, literally meaning "bite."

We spent the days appreciating the view, shelling, snorkeling, reading, and doing a minimal amount of expensive provisioning at the small grocery store. My loaf of Bobbi's Quick Whole Wheat Bread received a "great!" review.

In a little tourist shop specializing in items made from sharks' teeth, a simple pair of earrings, each with a dangling, white shark tooth, spoke to me. I loved those earrings and would be wearing them today if I hadn't lost one soon after returning to San Diego. They could be replaced with something similar from Ocean Beach or on the Internet, but they wouldn't be the same. A little bit of magic attached itself to things that came into our lives during our travels.

One afternoon when Annie, in shorts and a halter, and her dad were scrubbing down the deck, a 22-foot inflatable Zodiac from the nearby 100-foot motor yacht roared over to our boat. Two tanned, muscular young men, obviously crew and probably in their twenties, stood near Robb in their bobbing tender while holding onto *Sorcery*'s toe rail.

"Hi, we wondered if we could invite your crew to join us for an evening in town?"

Trying to make the boys feel as uncomfortable as possible, Robb asked in a gruff voice,

"You mean my fourteen-year-old daughter?"

"Oh! No! Sorry, sir! We had no idea! We … well, goodbye!" they stammered as they pushed off.

Our next port of call, Devil's Island, awaited 1,300 miles up the coast.

Devil's Island, French Guiana
A Week in Early April 1998

We anchored eight miles off the coast of French Guiana in an open roadstead sheltered by three tiny, tropical islands, St. Joseph, Royale, and Devil's. In 1852 the group became the site of a notorious, brutal French penal colony. The most famous inmate, Alfred Dreyfus, a French artillery officer, was convicted of treason in 1894, an event that rocked France. The case eventually ended with Dreyfus' complete exoneration, but not before he served five years on Devil's Island.

After closing in the early 1950s, the prison left behind deteriorating buildings sprawling over the three islands. In 1973 Devil's Island came to the world's attention with the release of the movie *Papillon,* a film I'd seen based on the autobiographical novel by a former inmate.

The morning after we arrived, we dinghied to an old wooden dock on Devil's Island. This was not a tourist spot. No guards or other travelers, minimal signage. A wide, smooth trail followed most of the perimeter of the ½-square-mile island, and offered a stunning view of the ocean. Sharp, lethal-looking rocks skirted the island and buffered crashing waves. Next to the path a cemetery for prison guards and their families held a sorrowful number of miniature graves for children. Most prisoners who died were thrown into the shark-infested waters.

Venturing off the trail, we stumbled over confused masses of tree roots, some as big around as a person, and vines, vines everywhere. The jungle began to reveal long stone hallways, small cells, and crumbling brick walls, some with rusting iron bars. Bright sunshine streaming through the lush green overgrowth kept the horror of the place at bay, until we came upon disintegrating heavy metal rings still secured to walls. Then I could visualize a wild-eyed man, dirty and bone-thin, chained there for who knows what crime or for how long.

On the second or third night after we'd gone to sleep, thundering noises from the wind and the boat brought us all up on deck. Here's Robb's account of what happened:

> When we anchored, I'd deployed the heavy Bruce, a claw-type hook, from the bow. Then I headed into the wind, and backed the boat down. Because a sizable swell came from the side, I also carried a smaller anchor out in the dinghy and dropped it off *Sorcery*'s stern.
>
> With the change in swell direction during the night, the boat groaned and strained to pull the stern anchor out. The force could have yanked the winch right out of the boat. We had to let the anchor go, and fast. Annie ran below to get the sealed empty plastic gallon jug we'd saved to be used as a float. Dianne started tying the float onto the anchor line. Then I had her and Annie stand clear as I finished tying, cut the line, and let it sizzle out into the sea. Almost immediately the jug popped off.
>
> For an hour or two the next morning, Annie and I crisscrossed in the dinghy over the area where the anchor should be. We dragged hooks in the 30 feet of murky, shark-filled water, hoping to snag the anchor line. Even though the water wasn't zero-visibility like it had been in Bundaberg after the flood, I wasn't about to go diving with sharks. We lost the anchor, chain, and rode.

On an excursion to the mainland we toured, of all unexpected things, a spaceport. Operational since 1968, the Guiana Space Centre is especially suitable as a location for launching rockets because it's only 311 miles from the equator. The spinning earth gives extra takeoff velocity to the rockets, saving fuel and money. In addition, with the ocean to the immediate east, lower stages of rockets and other debris won't fall on heavily populated areas. The launch trajectory is directly over the Devil's Island group, and the isles are evacuated when rockets take off, which may explain why the movie *Papillon* was filmed in Spain,

Jamaica, and Hawaii. The European Space Agency used the Guiana Space Centre to send supplies to the International Space Station.

***

Since we hadn't checked in or out of the country, before we left we paid $10 each to have "Devil's Island" stamped in our passports at the tourist shop.

On Saturday, April 11, we started our journey to the Caribbean. Close to the South American continent, the water turns a muddy brown from the rivers emptying into the ocean. Out farther, anywhere from a mile to several, a sharp line appears where the blue water takes over. As we left Devil's Island, Robb threw out two hooks so they'd be in the water when we crossed into the deep blue. About five miles out, as we crossed the line, a wahoo bit on each hook.

Near sunset after leaving Devil's Island, a silhouette appearing to be a swarm of giant mechanical insects with wings outstretched glided in the water toward us on a collision heading. As we got closer, we identified a 13-boat commercial fishing fleet drift-fishing, and easily motorsailed through the middle of the sprawling flotilla.

The Caribbean and Bahamas
Mid April to Mid June 1998

For two months, we zigzagged 1,500 miles through the island chains of the Caribbean and Bahamas, making 10 landfalls of the hundreds available. We usually preferred spending more time in one spot, rather than trying to see too many. Cruisers had warned us that with our 8½-foot keel, we wouldn't be able to get in close enough to anchor at many places, but we never had any trouble.

After stopping a few days at one island, we'd make a day sail, or maybe an overnighter, to the next place. I'm not saying when you've seen one island, you've seen them all. Still, the ones that were the green, rugged tops of submerged mountains in the Caribbean betrayed a family resemblance. The flat, coral islands of the Bahamas did the same. Probably each isle or islet had something special to see, but the urge to explore had deserted us. We walked the beach, and went into town, if there was one. Otherwise, we luxuriated in being at home on the boat with our simple routines, doing everyday things in spectacular and soothing surroundings – a life that would soon disappear.

The Caribbean

Martinique

Five days after leaving the South American continent we arrived at this French island. Talk about culture shock. Big party boats overflowing with noisy people filled the first few anchorages we passed. To our relief, not all islands or anchorages attracted the wild crowd, and we always found a quiet place to park.

In any case, we couldn't allow ourselves to be disappointed. These islands weren't a destination for us, merely stepping stones to North Carolina. We'd never seriously entertained the idea of transiting the Panama Canal, and slogging on up to San Diego, thus completing a true circumnavigation. Such a trip would have taken an extra year, and none of us, each for our own reasons, was up for it.

Guadeloupe

An old postcard to my mom from Guadeloupe reported experiences I'd forgotten, "Nice to be able to get in the water. First time since Cocos Keeling nearly two years ago. Great French bread baked over coals in brick ovens with wonderful wood-smoked flavor. You could live on it."

St. Barts

An enterprising local man motored around the harbor in the early morning selling freshly baked croissants. Had he known, he could have sold them to us for 10 times the going rate. Warm croissants delivered to the boat at a French island? Priceless.

Annie and her dad swinging off *Sorcery*

St. Maarten/St. Martin

When we pulled in to the Dutch, or maybe it was the French, side of the island, a raucous carnival, with an endless parade of women loaded with glitter, beads and gigantic feathers greeted us. Both sides held carnivals throughout the year. Caribbean music, food, and activities for young and old ran all day and long after we retired.

In the morning, Robb had a rare opportunity to scuba dive. Most places where he could have dived didn't have facilities for refilling air tanks. Without fail, he made certain we had full tanks when we started every passage, in case of an emergency on the boat. The best dive spot was quite a ways out, so he went out on a dive boat, rather than go by himself. The dive turned out to be "nothing to write home about," a disappointing beginner's tour with no time for exploring.

St. Thomas

At this unincorporated territory of the United States, the sweet sight of American flags fluttering against the blue sky welcomed us. For lunch we went in to Charlotte Amalie, the capital and only town on the island. To get to Zorba's white, blue-trimmed Greek restaurant overlooking the town and harbor, we ventured up Government Hill. Discreet photos and signs inside the modest establishment let us know President Clinton and his family had recently dined there, a fun fact adding to our happy memory of the meal.

The Bahamas

Turks & Caicos

At this first stop in the Bahamas we didn't stay in one of the luxury retreats built to accommodate people who'd come to see where their off-shore accounts were being held. Instead, we found a secluded area with no evidence of civilization. There we snorkeled and read the days away. As on other islands, we'd often jump into the clear water, soap up, and have our showers that way. Soap in the ocean. I know. Back then we didn't give it a second thought.

One evening's entertainment consisted of watching a Cape Canaveral rocket arc through the dark sky. We'd heard about the time of the launch, and sat in the cockpit with wine and snacks enjoying the show and evidence of civilization from that comfortable distance.

San Salvador

Scholars have long believed this tiny island to be the first land Christopher Columbus sighted, and where he went ashore during his expedition to the New World in 1492. We stood on the empty pearl-white beach, which must have looked essentially the same as it had to Columbus and his crew. The one sight more interesting would have been watching the authentic replicas of the *Nina, Pinta,* and *Santa Maria* when they visited in 1992 to celebrate the 500th anniversary of the landing.

In 1983, items confirming San Salvador as the landing place came to light: Spanish green and amber glass beads, D-shaped belt buckles, and a coin minted between 1454 and 1479. Columbus had reported giving all three trade items to the natives. Long before that find, a small museum had been created in the former jail, a room of no more than 12 feet square. A forlorn suit of Spanish armor stood in one corner guarding plenty of artifacts, few, if any, related to the event. If proper security can be arranged, the historic evidence will be displayed there. Otherwise, it will go to the new National Museum planned for Nassau.

Cat Island

At this admirable little island, we had the anchorage to ourselves, except for one small boat not far away. One morning, I sat on the foredeck in a sarong, eyes closed, face to the sun, a coffee mug held in both hands. The delicious feeling of contentment moved all the way up to joy when notes of my most-loved classical piece, "Pachelbel's Canon," floated across the water from the other boat. Either the music or the setting alone was marvelous, but the two together nearly moved me to tears. When the music finished, I called over asking for the recording to please be played one more time. It was.

Little San Salvador

Our penultimate stop, this island owned by The Holland America Line, was used occasionally as a port of call. Technically, cruisers weren't allowed, but as we sailed by the obviously deserted resort, we decided to stop. Anchoring away from the built-up part, we went snorkeling with a few sharks for company.

After the excursion, as we sat in the cockpit with our traditional butterscotch punch, I said, "The sharks were pretty big. I saw a 10-footer."

"Ten feet? No!" Robb and Annie guffawed, "The sharks were only about three to four feet long!"

"Well, the one I saw over by those tanks was bigger than that," I insisted.

"Mom, I saw that one too, and it was nothing like that long. Sharks always look bigger to you."

"That may be, but the one I saw was definitely more than four." Further bantering led to a compromise of six feet. They wouldn't go to seven.

Grand Abaco

Only 180 miles from Florida, this island had a Pizza Hut. There's more. The fast food eatery had its own dinghy dock. In San Diego we'd gotten a kick out of docking *Sorcery* at the Bali Hai restaurant on Shelter Island, then going in for lunch. Silly, but parking the dinghy at a Pizza Hut in the Bahamas seemed more exotic and fun. For years we'd eaten pizza all over the world. Most we'd made, some we'd bought, but none had real pepperoni. After stuffing ourselves with double cheese and double pepperoni, we took the dinghy to Marsh Harbor, and strolled around the old beach village with its white and pastel-colored clapboard houses and profusion of small stands with over-priced souvenirs.

Heading for Home

Our last passage before getting to the States would be 550 miles to the Cape Fear River in North Carolina. Hurricane season had officially started in the northern Atlantic on June 1, a date we'd already passed. Constantly monitoring the weather, waiting for a good window between us and the dangerous cape, Robb finally chose Monday, June 15, as the day to leave.

As we pulled out into the open ocean, a water spout like a mini tornado touched down to the water, only a mile or so away. Not a good sign in my book. We kept our eyes on it, ready to head another direction if necessary. The spout dissipated, and as we moved north two or three others danced and flirted in the distance.

* * *

Cape Fear got its name for a reason. Besides the frequent dangers from high winds and treacherous seas, sandbars known as Frying Pan Shoals, part of the Graveyard of the Atlantic, extend 28 miles out from the mouth of the river. Dozens of ships have sunk there, including 21 during the Civil War. Cruising lore told us people have gone around the world only to lose their boats at Cape Fear.

We'd chosen that intimidating port of entry because our friends, Catherine and Bill on *Brigadoon*, lived 25 miles up the river in Wilmington, North Carolina. Four years earlier, when we were all in Fiji, Robb and I had mentioned we might settle on the East Coast. Our friends encouraged us to have a look at their hometown.

Their suggestion gave us a focus, a place to start. From there we thought we might cruise the Intracoastal Waterway, a 3,000-mile stretch running from Boston to Brownsville, Texas. However, in the ensuing years, we recognized that though we might settle on the East Coast, the time would have come to sell the boat. Robb and I needed to work and replenish our funds and Annie had to attend high school. I yearned to put down roots, and the boat was too big for day sailing.

For much of the Bahamas to Cape Fear passage, the sky had been overcast with vaguely threatening clouds. Then, as we approached the Cape in the late afternoon, the clouds parted, just enough to expose the setting sun. Completing the unusual and glorious tableau, and further lifting our spirits, dolphins played near the boat, jumping clear of the water.

Shortly after dark, we dropped the hook just inside the entrance to the Cape Fear River. We had no idea that would be our last night at anchor on *Sorcery*.

The next morning, a brilliant, sunny, and breezeless day, we began our final trip on the boat, a concept none of us fully understood at the time. As we motored up the river, we behaved as if we were simply making another passage: monitoring the gauges for water depth and engine temperature, looking out for other traffic or any hazards, consulting the chart for landmarks, and readying the lines for tying up. A gorgeous 4-inch green dragonfly with gossamer wings hitched a ride on the black cover of the mainsail.

In spite of our various complaints over the years, the very idea of The End was too big and too sad to talk about. Besides, as usual, we really didn't know what was in store. The boat, for example, might not sell, changing everything.

To pass under the Cape Fear Memorial Bridge, we summoned the operator on the radio, and asked her to raise the bridge. The normal 69-foot clearance of the vertical-lift span wouldn't be enough for *Sorcery*. The mast rose 70 feet from the deck. And with the 5 feet from the waterline, the mast towered 75 feet into the air. We asked for the bridge to be raised to 80. As we moved cautiously underneath, we stared up, watching the mast clear the structure by what looked to be only a few inches. The captain reassured the crew, "The head room's more than it appears from our perspective."

Later, he amended that. "It didn't look as if we'd make it."

***

In the early afternoon we pulled into the Hilton Hotel dock in Wilmington. As soon as we'd tied up and gotten settled, Annie and I put on a Crosby, Stills and Nash CD with the song "Southern Cross." We played the rousing tune over and over at full volume, waiting for and singing along with the important words, "I have been around the world." Well, coast to coast, the long way. I don't remember opening a bottle of champagne, but I hope we did.

After a complimentary week or so at the Hilton, we moved to the dock at the Wilmington Marine Center, a facility claiming to be hurricane safe. On August 27 Hurricane Bonnie flooded the streets and toppled huge trees across roads, power lines, houses and cars. No one appreciated the irony of us having survived and avoided tropical storms for years of cruising, only to have one "as big as the state of Texas" come directly over our heads at the end of our trip.

People we hardly knew had invited us to stay in their homes, but we felt safer on the boat. For three days rain and high winds battered *Sorcery*, but we were snug inside with full water tanks, a generator for movies, stacks of books and games, propane for cooking, and plenty of food. Once a day we'd don our foul-weather gear to brave the tempest and stretch our legs on the dock.

⚓

Since we assumed we'd stay in Wilmington for at least a year while Annie attended school, we bought a car. Before school started, we drove to Robb's sister's home in Dallas to meet up with Alex, who flew in from San Diego. At the airport, a tall, handsome eighteen-year-old in sunglasses walked past us off the plane, and then turned back.

"Alex!" We shouted.

He grinned. "I wondered how long it'd take you to recognize me!"

Big hugs all around. So good seeing him, so much to catch up on. He filled in the details about crewing on a delivery through the Panama Canal to Grenada at the first of the year and announced he'd start at the University of San Diego in the fall. We couldn't have been more proud and happy for him.

Back in Wilmington we bought a second car and found pitifully low-paying jobs. To begin the months-long process of preparing the boat for sale, we moved into an apartment and rented a storage locker, then another, for all the stuff on the boat. Robb worked on repairs, while I looked after cosmetic details and dealt with routine family maintenance. At Christmas, a big treat, long-time friends Lisa and Ellen invited us to spend the holiday with them in New York City.

Goodbye to *Sorcery*

At Robb's suggestion, whenever the broker showed the boat, I baked bread, adding a homey and inviting scent to the interior. *Sorcery* sold rather quickly for a 61-foot has-been race boat that had also been hammered on by years of cruising. In January a man from Newfoundland, who knew and loved the boat, bought it, and planned to take his young family cruising as we'd done. Friends of his came down to crew, and for a couple of weeks familiarized themselves with the boat. Robb went down nearly every day to explain or help with something.

As far back as September we'd known North Carolina, with its mosquitoes and no-see-ums, heat and humidity, not to mention hurricanes and low wages, was not for us. At the end of February, before *Sorcery* left for her new home, Robb drove to San Diego to get work. As a union electrician, all he had to do was sign the book at the hall, and he'd get a good-paying job as soon as his name rose to the top. He left Wilmington early on a Monday, signed the book on Wednesday afternoon, could have had a job on Thursday, but chose to rest and start Friday.

After Robb left, the new owner called to have me explain things about the boat. Often, I surprised myself with how much I knew, and a wave of nostalgia would sweep through me.

As the time neared for *Sorcery* to leave, the new captain asked if Annie and I wanted to go with them as far as the mouth of the river. Part of me would love to have gone. Yet speechless with emotion, I could only answer by shaking my head 'no.'

"Do you want to come aboard?"

Another silent head shake. The boat, our boat, now someone else's, had taken us through hundreds of adventures. More than a boat, for years *Sorcery* had been our home. Alone on the dock I wished a silent, painful farewell to her and the life we'd known.

Epilogue

ANNIE hadn't been in an American school since third grade and wanted to do her 10th year over. After she'd been in school a couple of weeks, she said to me, "Mom, you know when I said I wanted to stop cruising?"

"Yes. Why?"

"I didn't know what I was talking about."

Annie and I thought we were done with cruising – Robb and Alex maybe not so much. What we hadn't reckoned on was how boring "real life" could be compared to our time at sea, when everything was extraordinary, in the literal sense.

Adding to our frustration and isolation, few people were interested in or, for that matter, believed what we'd done. That was true particularly for Annie. Many times, kids would ask her where she was from, and she'd begin telling her story of the places she'd traveled. Soon they'd interrupt and ask,

"Well, why were you in Australia?"

"Because my family and I lived on a boat and we traveled a lot."

"Why?"

"...I don't know. My dad likes sailing. To see the world."

"Oh, okay. What do you want to do this weekend?"

By the end of the school year, Annie had become entrenched and wanted to stay in Wilmington. But I hadn't settled in so happily. In any case, Robb wasn't coming to North Carolina, so we were going to California. As we packed our furniture and other belongings into a new

15-foot yellow Penske rental truck, another hurricane headed for Wilmington. With the car secured onto the truck's trailer, we headed west. Literally hours ahead of the storm, we didn't stop for the night until people said they felt certain the hurricane wouldn't come in that far.

In five days we drove 2,600 miles without backing up the unwieldy truck and trailer. Sometimes, my fifteen-year-old, with her new learner's permit, took the wheel, which goes to show even on land you can cheat death.

Robb had rented a place for us near Point Loma High School where he'd already enrolled Annie. Both he and Alex were there to greet Annie and me and the newest member of our family, Nuisance, the tabby kitten a friend had given Annie and we'd brought from North Carolina. Unless you count Jaws, the goldfish Annie won at a carnival when she was five, or Buddy, the dog given to her in Tuvalu, Annie had never had a pet. There was no going to California without this one.

Robb and I bought a little house and worked for many years before retiring. As a member in good standing of the International Brotherhood of Electrical Workers, he got credit for his time abroad and received his 40-year pin a couple of years after we returned. For the final 13 years of my working life, I landed a terrific position as a paralegal for Alexandra Kwoka, an awesome individual and family law attorney.

The kids both finished college and are living their grownup lives: Alex as a Lieutenant Commander in the Navy, and Annie as a Registered Dental Hygienist with a degree in Journalism. Go figure. We all continue to be world travelers.

So many things trigger happy memories of our adventure. Every day, when I look up at the sky and clouds, I'm reminded of seeing them stretching in all their glory from horizon to horizon – and of the excitement of spotting that pinpoint that will be our next landfall.

Land ho!

APPENDIX

Robb's Glossary of Sailing Terms

Cruising Life by Annie

Dead Reckoning and Celestial Navigation
Around the World in the 1990s
by Lee

Sorcery's Movie List

Boats We Met

Glossary of Sailing Terms

By Robb

Aft: the very back part of the boat

Beat: to sail as close as possible in the direction from which the wind is coming

Boom: horizontal spars or poles for extending the bottom of sails

Boom vang or vang: a sail control that counters the upward tension of the sail

Bosun's Chair: a seat with ropes and pulleys for hoisting a person up the mast of a boat

Bow: front or forward portion of a boat

Clew: aft lower corner of a fore-and-aft sail, usually used to control the sail

Companionway: a stair or ladder within the hull to go from the cabin to the deck

Dead reckoning: Please refer to Lee's description in the Appendix

Dinghy: small boat to get to land from the big boat

Dodger: shield erected on deck to protect persons on watch from weather

Fetch: distance seas can travel unobstructed by land

Fiddle rail: rail around edge of a table to prevent items from sliding off

Foredeck: forward of the mast

Galley: kitchen in a boat

Gunnel: upper edge of the side or bulwark of a vessel

Hatch: opening in the deck through which people or objects can pass

Haul out: move a boat from water onto the shore

Head sail: sail set forward of the mast

Heel: to lean over

Jibe or gybe: to change from one tack to the other

Jury rig: refers to makeshift repairs or temporary contrivances

Moor: to attach a boat to a mooring buoy or post

Motor sailing: motoring with some sail up

On the hard: on dry land

On the outside: in open ocean as opposed to an anchorage or bay

Palapa: an open-air, palm-thatched restaurant on the beach

Panga: small open boat with an outboard motor

Port: left side of a boat when facing forward

Reef: to temporarily reduce the area of a sail exposed to the wind

Roadstead: a partially-sheltered offshore anchorage area

Rode: rope or line attached to an anchor chain

Salon: the living room on a boat

Shroud: a cable serving to hold a mast up from side to side

Single side band radio: high-frequency radio capable of worldwide communications if conditions are right

Sloop: small to mid-sized sailboat with one mast bearing a main sail and head sail

Spar: pole used to support various pieces of rigging and sails

Splash: put boat back in the water after a haul out

Spreader: spar to deflect the shrouds to better support the mast

Starboard: right side of a boat when facing forward

Stern: rear part of a ship

S/V: sailing vessel

Tack: to sail at an angle to the wind

Taffrail: rail above stern

Tender: dinghy or small boat used to get from the bigger boat to shore

Topsides: the part of the hull between the waterline and the deck

Transom: a more or less flat surface across the stern of a vessel

Underway: sailing or motoring, not at anchor

VHF radio: Very High Frequency radio, limited to line of sight

Zulu time: world time, the same all over the planet

Cruising Life

By Annie

Remember the opening scene in *Fiddler on the Roof* when Tevye is belting out that glorious, toe-tapping ballad about traditions? Well, my family was nearly as passionate when it came to tried and true customs when we lived on the boat.

As a child cruiser, my world was an exciting yet ever changing scene of new people, new places, new languages, new schools. Sometimes there were kids my age; most of the time there weren't. I'm not complaining by any stretch, but the simple traditions of our family brought with them a cherished sense of stability.

For birthdays, everyone but the birthday person would wake up before sunrise, collect a pile of all the gifts and prepare the cake with candles. I'm not sure how my mom did it on a 61-foot boat, but she always managed to keep things very well hidden. Then the family would creep across our creaky floorboards to the birthday person's cabin and slowly start singing. As the recipient, it was always a joy to wake up to candlelit faces and that gentle chorus. And it was the one time we were allowed to eat in bed.

The rest of the day was less predictable, depending on whether we were at sea or anchor, and how the weather was. If near land, we'd go ashore and have dinner out – a big deal for our rather frugal family. At night the birthday person usually got to choose a movie to watch.

Watching a movie on a boat takes some preparation. First, there's the generator – a noisy contraption that might need to be filled with gasoline. One time, while trying to demonstrate that I was essentially self-sufficient at the ripe old age of eleven, I poured diesel into the generator instead. When it would only stutter and shake, I realized what I had done and nervously prepped myself for the moment of reckoning with my dad. I remember he took the news with surprising calm given the expense of the generator and the amount of time that later went into draining it. To this day, I'm still not sure why that was. Perhaps he thought it was punishment enough that a movie would be out of the question for a while.

Back to the noise of the generator. We always anchored a safe distance away from other boats to allow for the anchor dragging under heavy currents or a sharp change in the wind. So, the noise of the generator was never really a nuisance to our neighbors, and vice versa. I suppose it could be compared to living in a neighborhood with mild flight traffic. The drone of the airplanes taking off and landing become background noise soon enough and you hardly even notice it after a while.

But in order to clearly hear the movie, we usually closed all the hatches to block out the sound. If we wanted to watch a movie during the day, we would often have to place a dark towel over the window in the back hatch of our main cabin, so as to block the glare on our little 12-inch TV screen.

We only had a very small but prized collection of VHS movies. I probably saw *The Blues Brothers, Driving Miss Daisy,* the *Star Wars* trilogy, *Two Mules for Sister Sara, Frisco Kid,* an assortment of Disney classics, and, of course, *Fiddler on the Roof* each 200 times during our six-and-a-half-year trip.

I've seen *The Little Mermaid* close to a thousand times, and that's truly a conservative estimate. Before we left on our trip, I would wake up at five or six in the morning, put in *The Little Mermaid* and watch it once through before my parents and brother woke up. I'd watch at least two more times throughout the day.

Twenty-plus years later, I can still recite every word. More impressively, and not by choice, so can my brother. He once told me that in college he happened to pass by two girls in his dorm that were half-heartedly arguing about a certain line in the movie.

"It goes like this…," one girl said.

"No, it's this…," said the other.

"No, no, it goes like *this*…," my brother stated before reciting the line and continuing on to class. Major brownie points were scored.

When it came to Thanksgiving, the movie of choice was an old episode of Garfield that my grandma had recorded for me and sent in a care package. Whether we had the fortune of celebrating with others or not, we would watch *Garfield's Thanksgiving* without fail. As a kid, it was kind of a big deal when my parents sat down to watch a cartoon; and yet, I could always count on having them by my side for this and for the Christmas episode of Garfield, along with the recording of Will Vinton's *Claymation Christmas Special* and the *California Raisins* my grandma had sent as well.

It wasn't so much the genius behind the shows we were watching that attracted us, I don't think; but rather the familiarity and the tie to home that we clung to. Our life on the boat was charmed, without question. We experienced things most people only dream about, and we required far less in the way of material items than most Americans today can comprehend. We feel we are better, if not a little misunderstood, for it. But there were also many times when we missed the comforts and family back home, and a flight back or sometimes even a phone call wasn't possible.

Movies were a treat, but more often than not each of us had our own book that we were reading. On a boat, especially while at sea, there is often nothing to do but delve deep into a story to pass the time.

My brother and I read non-fiction more than we read fiction, though I remember getting really into R.L. Stine's teen murder mystery series. I probably collected around 75 of his books before moving on; and still have them to this day because of the endearing memories they engender. My dad, who is almost entirely a non-fiction reader of the historical genre, would read whatever mystery I was reading whenever I put the book down. He was a faster reader than me, so he could quickly catch up to my place, though he never tried to pass me. He always figured out who did it long before I did. But we would talk about the characters and the plot and, bless his heart, he seemed genuinely interested in them – even though I knew he was only reading them to spend time with me.

Another tradition, especially when we were traveling in the warm water of the South Pacific, was snorkeling. Usually my mom stayed on board, but my brother, dad, and I were always game for at least a couple hours in the water. By the time we were done, however, we'd be wrinkled and chilly and more than ready to get back to the warm boat and into warm clothes. The smell of hot chocolate, or when we were luckiest, homemade butterscotch punch, always greeted us, thanks to Mom. It was a race to get off our wetsuits and rinse off with fresh water before settling down to a steaming cup of pure heaven.

There were also a few meals that became the equivalent of secret family recipes though there was nothing too classified about them. One such preparation was a three-bean salad. No matter what, my mom made sure we had several cans of green beans, garbanzo beans and kidney beans on board. After that, it was just a matter of adding some Dijon mustard, oil, salt, vinegar and dill – one mustn't forget the dill.

The other meal that never yielded much in the way of leftovers was peanut butter pasta. It sounds disgusting, I'll grant you, but it's actually divine. Toss al dente linguine into a sauce of peanut butter, soy sauce, ginger, oil, sugar, vinegar, red pepper flakes, onion, and sesame seeds – and you had the perfect lunch, dinner or, in the case of my ever-growing and seemingly starving brother, midnight snack.

Those were some of the things that held our family together. Sixty-one feet is a big boat, unless you live on it full time with three other people. Like every other family that ever was or will be, we had our less-flattering moments. But the great take-away was an adventure of a lifetime filled with treasured memories and traditions that are, simply put, ours.

Dead Reckoning and Celestial Navigation Around the World in the 1990s

By Lee Pliscou
August 23, 2016

We trailed a taffrail log for miles traveled, for the dead reckoning part. With star sights, you usually shoot three stars, and you end up with three lines that cross and make a triangle. The smaller the triangle, the better. Your location is somewhere within the triangle. On good days, I was confident I could routinely fix our position within a couple miles. And, even the smallest atoll, if it has a palm tree, can be seen from about 10 miles away.

The routine with the sextant was a round of star sights at dawn (during the few short minutes you can see both stars and the horizon), a sun line in the morning (shooting a single celestial body gives you a single line—meaning that you're on (or near) the line. A noon shot, which gives you a decent position, both latitude and longitude, but it's not really a single shot. You have to take a series of shots starting about 15 minutes before the sun is at the highest point in the sky, and then corresponding shots right after noon. This is reasonable accurate way of fixing latitude, and it's not bad for longitude—but it depends on the accuracy of your clock. We had a cheap shortwave radio, and were able to get accurate time from station WWV. But around the equator, being off by four seconds translates to being off a mile in longitude.

Then, another sun line in the afternoon, and then shoot a round of stars, again, during the brief time when you can see both stars and the horizon. There's a decent amount of planning that goes into shooting stars—you have to know which stars you're going to shoot before you shoot them—so you predict where you're going to see them, and pre-set the sextant.

I never warmed up to moon sights. The moon moves so fast against the horizon, moon shots are not as accurate as other celestial bodies. And one person doesn't have enough time to get a round of star shots and a moon shot—so, I stuck with the stars. It's not quite a full-time job, but it occupies good chunks of the day.

So, here's the thing: clouds, fog, waves, and sails. You can plan a round of star sights, and one of the stars you need is behind a cloud. So, you've got to plan for a backup star. And it happens the entire sky is overcast, or there's fog, in which case you get no sight at all. We only ever missed one landfall—Niuataptopu—because we had three days of solid overcast, and when we got a sight finally, realized we had sailed past the island and had to beat back for a day to get there.

And then there's the practical problem of taking sights from a small sailboat. With even moderate waves, two hands are barely enough to hold on and get your sights. And with the boat pitching, rolling, and yawing, it happens frequently that just as your star—or your backup star—comes out from behind a cloud, and you have just barely enough horizon left, and you find the star in the scope of your sextant, the star suddenly disappears behind one of your sails. I believe this is the origin of swearing.

I'm not proud of the fact that I was occasionally anxious about making landfall. But I liked using the sextant, not just for celestial navigation, but for measuring distance off, and for being able to triangulate a position within an anchorage with horizontal sextant angles. We watched the birds which fly out from land in the morning, and back to land in the evening, to fine tune our course to an unseen island. I got to know some of the brighter stars fairly well, and I am glad for that.

If the most important thing is being safe, you definitely need a GPS, or two or three or four. But we ended up feeling that having this kind of relationship of dependence on the stars, sun, birds, was a higher value than the benefits we would get from having a relationship with a GPS device. I wouldn't recommend it for everybody else, but it worked for us.

Sorcery's Movie List
The treasured VHS tapes that kept us anchored to home.

Addams Family
Apollo 13
Around Cape Horn
Captain Ron
The Civil War series – Ken Burns
Das Boot
Driving Miss Daisy
Fiddler on the Roof
Frisco Kid
Grumpy Old Men & Grumpier Old Men
Hook
Hunt for Red October
Moonstruck
Mrs. Doubtfire
Mutiny on the Bounty
My Cousin Vinny
Nightshift
(Dianne always asked at the start of *Nightshift*, "Is this the right movie?")
Raiders of the Lost Ark
Searching for Bobby Fischer
Star Wars
The Blues Brothers
The Gods Must Be Crazy
The Little Mermaid
The Man Who Would be King
Two Mules for Sister Sarah
Who Framed Roger Rabbit
Yankee Doodle Dandy
Young Frankenstein
Young Sherlock Holmes

Boats, Boat People,
and
Where We First Met

Over the years we crossed paths with hundreds of boats and their crews. Some boats we met only in passing. Others came into our lives again and again, sometimes in more than one country. In that case, only the country of the first encounter is listed. A precious few people became our life-long friends. Most of the adventurers were American, but if they were from another country and we knew where that was, that's been added. Please forgive any and all errors or omissions.

About Time: Terry – Mexico
Adélaïde: Christian & Nicole, Adrien – Cocos Keeling, from France
Alba: Ascension, Victor 18 and Jose 16 – Fiji, from Spain
Alcatraz: Drew & Susan, Elizabeth – Mission Bay, San Diego
Alegria: Mossel Bay, South Africa
Alia: Lou, Loren and Dylan – Mexico
Alexandra Louise: Neil & Helen – Australia, from England
Allegro: Sarah – Mexico
Alley Cat: George – Tuamotus
Almitra: Gary & Lisa – Marshall Islands
Alrisha: Gene & Joanne – Mexico
Amanita: Monique – Mexico
Angelos: father and son – Cocos Keeling, from Germany
Antigua: Bruce & Kay – Mexico
Aquila: Trevor & Carrie, Morgan & Tamara – Mission Bay, San Diego
Aqua Symphony: Mike & Jane – Cocos Keeling
Ariadne: Henry & Diane – Fiji
Arlynn: Junior and Howard – Mexico
Astrid I: New Caledonia
Atom: James – Richards Bay, South Africa
Avatapu: Nancy Griffith – Rarotonga, Cook Islands.
Bag End: Don & Nancy – Mexico

Bageera: Rod & Hillary – Australia
Bardoo: Rob & Robbie – Richards Bay, South Africa
Bastante: Tom & Kay – Mexico
Beaudacious: – Marquesas
Bequia Chief: Janice, husband & kids – Mexico
Bilge Rat: – Mexico
Blaze: Lauren with crew – New Zealand
Blue Serenity: Chris and Skip – Mexico
Brigadoon: Catherine & Bill and cat Muffin – Cook Islands
Buffan II: Otto & Helen, Marika 15 and Garren – Australia
Capricious II: Steve, Woodie – Mexico
Carioca III: Alan & Gertrud, then Susan with cat Chelsea – Mexico
Casteele: Ed & Marilyn – Mexico, from Victoria BC
Cetacean: Mark & Cindy – Rarotonga, Cook Islands
Champagne: Mexico – up outside Baja coast 1st trip
Cheeky Hobson: Ken & Mo – Mexico
Cheshire Cat: Dave & Gladys – Australia
Chimera: Robbie & Grant from Australia
Chenoah: Robert – South Africa
Christel II: Sam – Mission Bay, San Diego
Cirrus: Rudy – Mexico
Coconut Express: Paul and family – Australia
Columbine: –Mexico, up outside Baja coast 1st trip
Comme un Cheval Fou: South African coast, from France
Companion: – Mexico, up outside Baja coast 1st trip
Con Todo: – Mexico
Constance: – New Zealand
Cruising Time: Mitch & Vicky, Brian and Ethan – Mexico
Crystal Wind: Marty & Chandler – Mexico
Damian: kids Bree and Josh – Mexico
Delia: Phil & Michele, Colin – Mission Bay, California
Destiny: Claude & Naomi – Mexico
Détente: John & Norma – Australia
Diario: Babs and husband – Tuamotus, from Italy
Diabolo: Manou, Soazic and toddler Thomas – Moorea, from France
Double Time: Mick & Debbie, Erica 6 – Mexico
Dream Merchant: Jim & Joan, then Luanne – Mexico

Dreamchaser: with Joanna, a girl Annie's age – New Caledonia
Drumbeat: Dennis & Drew – Mission Bay, San Diego
Dulce Vida: Rick & Shelly – Mission Bay, San Diego
Ecstasy: John & Lorenza – New Zealand
El Gitano: Peter & Val, Sven, Michael, Zoe, Nils – New Zealand, from Germany/England
Endless Summer: Rob & Lynn, and Jo-Jo – Mexico
Energetic: parents and 20-old girl w/dog – Rarotonga, Cook Islands
Ethereal: Al & Kathryn – Mexico
Etoile Polaire: Terry & Martha – Fiji
Fair Rover: Chris & Cindy, Celeste, Jeff – Tuvalu, from Guam
Fair Wind II: Chris & Liz – Australia
Fallado: Heburt & Meryle – South Africa, from Germany
Fat Cat: Megan – Fiji
Feisty Lady: – South Minerva Reef
Felicity: Jerry & Karen, Darren – Mexico
First Light: Gary and Donna – Marquesas
Flambouyant: Dennis & Kathryn – Mossel Bay, South Africa
Fradilira: – Cocos Keeling, the Indian Ocean
Free Spirit: Jim & Dee – Australia
Friendly Rival: Peter – Réunion
Frolic: Tom & Sarah – Mexico
Galadriel: – Mexico
Galatea: Archie & Margaret – Mexico
Galaxie: Ed & Trisha – Fiji
Gambit: – Mexico, up outside Baja coast 1st trip
Gannet: Jim & Joan – New Zealand
Gibbs III: Total loss going between motus in South Pacific
Gjoa: Sandy & Heather – Fiji
Go the Risk: Janet – Mexico
Gold Eagle: Tom & Linda, Dan – Mexico
Golly Gee: Don & Jan, then Lois – Mexico
Guinevere: Bert, Wilma, Olin 15, Elaine 13 – South Pacific
Gulliver: Lou Ellyn – Mexico
Gwenaskel: Bernard & Beatriz – Rodrigues, from France/ Brazil
Hagar: Stacia – Mexico
Halcyon: Jeff & Janet – Marquesas

Harmony: Tom & Shirl – Mexico
Hasty: Tom & Lynn, Tim – Fiji
Hawah: John & Jane – Tuvalu
Heart of Gold: Jim & Sue – Australia
Homespun: Matthew and Paulette – Mexico
Ho'o'nanea: Bob & Kay, Sheldon – North Minerva Reef
Insatiable: Jim & Ann – Mexico
Intercept: David & Shirlee – Australia
Interlude: Dennis & Doris – Australia
Ishmael: Jim and kids – Australia
Islander: Theo – Richards Bay, South Africa
Jacaranda: Chuck & Dianne – Fiji
Jennifer: Lars & Johanna – Fiji, from Sweden
Joan D III: Jenna – Mexico
Joanie C.: girls Vivienne and Carrie – South Africa, from South Africa
Just Do It: Walter & Joyce – Mexico
Kama Lua: Carl & Diane – Marquesas
Kaselehlia: Kase & Linda – Mexico
Kavenga: Parents, Anna, Claire, and Tani – Fiji, from Tasmania
Khamsin: Gillian & Michael – Fiji, from Canada
Kindred Spirit: Jerry & Gail – Australia
Kinship: Bob & Jan, Devin, Colin – Mexico
Kodiak: – Cocos Keeling, the Indian Ocean
Kona Star: John & Lena – Australia
La Mouette: Chuck & Gigi – Mexico
La Pinta: Parents and two young girls – St. Helena, from Sweden
Lady Ruth: Rod & Frances – Rarotonga, Cook Islands
Lena: Kirby and Lee – Mexico
L'Equipe: Stewart & Josie – Fiji
L'Escargot: Dick & Mary and cat – Mexico
Lobo: John and Jay – Mexico
Loke Lani: Jim & Janice – Tuvalu
Lookfar: Stu and cat – Mexico
Makaira: Gene & Maddy – Mexico
Malagueña: – Rarotonga, Cook Islands
Mano Bubna: two middle-aged fellows – Fiji, from Argentina
Marco Polo: Simon & Pauline, Simon – Mission Bay, San Diego

Mary T: Sig & Carol, Anna – Fiji
Maybe Tuesday: Dinghy named *Maybe Not* – Mexico
Mini-the-Mermaid: – Tuamotus
Mithril: Mike, wife & young girl – Up outside Baja coast 1st trip
Monte Cristo: Norm & Susan, Justin 5 – Mexico
Moon Shadow: Eric – Mexico
Moonshadow: Dave & Candia, Justin, Lana – New Caledonia
Moony: Dennis & Wolfgang – South Africa, from Germany
Moorings: Kids Megan, Josh, Samantha, Jennifer – Mexico
Morasum: Chuck & Linda – Mexico
Mushaugge: single-hander – Mauritius, from South Africa,
Music: Kenny & Mary, toddler Meg, baby Dylan – Ashmore Reef
Myste: Morice & Jacqueline, Morgan, Sarah, Anais, baby Joe –
    Marshall Islands, from France
Naiad: Craig & Sue, Laura – Fiji
Naomi: Roland & Marianne – South Africa, from Switzerland
Nautical Wheeler: Steve & Thames, Justin, Heather – Mexico
Nerissa: Tom – New Caledonia
No Problema: Mexico, up outside Baja coast 1st trip
Non Pariel: – Mexico
Ocean Angel: Larry & Adrianne – Mexico
Occam's Razor: Sherry & Ken – Mexico
October: Parents and Clara – Mexico
Ondine: two boys – Australia
Opal Eye: – Mexico
Orion: Rodney & Katherine – Marquesas
Otto: – Richards Bay, South Africa
Our Way: children Chris, Robin and Franni – Fiji
Pablo: Paul – Mexico
Panacea: Joe and Ron – Marshall Islands
Patuky: – South Minerva, from Germany
Perelandra: LeCain & Sheila – Richards Bay, South Africa
Perpetua: Jack and crew, Norman – Mexico
Petit Cheval: parents and Rafi and Jeremy – Australia, from Belgium
Pollen Path: Randy & Laura – French Polynesia
Potlatch: Michael & Kandis, Garrett, Jerrold –South Africa
Primo: Ron & Milly – Mexico

Querida: Rob & Terri – Australia
Rapunzal: Mark & Cindy – Rarotonga, Cook Islands
Razzle Dazzle: – Mexico
Reefer: Jim & Shannon, Savana and Marina – South Africa
Refrega: Marcelo & Nicia, Cuca –South Africa, from Brazil
Renaissance: Brian & Kathleen – Richards Bay, South Africa
Rosel: – Mexico
Royal Salute: Roy & Gloria – Richards Bay, South Africa
Rubiyat: girl Jessica – Australia
Rusuri: Winfield & Jillian, Saul, Dayl – New Caledonia
Saga: Gary & Julie – Mission Bay, San Diego
Sagittarius: Ron – New Caledonia
Samatas: Mike & Marie – Mexico, from Vancouver B.C.
Sannyasi: Al & Lisa – Tuamotus
Saoirse: Orla & Gar – Mossel Bay, South Africa
Sapo: Mary – Central Pacific
Savant: Kim & Deb and Kelly – Richards Bay, South Africa
Scout: Rob and Lynn – Mexico
Scrimshaw: – Mexico
Seapod: Bill – Mexico
SeaRider: – Mexico
Sendaya: Bill & Anne – Mission Bay, San Diego
Serenity: John & Eileen – Mission Bay, San Diego
Shackles: Deb & Kelly, Kim – South African coast
Shahrazad: – Mexico
Shinola: Jessie – New Zealand
Silke: John & Jo – Mexico
Siomi: Alan & Martha, Lisa and Amy – Australia
Skywave: Tom, Casey, Brandyn – Fiji
Solfrana: – Rodrigues
Solstice: Steve & Carmen, Aaron, Alex – Mexico
Southern Cross: Caroline, brother – Mexico
Spirit of Kalahari: Barry, Maureen, Dani, Kevin – Fiji, from Australia
Spice Sea: Hal & Kay – Mexico
Sprig: – Mexico
St. Leger: Mike & Doreen – Mexico, from Canada
Steeldiver: Don & Adele – Mexico

Still Crazy: Neil & Kaylin, Erin, Ian, Corey – Mexico
Storm: – Richards Bay, South Africa
Storm Along: Brian – Mossel Bay, South Africa
Stormy Weather: Mike & Tristan – Mexico
Stromer: Claus & wife – Rodrigues, from Germany
Sula II: Morris & Jenny – Fiji
Summer Rose: Julie – Mexico
Susan Bright: Michael & Susan – Mossel Bay, South Africa
Susitna: Marvin & Sue – Mexico
Swift: Garland & June – New Caledonia
Talofa: couple w/two small children – South Minerva, from Germany
Tamara-I: Karl and Winfred – South Africa, from Austria
Tambra J: Gene & Tammy, Jean – Mexico
Tenacity: – Mexico
Thesis: Jim & Rhea – Tuvalu
This Side Up: Dan & Pat – Mexico
Tiaka: Richard & Rita, Heather, Tanya, Ken – Fiji
Tieras: Fred & Esther, Rudy and Heidi – New Zealand, from Canada
Tinker: – South African coast
Triumph: Tony & Lynn – Mexico
Tshinta: Frank & Yvonne – Australia, from Australia
Tshuza: Darryl & Gayle – Tuamotus, from South Africa
Tusk: – North Minerva Reef, from England
Unforgettable: Fernando & Jan, Nathanial and Alisha – Mexico
Unicorn: Ernie & Annie, Osita – Mexico
Uwhilna: Vic & Trish, Justin and Simon – Mexico
Vagant: Ussel & Friedel – Mexico, from Germany
Valiant: – Mexico
Vamanos: Chuck – Mexico
Viking: – Turtle Bay, Mexico. Gave us a lobster as tall as Annie
Vitamin Sea: Paul & Melinda, Tawndi – Mexico
Voyager: Peter & Jeanette – Australia
Wadu Ryo: Klaus & Claudia – Marquesas, from Germany
Wanderer III: Thies & Kicki – South Africa, from Scandinavia
Wandinstar: Wayne & Leslie, cat Thunder – Mexico
Wave Dancer: – Mexico
Whia: several young divers – South Minerva, from New Zealand

Whirraway: Reg & Maggie – Mexico
White Heron: Frank & Jane – Australia, from Australia
White Tunny: Ami & Sharon, Yotam and Maya from Israel
Whitecap: Kurt – Fiji
Wind Journey: girl Cassandra – Mexico
Windfall: Victor – New Caledonia
Windfall: Lee & Beth – Australia. Daiva born aboard *Windfall* in
  Cocos Keeling, the Indian Ocean.
Windora: Phil & Lynda, Cliff and Luke – Darwin, from New Zealand
Windrose: Warren & Wendy – Marquesas, from Canada
Winsome: woman named Cat – Mexico
Witraway: Reg & Maggie – Mexico
Witchcraft: Norm & Gerri – Australia
Yellow Rose: Glen and Lee – Mexico
Zardoz: Jacques & Susan, Tamerlan – New Caledonia, from France
Zephyr: Dixie – Mexico
Zilonen (Stealaway): John – Mexico
Zingara: – Mexico. Bobbi was crew.
Zorra: Stu – Mexico
Other: three guys and a girl, all of whom went topless– Cocos Keeling,
  from Norway

Manufactured by Amazon.ca
Bolton, ON